WHY EVIL MATTERS

How Science & Religion Fumbled a Big One

ALEX TSAKIRIS

Copyright © 2021 by Alex Tsakiris

ISBN Paperback: 978-1-7367325-0-2
Ebook: 978-1-7367325-1-9

All rights reserved, including the right to reproduce this book or portions thereof in any form whatsoever.

The opinions expressed in this book are those of the author.

For information, go to or write Skeptiko.com

CONTENTS

AUTHOR'S NOTE	7
INTRODUCTION	9
1 - EVIL IS A LENS	**15**
Skeptiko	16
Looking Into The Abyss	17
My Muse Speaks	19
Evil Is A Lens	22
2 - FINDING SATAN	**23**
Forced Choice	24
Is Satan Historical?	27
Satan's Co-Creators	29
3 - FAILING THE GREATEST CHALLENGE	**31**
3.1 Materialism's Final Death Blow	34
Science's Contribution to Cultural Sickness	37
Mathematical Model of What?	40
Spiritual Precision	42
A Spiritual Map Versus The Territory	45
I Don't Need God to Explain It	46
A Vast Network of Conscious Agents	48
3.2 The Intrinsic Limits Of Science	50
Experiment Demonstrates Mind>Brain	54
Consciousness as a Disassociation Engine	55
3.3 Spoon Bending	61
4 - WHY SOCIAL SCIENTISTS BELIEVE WEIRD THINGS	**65**
Fake Fakery	67
Soft Science's Consciousness Dilemma	73

5 - WILL YOUR NDE SEND YOU TO HELL?   85
    The Nde Fear Factor   87
    Hellish Ndes are Underreported   89
    Encounters With the Light   93

6 - WHY IS THE BIBLE PRO ROMAN?   95
    The Chutzpah of Christian Apologetics   99
    Christian Complicity   105

7 - THE GOD PROGRAM VS. ECSTASY   109

8 - THE MOST EVIL ALEISTER CROWLEY   115
    Do What Thou Wilt Vs The Moral Imperative   119

9 - SATANIC PANIC   121
    Crowley Apologists   125
    Wink-and-Nod Satanism   131

10 - THE DEVIL IS A CONSPIRACY   135
    Project Stargate: Remote Viewing   137

11 - LUDDITES NEVER WIN   145
    Artificial Intelligence and Backdoor Materialism   149
    Outside the Matrix   155
    Strong AI, if They Can They Will   156

12 - THE INVISIBLE COLLEGE GOES OFF PLANET   159
    Breakaway Academia   166
    Left Hand Path   169
    Who Does ET Pray To?   170

13 GOOD ET VERSUS EVIL ET   175
    ET Consciousness   180

14 - STOP THE BASTARDS   189
    Helplessness   191

15 - HAVE WE FORGOTTEN ABOUT THE VICTIMS?   195

16 - WHISTLEBLOWER OF AN EVIL CHURCH   199
   Large-Scale Conspiracy   201
   When Institutional Evil Becomes Personal   203
   When The Church is Evil   204

17 - STATE-SPONSORED EVIL   207
   The Finders Cult   210
   Satanic By Any Other Name   219

18 - BARGAINING WITH THE DEVIL   225

19 - THE DIFFERENCE BETWEEN DARKNESS AND EVIL   231
   The Protocol   245
   Evil and the Darkness   250
   Suicide   255

20 - TRANSCENDING EVIL   259
   The Spiritual Path   261
   Dead   263
   Reincarnation And Science   264
   Darkness Vs. Light   266
   Higher Evolved Beings (Hebs)   266

21 -CONCLUSION   269
   You are More   269
   You are Good   270

SOURCES   273

INDEX   279

AUTHOR'S NOTE

Some audio interview transcripts have been edited for clarity and size limitations. Complete audio versions of the interviews are available at Skeptiko.com.

INTRODUCTION

People have different beliefs about evil. And no matter how sure you are about your beliefs, there are others who think you're the crazy one. Throughout time, people have watched as politicians, philosophers, theologians, spiritual teachers, and Netflix told us what they thought, but maybe we ought to start with a different question: does evil matter? Is it something we even need to worry about defining, avoiding, or, as some advocate, marshaling to our advantage?

I've tried wrestling this question to the ground by interviewing hundreds of respected, and some less respected, scientists and thinkers around the world. We have explored science, religion, and the outer fringes of both. What I found may surprise you. What I didn't find may surprise you even more because solid, deep thinking about evil seems to be in short supply. We find a lot of I-wouldn't-believe-it-even-if-it-were-true scientific chatter. We find a lot of because-the-bible-tells-me-so religious dogma. We even find a lot of "evil is cool" media messaging, but there doesn't seem to be enough deep, nuanced thinking about what evil is, and what we should do about it. This book is an attempt to nudge us in that direction.

Nailing down a firm definition of evil is difficult. Are drone strikes on a wedding party attended by suspected terrorists evil? How about government sanctions that kill thousands of innocent children? What about the crimes of Ted Bundy? Evil may be hard to pin down, but most of us have a I-know-it-when-I-see-it sense evil exists.

This is the starting point for Chapter 1: EVIL IS A LENS. I use undeniably evil crimes as a shock therapy entry-point into our discussion of evil. I also look at those parts of human consciousness beyond our here-and-now reality and ask if they need to be part of the evil discussion. Evil may be more than the "social construct" science would have us to believe. In fact, evil is a lens into a scary-but-true extended consciousness science lacks the wisdom, or maybe just the will, to understand.

When it comes to talking about evil, religion owns the mic. Even those who take a secular approach to the topic find themselves operating within, or pushing against, religious ideas. And none of those ideas about evil are bigger than Satan. The idea of an ultimate bad guy is ingrained deep into our collective psyche and has to be part of any discussion about evil. Particularly because, as we'll see in Chapter 2: FINDING SATAN, when you go looking for a historical Satan he has a way of sliping through your fingers.

With Satan out of the way, or at least sidelined for a minute, we can begin to look at how science has handled the question of evil. Science's role in our discussion of evil begins with that little voice inside our head we call consciousness. After all, if consciousness is an illusion as some curiously outdated scientists claim, we have nothing to worry about. But as we'll discover in Chapter 3: FAILING THE GREATEST CHALLENGE, consciousness is not only real; it's the only thing we can be certain *is* real.

Mention science and most of us think of lab coats and microscopes. But the social sciences have a dog in this evil fight as well. How have other cultures understood and dealt with evil? How have beliefs about evil changed over time? How can we help those who feel they are being influenced by evil forces? These are questions we look to the social sciences to answer. Obviously, they are predicated on whether evil exists. This is the dilemma that the social sciences find themselves in. Physics and neuroscience may be responsible for sidestepping the evil problem but the social sciences have propped it the sidestepping with a gusto that's hard to explain. I cover this in Chapter 4: WHY SOCIAL SCIENTISTS BELIEVE WEIRD THINGS.

The idea of an extended consciousness realm beyond our ordinary experience of consensus reality is central to this book. The scientific evidence for such realms includes evidence from near-death experience science, reincarnation research, parapsychology studies, and even the edges of mainstream science's work in neuroplasticity, epigenetics, and psychedelics. In Chapter 5: WILL YOUR NDE SEND YOU TO HELL? I look at the most compelling evidence for the existence of an extended realm of human consciousness.

In case you haven't realized it by now, this book is going to drift into the muddy waters of conspiracy theory. If you're uncomfortable with the idea that not all players in the game are listed in the program, you might have a problem with Chapter 6: WHY IS THE BIBLE PRO ROMAN? However, if you can make it through Chapter 6, then you might be surprised to find the ultimate conspiracy theorist has one of the clearest, most level-headed approaches to religion you'll find anywhere. That's in Chapter 7: THE GOD PROGRAM.

Our culture's fascination with evil is hard to explain. We like to believe we're a science-centered, "get the job done" culture, but our art and entertainment is brimming with an unmistakable wink-and-nod acceptance of a greater occulted reality many associate with evil. I explore this situation in Chapter 8: THE MOST EVIL ALEISTER CROWLEY and Chapter 9: SATANIC PANIC.

Did I mention that this book has a lot of conspiracy theory stuff in it? Take, for example, the government's alleged use of psychics to spy on the Russians because they were doing the same against us. Well, you can call it a conspiracy theory if you want, but the FOIA-documented remote viewing program (codenamed "Project Stargate") is part of our Cold War history. One of the reasons the program is important is because its 20-year history is "case closed," answer science's doubts about extended consciousness. As you'll see in Chapter 10: THE DEVIL IS A CONSPIRACY, our remote viewing program not only presupposed extended consciousness realms, it weaponized them. You'll also see that once scientists cross the border of extended consciousness, they run head-on into the evil question.

There's a strange relationship between technology and evil. The undeniable advancements in computer technology, virtual reality, and artificial intelligence propel us towards fundamental questions about who we are as human beings. As I explore in Chapter 11: LUDDITES NEVER WIN, the answers to those questions are pivotal to coming to grips with evil.

As with our examination of artificial intelligence in the previous chapter, the relationship between evil and the UFO phenomenon seems tenuous. But as you'll see in Chapter 12: THE INVISIBLE COLLEGE GOES OFF PLANET and Chapter 13: GOOD ET VERSUS EVIL ET, the same evidence that compelled us to look past science's stuck-on-stupid definition of consciousness compels us to confront the now confirmed reality of the UFO phenomenon.

Evil is dark, and staring into that abyss comes with the risk of falling in. However, as we'll see in Chapter 14: STOP THE BASTARDS and Chapter 15: HAVE WE FORGOTTEN ABOUT THE VICTIMS? looking away doesn't work either. Believe it or not, satanic ritual abuse is a real thing. There are real crimes. Real victims. We need to hear and to understand their stories.

Coming to grips with the reality of such heinous crimes and the lifelong impact they have on victims is tough stuff. Wrapping our head around the fact that our most trusted government and religious institutions have been complicit in perpetuating evil is even harder to take. After all, their complicity is our complicity. As we'll see in Chapter 16: WHISTLEBLOWER OF AN EVIL CHURCH and Chapter 17: STATE-SPONSORED EVIL, and 18. BARGAINING WITH THE DEVIL, institutionalized evil is more prevalent than we could imagine.

I was about halfway into this evil project when I got an email from a *Skeptiko* listener that changed what I thought I knew about evil. As you'll see in Chapter 19: THE DIFFERENCE BETWEEN DARKNESS AND EVIL, clinical psychologist, Dr. Tom Zinser, developed a protocol for helping his clients transcend evil. And whether you agree with his assumptions, or his methods, his work points towards a path we might take to understand this topic we've fumbled so badly.

Ultimately, any discussion about evil comes down to our personal relationship with it. In Chapter 20: TRANSCENDING EVIL, I examined the spiritual path of those who commit to understanding and transcending evil.

Interacting with some of the great thinkers who have contributed to this book has given me a unique perspective on evil. It's allowed me to peek beyond the shallow chatter about the topic and explore the sometimes scary but worldview-enriching realm we call evil. I can't wait to tell you what I've learned. I'm sure you won't agree with everything I have to say (where's the fun in that?), but I'm excited to have you along for the journey. Let's see if evil matters.

1
EVIL IS A LENS

"There is something addictive about secrets."
— J. Edgar Hoover, *former FBI director and longtime victim of sexual blackmail.*

> **IN THIS CHAPTER**
> - an FBI agent knows evil when he sees it
> - spirits on the other side of what?
> - can/should science tackle the evil question?

There was a noticeable shift in the tone of former undercover FBI agent Bob Hamer. Up to this point, he seemed professional but a little detached. About what you'd expect from someone who had seen it all while posing as a drug dealer, contract killer, and international weapons peddler. We were talking about the three years he spent infiltrating a group of pedophiles who formed a political front organization called the North American Man/Boy Love Association (NAMBLA). I sensed his outrage:

> **Bob Hamer:** Had I not been undercover, had I walked past them and heard these men talking like that, I would have thrown them off the railing. I mean, it was so disgusting. It demonstrated to me that parents were providing eye candy for these pedophiles and these sick perverts. I don't know how anyone, just as you said earlier, Alex, how can anyone say that is not evil?

Agent Hamer's story about this group of mostly middle-aged men who were plotting to abduct, torture, and rape 8 to 12-year-old boys was gripping, but I wanted to know about the "evil" part.

I had been talking to a variety of experts, researchers, and deep thinkers about the evil question. Now, I was turning my attention to the sadly horrible issue of sex crimes against children because it cut through the cultural head trash about "defining" evil. Everyone seemed to agree that these violent, soul-crushing crimes against children were evil.

I had stumbled on a very tragic way to get at the questions I was interested in, but I was also running into barriers. First, there was religion. Mention evil, and folks look for a bible behind your back. Secondly, I seemed to be bumping into the very thorny topic of morality. The existence of evil implies the existence of good. This duality implies a moral imperative. It implies we should choose good. While this sounds simple enough, it's been a sticky topic for social scientists, philosophers, and even neuroscience types who challenge the notion of free will. I was beginning to understand why so many really smart people wanted to look away from evil. I could understand it, but I couldn't accept it. The more I looked, the more I realized evil matters.

SKEPTIKO

My interview with Bob Hamer was number 357 in the *Skeptiko* podcast series. I had started podcasting in 2007 and immediately loved it. The show's focus has been to look for science-based answers to life's big questions – Who are we? Why are we here? For me, this meant spending hundreds of hours talking to experts in parapsychology, philosophy, religious studies, physics, and particularly consciousness science. The interviews tended to focus on what is politely referred to as "frontier science," but included many mainstream scientists, and even those who identify themselves as Skeptics. Eventually, the interviews took me into areas like UFOs, conspiracy theories, and deep spirituality, topics I had never before considered credible. These interviews are the core of this book.

While some of the topics on *Skeptiko* changed, the show remained rooted in the ethos of its name. Skeptiko comes from the ancient Greek philosophy of *skeptikos*, and refers to the teachings of a school of philosophers who sought "inquiry to perpetuate doubt." I'm an equal-opportunity doubter.

Maybe podcasting was my destiny, but my path to *Skeptiko* was unconventional. After working as a computer programmer and then a Ph.D. student studying artificial intelligence, I had become a tech entrepreneur in Texas. Ten years later, I was lucky enough to cash out when the company I started was acquired. A few years after stepping away from the tech world, I grabbed a microphone and began looking for answers to the big stuff.

DECODING: NAMBLA

South Park, Season 4 ep. 6, 2000. Cartman decides he is too mature to hang out with Stan, Kyle, and Kenny, so he starts to look for older male friends in an Internet chat room. He stumbles upon the topic "Men Who Like Young Boys" and talks to some eager men whom Cartman believes want to be friends with him. In reality, they are Internet predators who prey on young boys. Before being arrested by the FBI, the NAMBLA leader gives a speech claiming pedophiles are an oppressed minority, but Stan and Kyle say they believe in tolerance and equality. But members of NAMBLA are criminals who molest children and therefore deserve to be treated as such.

LOOKING INTO THE ABYSS

The NAMBLA crimes FBI agent Hamer investigated have become a joke. A cultural meme remembered as a *South Park* episode. The outrage they generated has been replaced by outrage over the evil deeds of Hollywood elites, high-ranking members of the Catholic Church, and sexual blackmailers like Jeffrey Epstein. And while looking into the grimy abyss of sex crimes against children continues to be off-putting for almost everyone, maybe our impulse to look away is why we shouldn't. Here's how I explained it in my introduction to the interview with Bob Hamer:

Alex Tsakiris: The topic of today's show is not what you'd expect to hear on a show about consciousness science. I know because I get plenty of emails asking me when I'm going to get back to psi research and near-death experience science.

But I think this interview gets to the heart of what this show is about. As you know, my primary finding from my interviews with leading consciousness researchers and thinkers is -- we are more. That is, we're not biological robots in a meaningless universe as materialistic mainstream, science-as-we-know-it types insist. We are more.

So, all questions beyond that are about what that "more" is. What is this stuff we call spirituality? What is this extended consciousness? How do we know it's there? Where did it come from? What is its purpose?

DECODING: DEATH

Dr. Sam Parnia is one of the leading resuscitation experts in the world. In a recent interview, he explained, "So rather than a near-death experience, I prefer to describe these cases as — actual-death experiences... because according to all the criteria we have ever used these people were dead... the problem is not death; it's our reliance on an outdated philosophical, rather than biological, notion of death."

More from my introduction with Bob Hamer:

Alex Tsakiris: Step back and look at the near-death experience for a minute. The overwhelming conclusion from this science is that consciousness survives death. Every significant near-death experience researcher has come to this conclusion. The data from hundreds and hundreds of published studies come to that conclusion. And the accounts of thousands and thousands of survivors confirm it.

But the next question about NDE research is, what does the experience seem to be telling us about the nature of this consciousness that survives death? And notice how I pose this question because that's really the rub here. Now we're talking about an experience people had when they were dead, or at least, when their brain was so severely compromised, we can't come close to explaining how it would generate consciousness as defined by our existing neurological models of how the brain works.

So that means we have to look at the near-death experience "experience" and ask, "What does this say about extended consciousness (i.e., experiences that seem to transcend our immediate time/space reality)?" One of the conclusions that's pretty clear... there appears to be a hierarchy to this consciousness... an order... a structure.

Now again, for the atheistic science types who thought they could dance around the God question and the evil question, this is a problem. Is evil something we just cook up in our consciousness-is-an illusion brain, or is it somehow related to the hierarchical nature of consciousness that near-death experience science is pointing toward?

DECODING: IGNORE-ANCE

from Skeptiko #164 with Dr. Janice Holden University of North Texas

Alex Tsakiris: Let's get to the meat of their paper—I'll give you this quote: "Contrary to popular belief, research suggests that there is nothing paranormal about these experiences. Instead, near-death experiences are the manifestation of normal brain function gone awry."

Dr. Holden: The material that's out there actually supports a different conclusion. To quote my colleague Bruce Greyson, "If you ignore everything paranormal about NDEs then it's easy to conclude that there is nothing paranormal about them.".

MY MUSE SPEAKS

In the introduction to my interview with Bob Hamer, I referenced Pizzagate, the 2016 controversy surrounding the occult-themed emails of Hillary Clinton's top aid John Podesta. References to "spirit cooking" in these emails drew attention to the fact that many of the most powerful people in the world are engaged in practices purporting to make contact with realms beyond our ordinary consciousness. They don't call it "spirit" cooking for nothing. At the same time, this wink-and-a-nod acknowledgment of a reality extending beyond our minute-by-minute, "exclusively brain-driven" experience stands in direct opposition to the prevailing "you're just a biological robot in a meaningless universe so get over it" meme of science. It's a hidden in plain sight contradiction that may point to a larger conspiracy. Of course, conspiracy is one of those words that seems to send folks reeling. But over the years, I've found it's more a matter of "which conspiracy." For example, most people have no problem accepting that the bombshell spirit cooking emails mysteriously leaked four days before the 2016 US presidential election were some kind of political conspiracy aimed at derailing Hillary Clinton's presidential campaign.

DECODING: SPIRIT COOKING

> "Spirit cooking" refers to 'a sacrament in the religion of Thelema, which was founded by Aleister Crowley and involves an occult performance during which menstrual blood, breast milk, urine, and sperm are used to create a "painting." According to Marina Abramovic, if the ritual is performed in an art gallery, it is merely art, but if the ritual is performed privately, then it represents an intimate spiritual ceremony.

The spirit cooking emails and Pizzagate had become taboo topics when I published the interview with Bob Hamer. I was feeling pushback from all sides for covering it. For example, here's an email I received from my friend and creator of *Buddha at the Gas Pump*, Rick Archer. Rick's show has become an awesome library of interviews with some of the world's most profound spiritual teachers. I have a ton of respect for Rick, but we sometimes clash over culture and science issues. As a result, Rick has become my muse to understand how some information I cover is processed by people unaware of how deep spirituality relates to our conspiracy culture. Here is the email Rick sent me after listening to my interview with Daniel Pinchbeck (*Skeptiko* #343) in which I said, "if you don't think there's something to Pizzagate, you're just not paying attention."

EMAIL FROM: RICK ARCHER

> Alex, you're a great guy and I love you. You've created something wonderful with Skeptiko.
>
> (Okay...wait for it...)
>
> Buying into this crap (Pizzagate) will cause sensible people to abandon your podcast in droves and leave you with an audience of wingnuts. It will also dissuade some important guests from coming on your show. You have an important role to play. Every time you voice your support for something like this, you erode and marginalize your legacy.

My muse had spoken, so I spent the rest of the introduction diving into Pizzagate:

Alex Tsakiris: Pizzagate is interesting because it helps us understand how extended consciousness realms relate to culture and conspiracy. It brought all the players onto the field. First, it stirred up Christians heading to the voting booths. The emails were released four days before the 2016 US presidential election, and when it comes to presidential elections, voters do not stray too far from the Christian motif. Any hints of occult-related "Spirit Cooking" stuff was probably enough to sink Hillary. If not, the innuendo of sex crimes against children among her staff sealed her fate. This is a conspiracy. I don't know who's behind it, but if the goal was to rally voters with Christian sensibilities against Hillary, it worked.

Second, it drew attention to a small but influential subculture of Satanists, occultists, and magick folks. Pizzagate and spirit cooking turned out to be accelerators for the ongoing occult revival.

Third, Pizzagate drew media attention. They may have spun the story as "people believe weird things, so let's control what they believe," but they were in the game too.

Fourth, a group that wasn't in the game was the atheistic/scientific/I-wouldn't-believe-it-even-if-it-was-true types. They stood where they always stand on issues of extended consciousness...on the outside looking in because their worldview requires none of this to be real.

And finally, we had the most important players of all, the ones we know almost nothing about. The gamemasters. The behind-the-scenes influencers playing an information/disinformation game of deception. They were running Pizzagate.

I had a lot more to say about Pizzagate in the introduction to my interview with Bob Hamer. It turned out to be a controversial topic among guests and listeners. It was also a springboard into my investigation of why evil matters.

EVIL IS A LENS

This isn't a book about evil. It's a book about why evil matters, and to get there, we have to look into the evil abyss. I understand the dangers. Focus too much of your attention on something and you risk becoming a part of it. But there's a price to pay for looking away as well. Our culture is crowded with evil deniers who insist science is the answer, sizing the evil question down to a small-scale talking point. At the same time, we're surrounded by "do what thou wilt" evil apologists who continue to pump an "evil is cool" message into music and the visual arts. For a counterbalance to this strange alliance of scientific materialism and wink-and-a-nod occultism, you might look to our religious institutions. They have failed in this is as well. We're preached at by narrow-minded religious believers who trade free thought for crazy, authoritative dogma. Maybe there's another path. And maybe evil can be the lens that helps us find it. A shock therapy entry point to understanding those parts of human consciousness that extend beyond our minute-by-minute ordinary experience. A lens to a scary-but-true reality science lacks the wisdom/will to understand. Maybe we can nudge a little closer to the truth. Maybe we can look into the abyss without falling in. But first, we'll have to confront Satan. We will do that in the next chapter.

2
FINDING SATAN

What's this war in the heart of nature?
Why does nature vie with itself?
The land contend with the sea?
Is there an avenging power in nature,
not one power but two?
-- **Terrence Malick**, *from the opening scene of the movie,*
The Thin Red Line.

> **IN THIS CHAPTER**
> - a "ridiculous" cosmology
> - religion's forced choice
> - the history of Satan

If you're going to talk about evil you pretty much have to start with Satan. I'd like to put Satan off until later. I'd like to explain how science's misstep regarding consciousness condemns them to be "more wrong" about evil than the religious folks they rail against. I'd like to explain how the social sciences have followed suit by ignoring consciousness and painting themselves into a postmodern, relativistic, "wokeness" corner. And I'm really itching to show you how all of this is more than accidental and seems to be part of some socially engineered agenda we can't quite pin down, but I can't. I can't because any discussion of evil has to start with the Christian understanding of evil that's deeply woven into our collective psyche. When it comes to evil, they have the mic. So, let's dive into a historical look at Satan and see if we can grab it from them.

I grew up in a Greek Orthodox Church in the western suburbs of Chicago. It was a scary place. Partly because YiaYia (my adoring but strict grandmother) was willing to use the sharp end of a straight pin to keep her grandsons in line, but mainly because of the over-the-top ritualistic icon-waving, incense-burning, scary-by-design ceremony that is mass in a Greek Orthodox Church. I wish someone could have offered me a different perspective. Fortunately, I grew up and met some deep thinkers like religious scholar Richard Smoley and author/podcaster and creator of Aeon Byte Gnostic Radio, Miguel Conner.

Alex Tsakiris: [from *Skeptiko* #446 and my interview with Miguel Conner] I want to play another clip from an interview you (Miguel Conner) did with the very excellent Oxford and Harvard trained religious scholar Richard Smoley. You asked him about Christian cosmology and his book, How God Became God: What Scholars Are Really Saying About God and the Bible:

Richard Smoley: ...what are we supposed to believe? God got mad at the human race for eating a piece of fruit in Armenia 6,000 years ago? He got so mad at the human race he condemned everybody to eternal damnation, except he kind of felt bad about this afterward, so he sent a part of himself down to have it tortured to death, which somehow made it all right. Except not really, because if you don't buy this story, you're still going to fry forever. Does that make any sense? Of course, it doesn't. It's phrased in, of course, elaborate theologies and rituals and doxologies, but it's still a ridiculous story

FORCED CHOICE

You already know the Adam and Eve story isn't a well-reasoned explanation for human origins. You know the Bible is inconsistent, historically inaccurate, often mistranslated, and open to interpretation. That's not the problem. The problem is you've been forced to choose between "Bible" dogma or science's "biological robot, meaningless universe" dogma. This is something I talked about with Miguel:

Miguel Conner: I do not know whether the gods are faces that we give to that which is faceless in order to comprehend it and be close to it as human beings. If they are manifestations of distinct powers arising from an unknowable immensity or supreme reality or oneness. If they are mediators or messengers between us and God, who is beyond comprehension. If they are aspects of nature and the world personified. If they are archetypes or forces of consciousness both within and without man. Or if they are at the highest human expression of being beyond mortality. Perhaps they're a combination of all of the above. What I do know is that the gods are mysteries and that we as human beings are ultimately drawn to them, and I know that they respond if one calls out to them.

Alex Tsakiris: I love this as a jumping-off point into this nature of the evil question.

Miguel Conner: It's no secret that our minds are wired to have mystical experiences. Science has shown how even chimpanzees will build temples. There is something with us that wants to, as you say, go into the extended consciousness realms, into the metaphysical.

DECODING: CHIMP TEMPLES?

Biologists working in the Republic of Guinea found evidence for what seems to be a "sacred tree" used by chimps for some sort of ritual. Laura Kehoe of the Humboldt University of Berlin, Germany, set up tree cameras beside trees marked with unusual scratches. What she found maybe the first evidence of chimpanzees attempting to connect with extended consciousness:

"Maybe we found the first evidence of chimpanzees creating a kind of shrine that could indicate sacred trees," Kehoe wrote on her blog. The "shrine trees" comes on the heels of evidence of chimps displaying strange ritual-like "rain dance" behavior during rainfall.

Alex Tsakiris: [What about] somebody trying to reach into the extended consciousness realm to do something especially wicked, that seems to be of a different ilk?

DECODING: EXTENDED CONSCIOUSNESS

I coined the term "extended consciousness" because I was frustrated by the fact that all of the theories about "consciousness" and "the hard problem of consciousness," and "consciousness is fundamental," and "pan-psychic conscious agents," seem determined to leave all the interesting stuff like near-death experience, out-of-body experience, after-death communication, life between life regression, remote viewing, ET encounters, and psi off the table.

Miguel Conner: I would certainly say so. And the worst is when people go into some sort of state of denial, "Well, there's some greater purpose for it." We've gotten used to turning a blind eye to it.

Alex Tsakiris: ... on a personal level, how does that shadow work impact your view of Gnosticism?

Miguel Conner: What did Jung say, "A shadow is everything I do not wish to be." But what I do not wish to be, means it's inside me. I mean, all of us have a dark side. We are both a mixture of darkness and light, and we have the ability to commit great atrocities. History shows it over and over.

Alex Tsakiris: ... in terms of the agency of malevolent forces in the extended consciousness realm, that's a controversial topic in the communities we are part of. Is evil just a manifestation of our shadow? Or is there a connection with something "real"? But maybe "real" isn't the right word – are spirit entities looking to commingle with us in a malevolent way?

Miguel Conner: Yes... In our culture, you always ask, how did evil come into the world? In Gnosticism you start with, how did good come into the world?

IS SATAN HISTORICAL?

More from my interview with Miguel:

> **Alex Tsakiris:** I had a guest on *Skeptiko* recently. I like and respect him. His name is Russ Dizdar. He's an Evangelical minister and former police chaplain who has done some real boots on the ground investigation of satanic ritual abuse. Russ is dedicated to helping people recovering from this abuse (see my interview with Russ in Chapter 14), which can be really tough because no one wants to hear anything beyond "satanic panic"... but it's real.
>
> **Miguel Conner:** It is real, more real than we thought.
>
> **Alex Tsakiris:** That's where it gets interesting... because you have one side saying, "Not happening... couldn't happen... there is no evil, there is no Satan because we're biological robots in a meaningless universe." Then you have Christians on the other side saying, "Oh, it's real, and I'll tell you exactly how it happens... just let me just pull out this Bible here."
>
> **Miguel Conner:** Yeah, but their understanding of Satan makes no sense...if we read the Bible literally, Satan is in charge of the kingdoms of the world. And if we read Paul the way Paul should be read, the archons, the powers, and principalities are in charge of this world. Good has to come into this world in the form of Jesus. But most say, well, God is still in charge, and somehow, he gives Satan, this resentful angel, a little bit of free will to work his way here and there and then run back to hell, which makes absolutely no sense.
>
> And then the question I always ask, what happens if Satan gets his hands on the Book of Revelation and says, "Holy shit, I don't want this to end this way. It doesn't look good for me. So whatever the Book of Revelation tells me, I'm going to do exactly the opposite." Well, he has no choice. That goes right back to God. Right? So if Satan has no free will, then he's just a puppet within some divine plan...

Alex Tsakiris: Let's take it in another direction. I'd again reference biblical scholar Richard Smoley because I appreciate his book, *How God Became God*, where he traces the early Hebrew history of Satan, and it just slips right through your fingers. You go all the way back to the earliest Yahweh the thunder god stories, and there's no Satan. And then a few hundred years later, all of a sudden, the same story now has this evil Satan in it. What about the historical Satan?

Miguel Conner: No, I think you hit it on the head. If you read The Book of Job or even the stories of David, Satan is just God's prosecutor. He's sort of God's tester of humans, sometimes as an executioner, he's one of the angels. In early Christian texts, he's even called the firstborn. He's really God's right-hand enforcer.

Then you have, of course, an admixture of Zoroastrianism. Zoroaster came up with the idea that there is a force of good and evil who are basically evenly matched. You've got Ahriman the Lord of Darkness and Ahura Mazda the Lord of Light and they're in this fight. Of course, now we know that Mithras is sort of the God in between, working with it. The idea of an apocalypse, the idea of a higher self or guardian angels. Zoroaster came up with so much, a genius, and he definitely affected... When the Jews were in Babylon, and then the Persians came and liberated, Zoroastrianism came into their matrix, the Jewish matrix, and Satan basically got rebooted to a new figure. He became the bad guy. He became doctor evil or your Bond villain.

But again, Christians can't make up their mind. At least in Zoroastrianism, they're evenly matched, and we'll see who's the smartest one at the end of the day. We assume good will be. But in Christianity, again, Satan has no power close to God, but he still has his power to start wars and pestilences and seduce people. And then God sort of allows him to do his shit... so again, we get into a lot of theological acrobatics that haven't helped the sanity of Christianity for the last 2000 years.

SATAN'S CO-CREATORS

Perhaps we are co-creators of our reality as some of our cutting-edge physicists tell us:

> **Alex Tsakiris:** Let's close the loop on the satanic ritual abuse thing... so we have to deal with the realness of it, which means there are people actively engaged in trying to connect with this spiritual force for their gain in this realm, right? What do you think is going on? Is it a tulpa co-creation thing? Like, if you want to manifest Satan, you can?
>
> **Miguel Conner:** That's another wrinkle too. The whole idea of egregores or tulpas, that if we believe something, our psychic energy will create this entity and this being to do our will. So that's definitely another wrinkle to it, and if you have a lot of jerks doing it, then they will create everything.

DECODING: TULPA

Tulpa is the concept of a being or object which is created through spiritual or mental energy that then becomes autonomous. It was adapted by 20th-century theosophists but originated in Tibetan Buddhists traditions.

My discussion with Miguel Conner and Richard Smoley (*Skeptiko* #368) doesn't close the book on Satan, but it exposes some of the limits of a "Bible first" understanding of evil. But if we can't rely on religion for a tidy understanding of evil, where do we go? As we'll see in the next chapter, we sure can't look to science.

3
FAILING THE GREATEST CHALLENGE

"One of the great challenges in life is knowing enough to think you're right, but not enough to know you're wrong."
- **Neil deGrasse Tyson**, *science showman and entertainer*

> **IN THIS CHAPTER**
> - does science leave room for evil?
> - what's meaningless
> - leaders of the landslide

I respect Neil deGrasse Tyson as a science showman. He's entertaining, and that counts for something. On the other hand, Dr. Tyson doesn't measure up to what he calls "one of the great challenges in life" when it comes to the science of consciousness. And that's not just my opinion:

> **Dr. Neil deGrasse Tyson:** *So, what I wonder, Richard (addressing Dr. Richard Dawkins on stage), is whether there really is no such thing as consciousness at all...*
>
> **Dr. Bernardo Kastrup (on *Skeptiko* after hearing the above):** The idea that maybe consciousness is not there is probably the weirdest, stupidest idea ever conceived by human thought. I mean, where does thought take place? It takes place in consciousness... the fact that something like this is not only seriously entertained, but verbalized by

someone with the public exposure of the gentleman we just saw, is a worrying sign of cultural sickness, a very serious one.

As I explored in the first chapter, evil is a lens we can use to contemplate questions about the nature of that little voice in our head we call consciousness. If there's "no such thing as consciousness" as Dr. Tyson imagines, then we have nothing to worry about. But if we are more than biological robots in a meaningless universe, then we may be obligated to ask some deeper questions about consciousness. Of course, maybe that's what materialistic science has been afraid of all along.

This paradigm shift from scientific materialism to "something more" is a topic I explored extensively in my 2014 book, *Why Science Is Wrong About Almost Everything*. Let me recap.

There are two paradigms for explaining the voice in your head that is human consciousness. The first, and the one that has ruled the roost among science-as-we-know-it types, is scientific materialism. It insists that consciousness is 100% completely a product of the brain. Mind-equals-brain. For these folks, we're all "biological robots in a meaningless universe."

> **DECODING: MEANINGLESS**
>
> From Skeptiko 314: Dr. Sean Carroll is a Harvard-trained, Caltech theoretical physicist with a long list of fellowships, awards, bestselling books, and television and movie appearances. He's a bit of a science celebrity. All of which makes his ridiculous opinion on consciousness and the meaning of life noteworthy.
>
> **Alex Tsakiris**: Do you really believe that all human experience can be reduced to chemical reactions in our brain?
>
> **Dr. Sean Carroll**: Yeah, except I wouldn't use the word 'just.' And I wouldn't even use the word 'reduced.' I certainly wouldn't use the word 'illusion.'
>
> --Before directly addressing Dr. Carroll's answer to this question, I'd point out that throughout this interview, I used my pet phrase,

"biological robots in a meaningless universe," when characterizing Dr. Carroll's Naturalism philosophy. I wanted to see if he'd push back. He never did. The reason is, no matter how he spins it, that is what Dr. Carroll is saying. He may say, "Meaning isn't built into the fabric of the universe," or "Meaning and purpose are a social construct," but it still boils down to the idea that we're all just biological robots in a meaningless universe. He knows this, so he never challenged my phrasing. Ten years ago, guys like Carroll were just flat out saying, "Consciousness is an illusion." In other words, there is no such thing as human experience, so get over it. But somewhere along the way, they realized this message/meme doesn't sell. You can't tell a rational person outside the brainwashed halls of academia that everything about their minute-to-minute experience is an illusion. They'd laugh in your face. So guys like Dr. Carroll have changed the script. They now say your experience is a way we have of "talking about" this "emergent property" called consciousness that happens inside the brain. The trick is to give you something that sounds like something (i.e., that you really exist and are experiencing consciousness... duh) while sidestepping the really big questions of purpose and meaning. And also sidestepping the huge metaphysical assumption Dr. Carroll is making when declaring that consciousness is entirely a product of your brain.

Keep in mind, Sean is a physicist. He's not supposed to make metaphysical assumptions. But also keep in mind that Sean can't say when consciousness begins. He can't say when it ends. He can't say what's necessary and sufficient to cause consciousness. But he wants you to accept his metaphysics and jump through these tortured apologetics about the "fabric of the universe" because he's really, really committed to his cosmology, and he wants you to be committed too. Unfortunately for Sean, logic gets in the way of his argument. If the universe is meaningless and you are embedded in that meaningless universe, then there can be no meaning to your life. It can't be any other way. If there's real meaning in/to your life, then there's at least that much meaning in the universe. If the universe is meaningless, if there isn't even a tiny smidgen of it anywhere, then you have zero chance of ever finding meaning in your life. But again, this is not something Dr. Carroll can sell. He knows that, even with his Harvard Ph.D., you're going to laugh at him if he tries to tell you your life is meaningless, so he's putting up this elaborate "yes, but..." smokescreen.

Materialism posits a clockwork-like world "out there" that scientists can measure and control. iPhone apps and Big Pharma fit beautifully into this world. The "consciousness is fundamental" idea has been around for a long time, but it got a Western science reboot in the early 1900s when the world's leading physicists noticed the observation of their experiment (i.e., consciousness) affected the result. It might seem like a leap to go from these spooky double-slit experiments to "everything from the smallest subatomic particle to the Milky Way galaxy is a product of consciousness," but that was the unavoidable conclusion of Neils Bohr, Werner Heisenberg, Erwin Schrodinger, and others. Even Einstein eventually relented.

In *Why Science Is Wrong*, I explored the evidence of the latest frontier science and its implications for understanding consciousness. The evidence has mounted in the six years since the trend towards a post-materialism science is undeniable. Here are some excerpts from *Skeptiko* interviews with three scientists leading this transition:

3.1 MATERIALISM'S FINAL DEATH BLOW

Dr. Donald Hoffman is a highly-regarded University of California-Irvine physics professor who's authored a best-selling book and published a TED Talk with millions of views. People seem to like him. Even mainstream science types who should be uncomfortable with his radical ideas about the nature of consciousness find it hard not to like the rigorous mathematical models he's applied to the mind-body problem, evolutionary psychology, and consciousness. Hoffman is a Renaissance scientist attempting to offer a bridge to post-materialism science. He's also offering a bridge to the deeper spirituality that lies beneath this transition.

Alex Tsakiris: One of the recurring questions on *Skeptiko* has been, how can science be so wrong about consciousness? I mean, poll after poll shows 90% of people completely disagree with this biological robot, meaningless universe perspective... and historically, every civilization we've known throughout time, would reject out of hand...

...so the real question is, how can we trust science going forward? You're a great advocate of science. You speak eloquently about the scientific method, about how beautiful science is, but I guess I'd turn it around. Can we really trust science when they've dropped the ball so badly?

Dr. Donald Hoffman: I agree that the current theories of consciousness among my scientific colleagues really do drop the ball. They start with an unconscious objective reality of space, time, and matter, and they try to boot up consciousness from that, and of course, I disagree with them. That's not the right way to go about it. It's interesting to ask why they do that, what's the history behind it, and why I still have confidence in science?

So first, I should say that my colleagues who are physicalists, who assume that space, time, and matter are fundamental, they're well-meaning. They're doing the best that they know as scientists and human beings. So there's no conspiracy. It's not that at all. Here's part of the history about why they're thinking the way they do.

It has to do partly with Galileo and what happened between the Church and Galileo, right? So Galileo overthrew centuries of Church dogma that the Earth is the center of the universe with this telescope and his evidence for Copernicus, the Copernican theory that the Earth is not the center of the universe, that the Earth goes around the sun. The religious people didn't buy that, and they put Galileo on house arrest and threatened him with torture if he didn't recant. That sort of set the stage for this battle between science and spirituality way back then, and many scientists still have a feeling that "If that's what spirituality means, then I will have none of it."

The other aspect is they feel like, starting with Galileo and then especially with Newton and following him, science made great strides in using the assumption that space, time, and unconscious matter are the foundations, and it's truly stunning what's happened in the last three, three-and-a-half centuries. It has completely revolutionized our understanding of the universe, the technology that has come out has been remarkable, and it's raised humanity's level of life dramatically.

So, there's this feeling among the scientists that, "Look, the physicalist framework was our way of getting away from the weirdness of the spiritual traditions and breaking free. Look what it's done," and it has been dramatically successful. So that's part of where they're coming from. It's a big part of the whole culture.

But now, on the question of the origin of consciousness, how does consciousness arise? When I was a graduate student, that was not an acceptable topic. I was a graduate student at MIT from 1979 to 1983 in the Artificial Intelligence Lab, in what's now the Brain and Cognitive Science Department. And I knew that even if I was interested in consciousness, that was not a serious topic for a serious researcher.

But about 10 years later, it became a serious topic that was viewed as a genuine, worthwhile scientific endeavor, largely perhaps due to Francis Crick, who said we really need to take this quite seriously. When Francis said that, then the rest of the scientists said, "Okay, if a Nobel Prize winner says that it's legit, then we should jump in."

What we're finding, and I do have faith in science, all of the theories that my colleagues are proposing are, of course, physicalist theories. There's integrated information theory, there's the collapse of microtubules, we can talk about these, there's global workspace or global neuronal workspace theories. There are a variety of theories that are all physicalist, but we know they don't work. And when I go to conferences, I can actually say to my colleagues... And by the way, there's nothing personal here; I like these guys, and guys in the generic sense. They're brilliant, they're nice people. We disagree deeply, but it's not ad hominem. We're all trying by our best lights to understand what's going on.

I will say to [for example], Stuart Hameroff, "What is the collapse of microtubules that is the taste of vanilla?" And he can't do that. The thing about science is, at some point, because science requires mathematically precise theories and experiments, at some point, you can no longer fool yourself. You realize you just don't have the beef. You can't do it.

So, I know these guys. I'm friends with them, and I'm telling them, "You don't have the beef. I think in principle you don't have the beef, and you're going to have to do something different. You're going to need a deeper theory."

SCIENCE'S CONTRIBUTION TO CULTURAL SICKNESS

Next, I played Dr. Hoffman the clip from my interview with Dr. Bernardo Kastrup[1]. There's some nesting of clips, so it might get a little confusing, but I think you'll follow along:

Alex Tsakiris: ...Let me play a clip from Dr. Bernardo Kastrup, who you know, right? You know Bernardo, right?

Dr. Donald Hoffman: Sure, oh yeah, we're friends.

(begin clip from my interview with Dr. Bernardo Kastrup)

Alex Tsakiris: *(me speaking to Bernardo)* These people are generally regarded as scientists (as opposed to radical skeptics), as the mainstream scientists, we're talking about Richard Dawkins, Lawrence Krauss, Neil deGrasse Tyson. And Neil deGrasse Tyson, whether we like it or not, is the face of science for many, many Americans. So let's see what mainstream science has to say about consciousness.

(clip within the clip)

Richard Dawkins: *But you can say something about the question which you really would wish to know the answer to, and for me, it would be what's consciousness, because that's totally baffling.*

Neil deGrasse Tyson: *Richard, you know what I think, not that you ask, but what I think on this is, consciousness has, kind of, baffled us for a while and evidence that we haven't a clue about what consciousness is, is drawn from the fact of how many books are published on the topic. We're not really continuing to publish books on Newtonian physics. It's done. So, the fact that people keep publishing books on consciousness is the evidence we don't know anything about it because if we knew all about it, you wouldn't have to keep publishing.*

So, what I wonder, Richard, is whether there really is no such thing as consciousness at all and that there's some other understanding of the functioning of the human brain that renders that question obsolete.

Bill Nye: *To that, I've got to say like, oh wow!*

(end of clip within... back to my interview with Dr. Bernardo Kastrup)

Alex Tsakiris: *I'm laughing, but what is so funny about that? Of course, that last voice was Bill Nye, The Science Guy.*

Bernardo Kastrup: *He was astonished. Bill was astonished.*

Alex Tsakiris: *He was.*

Bernardo Kastrup: *The idea that maybe consciousness is not there is probably the weirdest, stupidest idea ever conceived by human thought. I mean, where does thought take place? It takes place in consciousness. So, here we have consciousness, speculating about the possibility that consciousness does not exist, and it may not be there. I mean, the very thought is an in-your-face contradiction, and the fact that something like this is not only seriously entertained, but verbalized by a* *person with the public exposure of the gentleman we just saw, is a worrying sign of cultural sickness, a very serious one.*

(end of clip from my interview with Dr. Bernardo Kastrup)

Alex Tsakiris: "A worrying sign of cultural sickness." I guess that's closer to my position regarding science. What do you think?

Dr. Donald Hoffman: I take a slightly different view. I'm more optimistic about it. I mean, I know these guys. They're my friends and what I see is the way they're thinking is physicalism, the idea that space, time, and matter are fundamental, has worked for so many other problems that we've got to try our best to make it work on this problem. So it's not like they're degenerate or anything like that; it's rather, "Look, this hammer has hit a lot of other nails. Hopefully, this hammer will hit the nail of consciousness, and we need to keep trying."

Alex Tsakiris: ... you said you were in the AI lab at MIT in 1973, right?

Donald Hoffman: I was yes, '79 to '83.

Alex Tsakiris: I was studying AI at that time too. I was in a Ph.D. program at the University of Arizona. We've now come to know that at this same time, at Stanford Research Institute, Dr. Hal Puthoff and Dr. Russell Targ were way past these materialistic assumptions about space, time, and matter. They were doing experiments with remote viewing… they knew the materialism/physicalism thing was falsified because they'd proven it over and over again in their lab.

So we have this kind of invisible college thing going on where there are some people in the know who have moved way past this, and they seem to really be closer to the folks who are in power. Then we have Neil deGrasse Tyson playing this lost in the woods kind of thing, and we can all laugh at it, but…

Dr. Donald Hoffman: Right. I think that's the way revolutions in science happen. You usually have a few people who are doing something different than the mainstream, and it takes a long time for scientists. We're a conservative group. We're very, very conservative in the sense that, if you're going to rattle a deep theory, you're going to have to really rattle it hard before we take it seriously...

Alex Tsakiris: Maybe.

MATHEMATICAL MODEL OF WHAT?

One of Dr. Hoffman's accomplishments is his rigorous mathematical model of consciousness that offers testable results. I asked him how such models fit in a post-materialism world:

Alex Tsakiris: ...I appreciate what you said earlier about science being driven by models best expressed as mathematical equations, but at the same time, those are abstractions of reality... I wonder if we gloss over that fact...

And before I let you jump in, I'd like to point out our history, where a hundred years ago all the great quantum physicists basically reached this same point and said, what Max Planck is famous for saying, "I regard consciousness as fundamental," which is very close to what you're saying.

But then we did the "shut up and calculate" end run on all of that... we decided to forget about the philosophical implications and just see what we could crank out in terms of dazzling technology.

And I guess that's my concern... are we preparing for another version of shut up and calculate where we don't really address the underlying implications of what you're discovering?

Dr. Donald Hoffman: Yes. First, I certainly agree with Max Planck that consciousness is fundamental and matter as derivative. Absolutely. It's well-spoken, and other great quantum theorists at the foundation of it thought that.

Wagner thought that. Von Neumann thought that consciousness was important and fundamental.

Many of the early quantum theorists were very interested in the broader implications of the theory. It seemed to be challenging our thoughts about reality, and they wanted to really explore that. And then World War II came along, and that really sidetracked everything because what happened was they needed all of these quantum physicists to help them with technology to win the war. And they did. They built the atomic bomb. It was revolutionary, and all of a sudden, there was big money.

So, that changed the whole framework of physics. It became a part of the military-industrial complex, and the shut up and calculate attitude came out of World War II and big money.

That was a big tragedy. World War II was a big tragedy in a number of ways. It stopped this deep philosophical inquiry into what the mathematics was telling us and it got us into this more military-industrial complex kind of attitude. And we're now slowly wrestling our way out of that.

And going back to trying to ask the deeper questions, the question you ask is a good one. What is the math about? One reason why scientists love mathematics is it forces you to be absolutely precise in what you predict. You can't hide. It's much, much harder to hide. And you know, when Einstein wrote down his equations, if he was off by 5% or 10% on predictions about where Mercury is, then that's going to be a problem for him.

So, you do mathematics in part to be precise. You can find out precisely where you're wrong, but also because once you write down a mathematical theory, the theory becomes smarter than the person who wrote it down. When Einstein wrote down the equation of general relativity, he had no idea that it was going to predict black holes. He didn't know that. But the equations do predict black holes, and he didn't like it. He didn't believe in them, but he was wrong, and the theory had a deeper, in some sense, a deeper insight into reality than the person who wrote it down.

Another reason why scientists do mathematical theories is because they surprise us, they become smarter than us, and eventually, we become the students of the theory. Now, of course, Einstein's general relativity is not the final answer. His equation, we know there has to be something deeper. We know that because his equation is so precise that we begin to get insights into precisely where it fails. That's the power of mathematics. It's so exact that it tells you when the mathematics stops and fails. So Einstein's equations have a singularity. It has a black hole. When you have infinity in your equations, that means you've got an error. That's a big, big error signal. So we know that general relativity can't be the final answer, and it tells it to us by saying, I get the answer infinity here. There's something wrong with the theory.

SPIRITUAL PRECISION

Dr. Hoffmann is a world-class physicist, and he can hold his own when it comes to deep spirituality as well:

Dr. Donald Hoffman: ... I recall giving a presentation on my mathematical theory of consciousness. At the end, I received a tough question from a member of the audience who quoted a famous spiritual teacher. He said, "The language of God is silence. All else is poor translation."

Of course, the point this person was making was that my mathematical model of consciousness is just math, and the reality transcends anything that math could possibly discuss.

If someone says to me, "The language of God is silence, all else is poor translation," then being consistent says nothing else, I would actually very much respect that. I'm not being facetious. If someone said, "Look, the reality transcends math and words, end of story. And you just have to be with the reality," I completely respect that. But when you look at the spiritual traditions, what most of them do is they write lots of words. There's the Bible, the Koran, the Bhagavad Gita, and so forth. So my attitude then is, if we're not going to be silent, then don't we want to use the most precise language we possibly can so we can find out as quickly as possible if what we're saying is nonsense or not?

And it turns out with mathematics, you can quickly find out if you're being inconsistent and you can actually quickly find out if you're making predictions that are false. It's hard to do that with everyday language. It's easier to hide and to say nonsense and not be caught.

Alex Tsakiris: ...spirituality, particularly this nondual understanding of spirituality, is really about creating space between our habitual consciousness and this "higher consciousness"... and I don't have a mathematical equation for that... I challenge this idea that experience doesn't matter... that's not exactly what you said, so I don't want to put words in your mouth, but I think we could turn that around and say experience is the only thing that matters...

One of the things we talked about previously is this idea we can't be anything that we observe, right? We observe the computer screen. We know we're not the computer screen. We're observing the computer screen. And in the same way, when we observe consciousness, when we observe the habitual mind, we know we are not the habitual mind. And yet, that habitual mind, as well as the higher mind, is residing in what we call consciousness.

Let me share with you a guy who's done a pretty good job of summing up these ideas, Eckhart Tolle.

Eckhart Tolle: *So you give up: all knowing, accumulating knowledge, the mind-made self that consists of accumulated* thought-forms. As we sit here, we are dying a little death and realize that nothing real actually died. Only the illusion of a false self. What remains is consciousness, the very bare fact that you are. So at this moment is the opportunity of sensing something much more fundamental than the history of who you think you are in the mind, my past, your sense of identity but who are you really beyond the story?

Dr. Donald Hoffman: Yes. I like Eckhart Tolle's ideas very much. I've listened to a number of his talks, and I do agree that consciousness is the fundamental reality and that it transcends any of our theories, including my own scientific theories, my own mathematical models. And that going into silence and letting go of our thoughts and getting a direct connection with that conscious experience is very, very important. I actually spend time every day in meditation doing exactly that.

Alex Tsakiris: How would you explain it in terms of your model?

Dr. Donald Hoffman: ... when you're letting go of your thoughts and emotions you are in some sense letting go of your interface [to reality]. Instead of having this virtual headset on by which you're interacting with reality, you're slowly learning to let go of that and appreciate consciousness on its own terms, to be the consciousness, and be aware of the consciousness. And I think that there are fundamental limitations to mathematics and what it can model... every scientific theory always has to have certain assumptions...

Alex Tsakiris: Incompleteness.

Dr. Donald Hoffman: That's right. It's always going to be incomplete... the quest for mathematical models is never-ending and it will never fundamentally reach the bottom. There'll always be the deeper reality that goes beyond any mathematical quest.

...this goes back to the silence versus non-silence issue. If we, as Eckhart Tolle was encouraging, go to that meditative place...if we let go of all of our models and mathematics and go into the silence and face reality without the screen of mathematics or ideas, I think that's very legitimate. But in our everyday life, we do talk. We're doing it right now. And so my attitude is, if we're going to talk, then let's be as precise as we possibly can... because we don't want to spin around in silly circles. I do believe there are many deep insights from spiritual practitioners and spiritual traditions but they're not infallible.

And the question is, how do we find out what are the genuine insights, and what is the nonsense? And there's always going to be nonsense. Again, I think it's the precision. So I absolutely agree. If someone doesn't want to do the mathematics at all and just wants to be silent, I'm on board. But if we're going to talk at all, then I say be precise.

A SPIRITUAL MAP VERSUS THE TERRITORY

Next, I asked Dr. Hoffman about his path within the spiritual territory of extended consciousness:

Dr. Donald Hoffman: ...a little bit about my own personal history. My father was a fundamentalist Christian minister, so I was raised in that. It was very narrow... my way or the highway... you turn or burn. Meditation was definitely not something that was encouraged. If you meditated, it opened you up to the devil. And who knows what would happen. It was an interesting experience. I'm in recovery from it...

Alex Tsakiris: I take what you just said, literally. And I'm glad you said it... because one could make the case, and I have on this show, that the cultish practices that go hand-in-hand with Christianity, really need to be viewed for their mind control aspects. And that's not judging, we have other things in our society based on mind control techniques, but the fact we're doing this to kids is especially [troubling]...

I know from my own experience being brought up in the Greek Orthodox Church and having to walk up to communion and kiss the hand of some old man as he dropped bread into my hand to feed me. I mean, there's some deep symbology there...

Dr. Donald Hoffman: I agree with you completely on that. I felt that the institutions I was subjected to were not there to help me to explore and find out who I am. They had the answers. I needed to understand their answers and believe their answers. To question anything, they said was to be a non-believer and therefore be subject to hell.

And so it really is a mind control thing that goes deep into our limbic system and gets at your emotions... when you're young, you're defenseless against that.

It's taken me a long time to deprogram myself. Knowing it intellectually, of course, it wasn't that hard, but deprogramming emotionally is a very different thing.

And so I've had to let go of that programming. And one thing I do is meditate... by being in silence I'm facing all the fears and anxieties that were programmed into me... I have to let that healing take place. So I spend time every day in silent meditation. I have for the last 17 years.

I DON'T NEED GOD TO EXPLAIN IT

One thing you hear from atheistic science types is, "I don't need God to explain that." Hoffman offers a different perspective:

Dr. Donald Hoffman: Many of my colleagues will say there is no God because we have a physicalist framework that can answer all of the questions...

Alex Tsakiris: ...I often hear, "I don't need God to explain X." For our purposes, we can replace the X with reality. I don't need God to explain reality. And I think your theory blows that off the table. It says, "You have not explained reality in an adequate way with your science as we know it."

Dr. Donald Hoffman: Absolutely. The problem with God is that as science advances, it's only become more and more clear that our standard explanations cannot deal with consciousness. The thing that's most important to us, my feelings of emotions, the taste of chocolate, a headache, the feeling of velvet, all these things without which I wouldn't even really be here if I didn't have any experiences. And for this central thing (consciousness)… science is woefully inadequate. Scientists are beginning to understand that their mathematical models don't cut the mustard [when it comes to consciousness]. They're being forced by their own mathematics to say, this doesn't work. And I'm helping them, I come along as a gadfly and say, "it doesn't work." If we're going to get an understanding of consciousness, we're not going to be able to get it started with a physicalist framework, it just won't happen.

And so now the word God is a loaded word, right? Everybody uses the word, but it's never defined. It's the infinite consciousness or the consciousness that includes all the other consciousnesses. And maybe we're stuck with that, But as a scientist, I've got this theory of conscious agents… and the mathematics indicates this can go on to infinity.

Of course, I'm probably wrong, but I have proposed a mathematically precise definition of God. It's conscious agents that have an infinite set of possible conscious experiences.

So, for the first time that I know of, we have a proposal for a precise definition of God, and of course, I'm probably wrong, but the point is to be precise so we can now start the conversation. Where is it wrong? How is it wrong?

It's also open to someone saying, "God transcends any science, any experience, and any description." And again, if someone says that, I completely respect it, but that means we're not going to argue back and forth about your God versus my God.

A VAST NETWORK OF CONSCIOUS AGENTS

You can see why scientists like Donald Hoffman support a gnostic understanding of consciousness. He speaks their language. You can also see why dogmatic materialist scientists don't. Hoffman's not willing to settle for the "consciousness is an illusion" silliness they're peddling. He's committed to following the data wherever it leads. Even into extended consciousness realms.

> **Alex Tsakiris:** Let's talk about extended consciousness. It's a topic we've spent a lot of time covering on *Skeptiko*, literally hundreds of episodes at this point, so if we're talking about near-death experience science, remote viewing, out-of-body experiences, after-death communication... there are literally hundreds of peer-reviewed papers on this stuff... and I also have to throw E.T. in there. I don't want to leave it off just because people are uncomfortable with it. The point is, there does seem to be a reality to these extended consciousness realms. How do we fit those back into your model?
>
> **Dr. Donald Hoffman:** That's right. There's a lot to say here. Things like out-of-body experiences are interesting because we can induce them at will. Now, if I take a transcranial magnetic stimulator, a TMS unit, and touch it to the right temporal-parietal junction, you will have an out-of-body experience. We now know how to induce those at will with a magnet. So the question about these paranormal phenomena and psychic experiences [leads to more inquiry]. If you're a physicalist, there's no room for it, right? Space, time, and matter are fundamental. There is no consciousness outside of space and time. They're pretty much required to reject all this. And most of my colleagues reject this stuff out of hand. Now, my framework absolutely allows it. I'm

saying objective reality is a vast social network of interacting conscious agents.

Think of it like a Twitterverse. There are all of these conscious agents interacting. They're tweeting and following and communicating with each other. What we call space and time is just our visualization tool that allows us to understand this vast social network that would be too overwhelming without the visualization tool.

So there's lots going on outside space and time. These kinds of paranormal phenomena are absolutely allowed, but...here's the thing, most of my friends who are doing paranormal experiments have a view that fundamental reality does have space and time and physical stuff, but in addition to this physical reality, there's a ghost in the machine. Now, it's a fairly wimpy ghost. It doesn't have very strong muscles. You have to do long experiments and then you find something that's second or third decimal place effect. It's a dualist framework. My attitude is very, very different. I don't need the ghost in the machine. Consciousness is everything. And what I, what we call space and time and the laws of physics is exactly how we perceive our interactions with other conscious agents. I want to show that all of the laws of physics are in fact a projection of the laws of dynamics of consciousness.

Alex Tsakiris: I'm glad you're headed in that direction and you make some great points. That kind of rigor of science is also about this process of observing and explaining. There needs to be some observing going on. Take near-death experience science, it's at the beginning stages of observing a phenomenon so we can start testing some of the assumptions. I'm not sure we can really blow past that, especially when we look at how miserably poor a job science-as-we-know-it has done. Aren't we still dealing with some of these fundamental "meaning" questions? What does it mean to survive bodily death? What does it mean to encounter the hierarchical nature of consciousness? What does it mean to have experiences that seem to transcend any experience you've ever had? Isn't there a lot of territory that we need to map out?

Dr. Donald Hoffman: Absolutely. I completely agree with you. And in my framework, death is not the end. So think about it this way. Suppose that you go with some friends to a virtual reality arcade to play safe virtual volleyball, and you put on your headset and bodysuit, and you and your friends find yourself immersed in virtual volleyball at the beach. So you see sand and a net, and palm trees and you start playing volleyball for a while. And then one of your friends takes off his headset and his avatar collapses motionless on the sand. Well, from the point of view of the interface, it looks like he's dead, but he's just stepped out of the interface.

... I'm saying that when you die your avatar is motionless from the point of view of the interface, but it doesn't mean that your consciousness is gone.

3.2 THE INTRINSIC LIMITS OF SCIENCE

I appreciate Donald Hoffman's gentle but firm approach to materialistic science, but playing nice can only take us so far. That's not to say Dr. Bernardo Kastrup isn't nice; he's just more direct.

Bernardo used his Ph.D. in computer science to shoot up the ranks of the corporate high-tech world, but his passion for knowledge has led him to seek a Ph.D. in philosophy and publish highly regarded scholarly papers and books on consciousness. From *Skeptiko* #378:

Bernardo Kastrup: ... they are trying to explain consciousness in terms of something that isn't consciousness. And that is indeed a baffling question, because who is trying to answer? It is consciousness trying to answer. So, you get the self-reference there that makes the question very baffling if you're framing it that way. If you're trying to reduce consciousness that's where it goes wrong. Nobody, well, very few people have stopped to think that, "Maybe we shouldn't formulate the question that way. Maybe what we have to ask is, how can we explain everything else in terms of consciousness?"

Alex Tsakiris: I'd almost suggest that's step two. Step one is to properly frame the borderline between science and philosophy. Let me share a quote from your book, *Why Materialism is Baloney*[2]:

Bernardo Kastrup: *Capturing observable patterns and regularities of elements of reality, relative to each other, is an empirical and scientific question, but pondering the fundamental nature of these elements is not, it is a philosophical question.*

Bernardo Kastrup: The scientific method is largely an empirical method. It's based on observation and when we observe nature, what we are observing is the behavior of nature. When we see a billiard ball hit another, that's a behavior of matter and what science then does, it analyzes these observations and tries to exact the patterns and regularities of the behavior of physical nature, as it presents itself on the screen of perception, conscious perception.

So, at the end, we end up with predictive models of nature's behavior. We know that if we put things together this and that way, we will get this and that effect, and these predictive models are the heart of technology. We use these models to develop technology because we know how nature behaves, and then we can put that behavior to use, to our advantage. Because of the success of technology, science has acquired an enormous cache in our culture as the enabler of the technologies that extend and improve our lives.

This is all fair enough, but science says nothing about the intrinsic nature of the physical, it only analyzes behavior in differential terms, in terms of patterns, of differences, bare differences. For instance: What is a positive electric charge?

Is it that which is not a negative electric charge because it behaves in a symmetrical opposite way? That's all science does. But what is a charge, intrinsically, what is the nature of a charge? Science has nothing to say, it's fundamentally outside of the scope of the scientific method.

(later)

Bernardo Kastrup: Before we even get to extraordinary experiences and the paranormal, there is a challenge to explain the normal, the ordinary, because the ordinary and the normal are not explained under mainstream physicalism or mainstream materialism. There is no explanation for why we feel the qualities of experience, why we see red, why we feel warmth, why we feel disappointment. There is nothing about mass, momentum, charge, or spin in terms of which we could deduce phenomenal properties, what we experience in consciousness.

So, there is an enormous gap for explaining the normal. That's why I focus on the normal. Since the paranormal is the next step, we haven't even explained the normal yet.

Alex Tsakiris: I'm totally with you, until the last part, I might take issue with that. But I take it one step further and point out something like memory because we really don't understand memory, right? We don't understand what's going on, and memory is tricky because it's something that all the neurology folks, all the mind-equals-brain, materialist scientists say, "No, no, we really do have a handle on memory, we just need to drill down a little bit further."

So, if you can, speak to memory being another [unknown]. Yes, we don't understand how we experience red or how we experience love, but even this thing called memory, they think they've nailed it, but they don't understand it.

Bernardo Kastrup: If you look at the literature coming out, claiming to explain memory, it's all self-contradictory. Some explain memory in terms of large networks of neurons. Others try to explain memory in terms of interneuron processes. Things are all over the place.

I can mention one concrete example. There was a study published a couple of years ago, claiming to have found the key to memory based on experiments with mice. They exposed the mouse to a certain experience in one environment, moved the mouse to another environment, then they would trigger that memory artificially and the mouse would behave as if it were in the first environment, then [they concluded], "Oh, we've figured out how memories are created."

If you go through the details, they grew cellular switches in the brain of the mice, so they could identify which neurons fired up when the mouse was exposed to the first experience in environment A. So, they had the map of all of the neurons that were activated in environment A. Then they moved the mouse to environment B, and with a specific technique using light, they could artificially reactivate the same neurons as if the mouse was in environment A, and guess what? The mouse behaved as if it were in environment A.

Now, who recorded and recalled the memory? The scientists, through this cellular technique, through exposing the neurons to light, creating the cellular switches in the neurons, recording which neurons that were activated in the first situation, and then reactivating them artificially in the second situation. That doesn't show at all how memory works. To show how memory works, we would have to figure out where the mouse stores the pattern of activated neurons without these *artificial* cellular switches and exposure to light that the scientists created.

What you see being claimed in the science press about having "understood" memory, it's extremely exaggerated. We don't understand memory.

EXPERIMENT DEMONSTRATES MIND>BRAIN

I'd like to think I've pounded on the limits of science's mind-equals-brain explanation of consciousness, but I know from experience it's a difficult idea to get past. One experiment that makes it more tangible is the work of Dr. David Nutt:

> **Bernardo Kastrup:** There are several papers published by Imperial College, the group of Dr. David Nutt. They measured brain activity in an fMRI brain scanner, that's the baseline brain activity, then they inject folks with a psychedelic substance, it could be psilocybin or DMT or LSD, and they continue to measure brain activity as the substance takes effect and ask people to report on their experiences as their brain activity is being monitored. So, they can correlate the original baseline with the drug-taking effect, with the subjective reports of the participant describing the intensity and richness of their experiences.
>
> What they found is that the richer and more intense the experience they reported, the lower the brain activity that's measured, to the point that one can predict the other. We can predict how much lower brain activity is based on how rich and intense the report of the experience.
>
> **Alex Tsakiris:** Why is that a surprise? What does that fMRI normally look like when we're super excited?
>
> **Bernardo Kastrup:** Well, there has also been a neuroimaging study, a few years ago, done in Japan. They put people having dreams inside an fMRI. It turns out that even simple dream experiences, like a dream of watching a statue, leads to identifiable activations in brain activity. Brain activity goes up when you experience something, to the point that you can even predict what the experience was, and with psychedelics, which are incredibly intense experiences, the opposite seems to happen, which is surprising.
>
> Before all of this came out in 2012, we thought that psychedelics would light up the brain like a Christmas tree

because under materialism, experience is brain activity or at least generated by brain activity. So, if you have a richer and a more intense experience, you would expect more intense brain activity. The opposite is what is observed in a psychedelic trance.

And it's not only psychedelics, I already mentioned a couple of other examples. There's also been a study in Brazil of spirit mediums, which is a subject I know you're interested in. They took experienced mediums who were willing to do psychography, in other words, to write down information that supposedly comes from a transcendent source, from the spiritual world, whatever it is that they claim. They realized experienced mediums, when they are psychographing, their brain activity in areas involved with thinking and writing is reduced. Then they did controls. They asked these mediums, without psychographing, just to write text in the same brain scanner and the text they wrote scored lower in a measure of complexity than the text they wrote while they were in a trance. It should have been the opposite because in the trance, the areas that would activate for you to write complex text were actually deactivated while they were in trance. So again, you have this correlation of richer, more complex experiences associated with reduction of brain activity in key cognitive regions.

CONSCIOUSNESS AS A DISASSOCIATION ENGINE

Dr. Kastrup returned to *Skeptiko* in 2020[3] with some insights regarding the nature of disassociation of ego states. It's a topic relevant to a later conversation that I had with Dr. Tom Zinser in Chapter 19:

Alex Tsakiris: Can you lay out for people the position you're taking, and who you're taking a position against?

Dr. Bernardo Kastrup: ...since 2016, I've really been going for the mainstream, publishing mainstream philosophical journals, mainstream scientific journals, mainstream science, in popular science journals like *Scientific American*, and engaging mainstream people in debates, philosophers and scientists. That's the move I am making now.

In the early years I tried to speak to the general public, and I think to some extent I was successful, but I grew more ambitious. The case for metaphysical idealism is so strong that it deserves a very serious hearing in the mainstream. We just have to overcome the inertia, the momentum we have going with materialism so that we can hear out the story of idealism in an unprejudiced way.

Alex Tsakiris: Excellent. That might be a really nice segue into kind of this dissociative identity disorder (DID) subject I wanted to talk about, because it both launches us into one possible evidential element, but it also gives an example of how you're trying to engage. You recently co-authored a paper in *Scientific American* titled, "Could Multiple Personality Disorder Explain Life, the Universe and Everything?"[4] Tell us about this.

Dr. Bernardo Kastrup: There are three metaphysical alternatives. There are many more, but three main ones today. One is materialism, but it can't explain consciousness. You cannot bridge the gap from mass, charge, momentum, etc. to what it feels like to see red, to have a belly ache or fall in love. That's the problem.

Then you have panpsychism, which says that matter is inherently conscious. So you don't need to explain consciousness, it's a brute fact of nature. Every electron is conscious, every quark is conscious. And now the macro level of consciousness is formed by the combination of these little micro level consciousnesses of the subatomic particles in our brains. Now that fact is the so-called combination problem. There is no coherent way to explain at least in principle, how subjectivities can combine to form compound subjectivities. It's a problem just as hard as the hard problem.

Then the other alternative, which is a form of idealism, the one I endorse, is that there is only one universal consciousness, so we don't need to combine anything. But then you face the decomposition problem. I can't read your thoughts, presumably you can't read mine. So how can we both be this one universal consciousness? That's where dissociative identity disorder comes in because this is an empirically validated condition. We know it exists. We have brain imaging studies of people with this disorder. We know they're not lying. Clinical evidence for this goes back as far as you can look into the journals.

Alex Tsakiris: 1880s. 140 years ago.

Dr. Bernardo Kastrup: Yeah, late 19th century. But a lot of people still felt skeptical, they thought people were lying, they were just making this up to get attention. But since at least 2014, that doesn't hold anymore because of brain imaging research. One was done in 2014 here in the Netherlands by Yolanda Schlump and others[5], which could identify the patterns of activity that correlated with dissociative identity disorder and the controls were actors pretending to be dissociated. And guess what, the patterns of brain activity were completely different. Clearly there is something dissociative identity disorder looks like on their brain scanner...

Alex Tsakiris: .. So next talk about the other experiment because it removes any criticisms someone might have about using actors.

Dr. Bernardo Kastrup: That one is tough to dismiss. That was the year after 2015 in Germany. A woman claimed to be several different alters, different dissociated identities or personalities, and some of them, some of these altars, claimed to be blind, to not be able to see. So the psychiatrist had this brilliant idea of just hooking this woman up to an EEG to take brain readings at different times when different alters were in control of her body, at least that was the claim[6]. And when a sighted alter was in control, they could read normal brain activity patterns, here at the back of the brain, the visual cortex, the area associated with vision. And lo and behold when a blind altar was in control, even though the woman's eyes were wide open, activity in the visual cortex would disappear. Now that's something you cannot fake, you cannot pretend that.

Alex Tsakiris: Because, of course, there are critics of the conclusion that you just made, that maybe the study wasn't as solid as you think. But just so we cover the basics, the neural correlates of someone being blind is not something that we consider in our current model of consciousness, which is what your example is all about. I think this forces the issue, Bernardo.

(later)

Alex Tsakiris: ...one of the things that is interesting about multiple personality disorder, dissociative identity disorder, is that it suggests consciousness working to self-construct itself. And in this splitting and forming these almost conscious entities, for lack of a better term, are inside of our consciousness. And evidence of that, which comes through like you said, both clinically and then experimentally, if you were just going to place a bet, it would push you towards idealism.

Dr. Bernardo Kastrup: I don't even think it's the best evidence against materialism. Certainly, it's very handy to idealism because it allows the idealist to solve the decomposition problem. Now, look at the opposition. The opposition has the hard problem of consciousness. We have no idea how to even approach it, let alone solve it. And the subject combination problem, which we also have no idea how to approach it.

So the third option has an empirically, consistent avenue for tackling its own challenge, which is the decomposition problem. But if you want evidence against materialism, there is better stuff than dissociative identity disorder.

Alex Tsakiris: Agreed, and you know what? I'm really kind of leading you into some different waters, if you will, because what caught my attention about DID was the twofold aspect. One, it strikes another blow against materialism. It points out the inadequacies of psychology to really handle and fully fold in like clinical work, and they just deny it. I think that's an important element of this.

But what really struck me had to do with a rather amazing bit of research that I found. I interviewed this guy named Dr. Tom Zinser. He's a clinical psychologist from Grand Rapids, Michigan. Now retired, but was in the field for 25 years working with hundreds of patients. And many of his patients had DID, or other dissociative disorders. His work with those patients wound up evolving into spiritual work. He was finding that the ego separation of those "altars" were not only real in the way we were talking about, but sometimes had relationships with spiritual entities in the extended consciousness realm.

Now, that's a lot to take in, but there are some metaphysical speculations we might have to address.

Dr. Bernardo Kastrup: Oh, how do I comment on this? I don't know him, so I will be stepping on eggshells here because it's a subject I'm not familiar with. The baseline of what I'm saying of the position I put forward is that what we call life, organisms, metabolism, is the image of dissociation in spatially unbound, transpersonal consciousness.

Alex Tsakiris: ... break that down for me.

Dr. Bernardo Kastrup: Okay. Suppose that universal consciousness has something akin to DID, so it also forms alters. What would an altar look like from the point of view of another alter? I would say it will look like what we call life, a body, a metabolizing organism. From that perspective, the baseline is all alters are visible because the image of an altar is a visible body. If you're alive, you are dissociated, when you die, you are reabsorbed into that spatially unbound transpersonal consciousness.

Now, the question that you're probably alluding to is could there be dissociated alters of universal consciousness that do not correlate with the physical body?

Alex Tsakiris: Hold on, that isn't exactly what I'm talking about, because you actually kind of pulled us into the water. You just wrote a book on the metaphysics of Jung, right? Jungian metaphysics, something along those lines?

Dr. Bernardo Kastrup: Correct, yeah.

Alex Tsakiris: So Jung is talking about the shadow and he's open to the idea that... and you're also versed in many of the spiritual traditions. You understand the Tibetan Buddhist concept of the Tulpa and that as we have thought forms, those thoughts...can become ego states/alters. The language becomes very fluid there, in that it sounds like we're talking about the same thing. What does it, [unclear] the same kind of thing; thought forms, ego states, alters. And in particular with Jung, he's kind of playing both sides of the street. He's saying, "Well, you know, I work with clients and we can kind of treat them just like they're separate, but they're really not," and then he switches over and says, "Yeah, but they are." He's saying both.

Dr. Bernardo Kastrup: That's right. I think if you study Jung's corpus as carefully [as] I have, I've studied it three times over. There is no doubt that Jung did think certain dissociated complexes of the self, which is his word for universal consciousness, could be disembodied, that you could have a subject that is not correlated with the physical body. There is no question that Jung thought that was possible, despite all his tiptoeing and sort of contradicting himself. When you go really deep into it, it's pretty clear that's what he thought.

From that perspective, it aligns with the thought-forms of Buddhism, it even aligns with what some religious traditions would call disconnected personalities. Jung explicitly associated these dissociated complexes, he associated them with what in the tradition has been called the angels and demons.

3.3 SPOON BENDING

Dr. Dean Radin[7] is recognized as a world leader in parapsychology and psi research so the bent spoon on his desk is almost cliche. I mean, here's a world-class scientist who has dedicated his career to exploring what most consider impossible and he has a statue of the impossible on his desk. If you do a search for a photo of the spoon in question, you'll see what I mean. First off, it's a big thick old-fashioned soup spoon. Like the kind your grandmother owned. These things don't bend easily. Secondly, it's bent in some very strange ways including the ladle, which is folded over on itself in a way that would be impossible to do without tools and a good deal of force. But what's truly impossible is Radin's claim that the spoon was always in his possession during the spoon-bending party when it suddenly became so soft that it yielded to the gentle push of his thumb. Of course, maybe this renowned scientist who has published hundreds of peer-reviewed papers in some of the world's top science journals and written numerous bestselling books is misremembering, but then again, he still has that spoon on his desk.

Alex Tsakiris: ... when I interviewed you years ago, I remember asking you about these respected scientists, Dr. Ray Hyman, from the University of Oregon, and Dr. Steve Novella, from Yale, Neurology... who had done an interview in which they were laughing at you. They were literally mocking you and laughing at the research you'd published (in a subsequent interview on *Skeptiko*, Novella was forced to retract his claims/criticisms). But I can't help but wonder how this history is going to look years from now. Because, when we write this history, there's no way you're not right in the middle of this paradigm change that is happening.

We can't even say it's about to happen, it's happening. I mean, materialistic, mind=brain, "consciousness is an illusion", that science is gone except for a few diehards. How do you think you are going to be viewed in the longer lens of science history?

Dr. Dean Radin: I think Sibelius, the composer, said this, "No one has ever erected a statue to a critic." So, from a historical perspective, every advancement in every domain of human performance, of any type, has always attracted severe criticism. So, it's simply par for the course. Some people can take it and others can't. I guess I can take it.

Alex Tsakiris: One more question on this legacy thing. Let's speculate for a minute, what do you think the writing of this chapter of history, this post-materialism chapter, is going to look like?

Dr. Dean Radin: ... you asked about post-materialism. Post-materialism, as a word, actually isn't very good because it's a promissory note. So, the way I would put it, is you have to see what's happening in historical context, that there's a pre-materialism and then materialism, and then a post-materialism.

So, this evolutionary strand is that pre-materialism, we can think of as before the middle-ages, where everything was considered supernatural and everything was created by the Gods and so on...That was before science, so there wasn't any way of grasping, in any detail, what was going on. Everything was supernatural.

When science began, it flourished, say in the Enlightenment, between the 1500s and the 1700s. In that period, a method was developed which allowed us to look in much more detail, at the nature of nature, and that is materialism. It's both a philosophical stance and a set of tools to be able to understand things, and we know that it works really great because it allows us to make things like this, which has more computing power than any computer in the world 20 years ago, and that will continue. So, it becomes very seductive to imagine that everything can be explained using that philosophical basis.

But what's happening now, and this is largely driven by puzzles about the nature of consciousness, materialism is really good at looking at the world from the outside. It's good at objectivity, both from quantum mechanics and also in philosophy, mathematics, and physics in general, yet there's this puzzle of how does a material object give rise to an interiority? How does all of this objective stuff that we see and feel, have an inside experience that doesn't seem to be physical?

Well, there are people who are trying to come up with ideas that say how matter can turn into mind, but a growing number of scientists and scholars are saying, "maybe not," and this is why ideas like panpsychism are becoming more popular now. It's very difficult to figure out how a three-pound lump of tissue is giving rise to what amounts to our entire experience, including all of our ideas about the universe, all of our laws, all of our physical laws...everything is due to the inside here that is somehow coming out of this matter.

So, post-materialism is saying, "Maybe we've jumped the gun a little bit and set aside consciousness as an epiphenomenon that wasn't very meaningful, and actually it looks like it might be much more meaningful than we originally thought."

Science-as-we-know-it may be headed towards a more enlightened view of consciousness, but it's sure taking its time getting there. Meanwhile, and as we'll see in the next chapter, their little brothers in the soft sciences have completely lost the trail.

4
WHY SOCIAL SCIENTISTS BELIEVE WEIRD THINGS

"It is characteristic of the whole of modern literature that it speaks so little of evil; materialism simply does not concern itself with evil. A materialistic explanation can apparently be found for suffering, illness and death; but not for evil. "
-- **Rudolf Steiner,** *November 1906.*

> **IN THIS CHAPTER**
> - social science's evil dilemma?
> - academic naivete
> - a new approach to studying evil

The paradigm shift from "biological robots in a meaningless universe" to "we are more" might seem obvious, but we shouldn't expect it to be curated into Wikipedia anytime soon. And while many otherwise smart physicists and neuroscientists look pretty dumb when it comes to consciousness, the problem is even worse in the "soft sciences." Sociology, anthropology, religious studies, history, and psychology would seem to be well-positioned to answer some of the fundamental questions we have about evil. They've collected some good data across time and across cultures, but they seem to have painted themselves into a "consciousness is an illusion" corner they can't get out of. Consider my interview with Dr. Hugh Urban from Ohio State University. He came on *Skeptiko* to talk about his acclaimed book on

Scientology. Through his research into Scientology's founder L. Ron Hubbard, Urban had discovered proof that Hubbard, along with Jack Parsons, performed an occult sex magic ritual in the Mojave Desert that sought to give birth to the Antichrist. Here's a clip from an interview he did with Tom Smith on The Edge podcast:

> "L. Ron Hubbard and Jack Parsons became friends and began to engage in a series of rituals. The most important was called the Babylon working, which was based on [Aleister] Crowley's work and was intended to help identify a female partner who would serve as the whore of Babylon, and then through a series of sex, magical operations, they would conceive a being who would become effectively the [8]antichrist."

Jack Parsons was a famed rocket engineer and one of the founders of the multi-billion defense contractor Jet Propulsion Labs (JPL). Parsons was also the top-dog protege of Aleister Crowley, the famous occultist who reveled in his title of "the wickedest man alive." There's a lot more to Crowley's story we'll talk about Chapter 15 during my interview with William Ramsey, but what struck me was Dr. Urban's calm demeanor while we're recounting this history:

> **Alex Tsakiris:** ...the first thing that strikes me is you're pretty damn calm about all that. Most people wouldn't be shocked, and then they'd immediately want to know is this true.
>
> **Dr. Hugh Urban:** Well, you know, I've been teaching for 20 years and researching for longer than that, and I've seen a lot of weird stuff and so very little phases me at this point. And so my attitude in all the work I do is kind of what I call a radical agnosticism. So I try to just be as open-minded about anything that I look at and try to understand it without immediately passing judgment on it, no matter how bizarre it might seem at first glance.
>
> **Alex Tsakiris:** The part that concerns me is we have reason to believe that this stuff really did happen... and that the Jack Parsons and Aleister Crowley thing has direct connections to the MKUltra program (the illegal CIA secret mind

control program that came to light after a series of lawsuits in Canada and Congressional hearings in the United States) and has direct connections to the psychic spying program (Project Stargate, see Chapter 10 with Lance Mungia)... so it's not so much that I would immediately judge these practices, but I would want to drive a stake in the ground and say, there seems to be a reality to this extended consciousness realm they're trying to get to... because it looks like our government was trying to do the same thing...

Dr. Hugh Urban: ... the only reason that movements like these gain any traction is because people do take them very seriously and do believe... but I guess I would say that, I can't know, as a historian of religion, whether there's a reality to what they're talking about, but I can say that they certainly believed there was and took it very seriously. So that alone, I think, is worthy of study. Whether the psychic research they were doing was real or not, I can't say, but I can say that they certainly took it very seriously.

On one level Dr. Urban's response seems reasonable. No one, not even an Ohio State University History of Religion professor, can know everything. But should he know more about these extended consciousness realms he's studying? Is he unknowingly propping up this radically stupid "maybe consciousness doesn't exist" stuff we explored in the last chapter?

FAKE FAKERY

The sad state of the social sciences is more complex than simply ignoring the reality of extended consciousness. Consider my interview with respected archaeologist and anthropologist Dr. Brian Hayden who joined me to talk about his important contributions exploring the prehistory of religion, ritual, and our relationship with the supernatural.

Alex Tsakiris: ... I had a *Skeptiko* listener who contacted me and said, "Hey, there's this guy who's done some amazing academic research, looking at the prehistory of this evil sorcery, magic stuff," and he was referring to you Dr. Brian Hayden, and he said, "He's looked at secret societies, going back to prehistory and aggrandizement and all of this kind of stuff," and I was like, "Hey, that sounds great, but I'm a little bit skeptical because I know academics, particularly in Canada, often have to stay between some very narrow lines in terms of propping up this phony materialism stuff," and he was like, "No." And he sent me a quote from your book, a very excellent book, *Shamans, Sorcerers and Saints: A Prehistory of Religion*,[9] which you wrote a few years ago, and here's the quote from the book that he sent:

"I think that aspiring elites increasingly sought to restrict access to ecstatic contact with supernatural forces in order to claim privileged divine directives."

It's a mouthful, but it's really a powerful, powerful idea and I was like, "Wow, this is great. I'm on board. This is a guy I have to talk to."

Then literally, two days ago, I'm doing some more research and I'm trying to figure this stuff out and I ran across another quote I heard from a very nice interview you did on a podcast a few years ago called *Conversations From the Pale Blue Dot*.[10] Let me play this clip and then I think we're going to have something to talk about. *What seems to be an inherent pension, inherent proclivity for engaging in rituals and for believing in the supernatural, stems from a fundamental biological adaptation that may be a million or more years old.*

There we go. So then I kind of rocked back and said, "Uh-oh,, this is going to be another one of those typical materialists, trying to jam it back into a very narrow framework thing."

So, I sent you an email and I said, "Hey Brian, where shall we go on this?" And you sent me a really cool email back because I had referenced, for example, Dr. Dean Radin, Dr.

Jack Hunter, an anthropologist who calls himself a para-anthropologist because he's open to these extended consciousness realities and how they might affect our understanding of archeology. And I also sent you a link to a show we did with Jan Van Ysslesteyn, who studied the Ulchi shaman groups in Siberia for 30 years[11], and reports back all of these extraordinary extended consciousness, supernatural experiences.

I just want to lay out the groundwork for how we came to this interview because we have so many cool things to talk about and now, we just have to figure out where to grab onto this and launch into a conversation.

Dr. Brian Hayden: Okay.

Alex Tsakiris: So, where shall we begin? I think we should begin with those two quotes of yours, that I mentioned; one from your book and the other from the interview that you did. How do we resolve those two? How are we to understand what you're saying there?

Dr. Brian Hayden: Well, I have to say that both of those are really from, what you would call a materialist if you like, an ecological viewpoint. I don't think you can dismiss the materialist aspects, any more than you can dismiss physics from explaining how toasters work and how we get people to the moon and things like that, but it's not the whole picture either. So that's my background.

My personal feeling is that physics and materialism and ecology does not account for the entire universe as we know it. What I'm trying to say is that in academics, at least in my conception of academics, we have specific issues like getting to the moon or explaining human evolution or social evolution or cultural evolution if you like, and materialism and ecology is the best framework for dealing with those questions.

So that's the framework that I've used, just like physics is the best framework for getting somebody to the moon.

Alex Tsakiris: But Brian, I'm not sure I am with you on how science "evolves." Because in the case of quantum physics these guys were going down one path and then another group emerges, the shut-up-and-calculate guys, and they take things in a different direction, right? So you have Niels Bohr and Heisenberg and Schrodinger, and they start sounding very mystical. Then you have the shut-up-and-calculate guys say, which is your point. They say, "Look, we can sit here and have these philosophical arguments all day long, but in the meantime, we have some incredible formulas, powerful mathematical models that have fallen out of this work we've done in quantum physics, that could provide us just as huge a leg forward in technology." And they were right, and it did, it led to computers and cell phones and the communications system we have. All of this stuff is based on these very reliable quantum physics understandings that we have. But ithey sidestepped the philosophical question that mystics, like Schrödinger and the rest we're talking about.

I don't think the same actually applies in anthropology. So shut-up-and-calculate works in a limited sense, as does shut-up-and-excavate, if you will, for archeology. But when we start talking about the prehistory of religion and ritual and the rest of that, if we leave out our understanding of the relationship to the supernatural, we can't confine that to a materialist explanation that completely denies that consciousness even exists. Which is stunningly absurd..

I admire the work that you're doing, but you're inside of an academic bubble that has this dogmatic understanding of consciousness, that isn't just a shut-up-and-calculate thing, it's wrong, it's been falsified. The best evidence we have suggests that the preconceptions they have about consciousness, let alone extended consciousness, is just completely falsified.

Dr. Brian Hayden: I agree.

Alex Tsakiris: Isn't that a huge problem?

Dr. Brian Hayden: Well, no, it's part of the spectrum of scientific views that exist. I mean, Dean Radin is an academic, he's part of the spectrum. There are the shut-up-and-calculate guys, but they don't represent everybody, and they don't represent, certainly my perspective. I've worked with people who are, what I would call, hard scientists and they just don't have any [interest] with any of these issues of metaphysics or anything else. That's not my view, it's not Dean Radin's view. It may be pretty common, but it's not the whole thing.

Alex Tsakiris: Let's be careful there because in the same breath we can say, "Hey, there are a lot of people now that are very drawn to the flat earth hypothesis." We don't take those people seriously and when we hear the rest of their ideas we make further assumptions about where they're coming from. And the same is true with the materialists who don't believe in consciousness, or believe that consciousness is an illusion.

Dr. Brian Hayden: I agree.

Alex Tsakiris: I don't think we should equate those two and put them on the same level of saying, "Well, everyone has an opinion." Now, let me add quickly here Brian, because I don't want to misrepresent you... you and I are kind of on the same side. You've had to battle your entire academic career to get your voice in there that says, "Hey guys, do we maybe even want to look at the fact that all of these folks I'm talking to are reporting contact with the supernatural."

Dr. Brian Hayden: Yeah.

Alex Tsakiris: What was that like for you and where do you come down on something like that?

Dr. Brian Hayden: In the academic circle, I sort of skirted that issue. I've tried to frame questions that don't directly address that problem, but in my personal life I have experienced a lot of things and there's not too much doubt in my mind that there's synchronicity out there in the universe, and there are a lot of things that Dean Radin was talking about, like precognition and a lot of things we just can't explain yet. So I've tried not to deal necessarily with that and leave it, sort of as an open question from an academic point of view.

What I have tried to do is look at the way people use some of these innate feelings, innate proclivities to try to manipulate them and get more power for themselves in society.

What I tried to show is that some of these claims are pretty self-serving, like the claim on the Plains Indians that if I, as a leader of a secret society, have sex with your wife then you can get some of my supernatural power by your relationship with her.

(later)

Dealing with questions of the supernatural and what's real and what's not, is an extremely difficult question, because it's so complex. It's one of those questions that I've not tried to deal with in a comprehensive way, I've just tried to point out that at least part of the claims about the supernatural are bogus, especially from secret society perspectives. But there is an unknowable portion that may have some insights into ultimate reality in there, including these transcendent, ecstatic experiences, which may have opened up a window into other dimensions but the content that comes through is so varied that it's unreliable.

Alex Tsakiris: It may be varied, but in some respects it's important to the overall question. It kind of dwarfs everything else. Do we really want to talk about some Indian chief who's faking communication with the gods, or do we want to talk about his real communication with the gods?

Dr. Brian Hayden: That's the question, yeah.

SOFT SCIENCE'S CONSCIOUSNESS DILEMMA

Over the years, I've talked to a number of scholars who understand the dilemma philosophy, history, sociology, and anthropology professors face when it comes to consciousness. But no one has articulated it as clearly as Dr. Richard Greco did in episode #445 of *Skeptiko*[12].

> **Alex Tsakiris:** Today's guest is a former professional boxer, trained by heavyweight champ Floyd Patterson, and a former criminal investigator who's worked on many high-profile cases before becoming an instructor at the Criminal Justice Institute. Dr. Rich Grego is also a Professor of Philosophy and World Religion at Florida State College in Jacksonville, who earned his PhD with a dissertation on Krishnamurti and Thich Nhat Hanh...

One of the things I appreciate about Rich's background is his experience as a criminal investigator. Sometimes missing with academics:

> **Dr. Richard Grego:** ... I tend to be a both/and guy in my thinking versus either/or, and I try to reconcile, maybe seemingly contradictory views... I also understand the need for an investigator, whether it's a scholarly investigator or a criminal investigator, to be impartial and unbiased, and that's my big concern.
>
> **Alex Tsakiris:** You brought that up in a *Skeptiko* interview you did with Stanley Krippner. That was a good one, but I want to play a clip from another interview you did for us. It's with the past President of the Parapsychology Association, Dr. Hoyt Edge[13]:
>
> **Dr. Hoyt Edge:** *A number of parapsychologists, a lot of them perhaps, want to call the field a part of anomalistic psychology.*
>
> **Dr. Richard Grego:** *Why?*
>
> **Dr. Hoyt Edge:** *It's for two reasons. One, just as Bob Morris said, what we ought to do if we want to have parapsychology mean something and parapsychology be paid attention to, if we can contribute something to normal psychology, then*

they're much more likely to say, "Oh, these are good people."
One that he didn't like, I think he's also perhaps been a little unfair also.

Dr. Richard Grego: Just to explain it away?

Dr. Hoyt Edge: That's right. I like Richard, I know Richard. I like him. Susan Blackmore the same way. Susan has stayed at my home and so forth, I love Susan. These are good, good people.

Alex Tsakiris: He is, of course, talking about Dr. Richard Wiseman who, like Dr. Rupert Sheldrake, is a pretty measured guy and has that British, Cambridge kind of formality, called "intentionally deceptive" when referring to their research collaboration.

And then there's Susan Blackmore, who said she wasn't interested in near-death experience research anymore and she hadn't kept up with it, and then the next month after the interview, gave a public presentation reasserting her doubts about near-death experience science.

DECODING: SUSAN BLACKMORE

Join Skeptiko host Alex Tsakiris for an interview with often quoted near-death experience skeptic, Dr. Susan Blackmore[14]. During the interview Dr. Blackmore acknowledges that despite her reputation among near-death experience science doubters, she has not remained current in the field, "It's absolutely true; I haven't written about this subject for a long time and I haven't kept up with all the literature, either." Blackmore continues, "... I gave up all of this stuff so many years ago...if you are a researcher in the field it behooves you to read as much as you can of the best work because otherwise you can't be a researcher in the field. I'm not a researcher in the field. I have not been for a long time."

... so, it looks to me like [Dr. Hoyt Edge] is just naive. He doesn't understand that these people he says are "good guys" are not "good guys." He doesn't seem to understand that these people have completely undermined his field of parapsychology. I don't even know that parapsychology is relevant anymore. Which leads back to the first part of his quote where he says, "Gee, if we're just nice enough, then maybe science will let us in the door and get us a seat at the table." This just doesn't fly.

Dr. Richard Grego: It's interesting. Paul Smith, who I think you did a show with on *Skeptiko*, I met him at a parapsychology conference and talked to him about that issue in parapsychology. Paul Smith, being a remote viewing guy, worked with the Army's program, just to refresh anybody's memory. I remember talking to him about the very situation you're addressing and his response was, the need of the parapsychological community specifically to please the scientific community... reminds him of Stockholm syndrome, in the sense that these people who abuse you and don't understand you and are really out to get you, are the very ones you're just trying so hard to please. And I think maybe, to some extent, you see some of these guys bending over backwards in deference to that project.

Alex Tsakiris: I want you to weigh in on that further Rich, because as I was sending you these interviews that I've done, I was trying to come to grips with the complete disconnect in academia...

Dr. Richard Grego: I get where you're coming from. On the other hand, I'm looking at things from, say Hoyt Edge's perspective and thinking, what do you want him to do? What should he say about Richard Wiseman and Susan Blackmore?

Alex Tsakiris: He should say what Rupert Sheldrake [said about Richard Wiseman], which is, (paraphrasing) "I've looked at how he's handled the data, and he is being intentionally deceptive... and that doesn't speak well for him as a trusted researcher." I don't think you have to back off of any of that. Why would we trust someone who's intentionally deceptive?

I interviewed Dr. Daryl Bem on Skeptiko and he said the same thing. He said it in a little different way, but his conclusion was the same:

Dr. Daryl Bem: ...anyway, [Dr. Richard Wiseman] and Ritchie and French published these three studies. Well, they knew that there were three other studies that had been submitted and completed and two of the three showed statistically significant results replicating my results. But you don't know that from reading his article. That borders on dishonesty.

That to me is clear, and that's where parapsychology has completely run off the rails and why it's no longer relevant. And why Sam Harris says in a snarky email exchange with them that parapsychology is, "the backwater of science," everyone thinks, "well, it must be..."

Dr. Richard Grego: Yeah, I feel like for the sake of argument, I should disagree with you, but I think, certainly in terms of parapsychology, it's hard to disagree...

(later)

Alex Tsakiris: ...my concern is the social sciences, including philosophy, are headed down that same path parapsychology took... where they just become completely irrelevant. When I listen to Hugh Urban he sounds irrelevant.

Dr. Richard Grego: Really? It was that frustrating to you, the dialogue you had?

Alex Tsakiris: No, the entire dialogue wasn't that frustrating. But at the end of the day, I think his argument... sounds irrelevant.

(later)

Dr. Richard Grego: I think I'm even more sympathetic with the historian's perspective, because what he's trying to do is what the general public doesn't. If we allowed the fashionable trends in pop culture to determine what the truth of a situation is then why would we need courts? Why would we need scholars? Why would we need criminal investigators?

Alex Tsakiris: ...you're playing the slippery slope game here. I think we can have both. Here's a clip from an interview I did with (former Scientologist) Chris Shelton:

Chris Shelton: ...if you're going to publish an academic paper about Scientology, you better have something to say and if what you have to say is simply regurgitated Scientology promotional materials -- and I am intimately familiar with Scientology's promotional materials because I wrote them... what Scientology presents to the world is very different from what actually goes on in Scientology. Academics stop at the propaganda level, they don't go any further. [15]

(later)

Alex Tsakiris: ... Let me approach this from a different angle [from another clip from my interview with Dr. Hugh Urban]:

Alex Tsakiris: ... if you can't get consciousness right, if you're playing within "the consciousness is an illusion" paradigm as the atheist colleague you mentioned no doubt believes, then you're not even in the game.

Dr. Hugh Urban: *That's an interesting point. I guess I would say that, well, there's a couple of answers to that question. There is a movement in religious studies and other fields that is extremely interested in consciousness from different perspectives. But in my own work, I'm a historian, so I look at what people do and the texts they leave behind and what we can sort of see.*

Alex Tsakiris: If you listen to the whole interview, when you really hold his feet to the fire and he sounds like so many of the other academics I've interviewed, they go, "Look man, I can't publish that. I may believe that's true, but

I can't get that published." Listen to Hugh Urban's story and you'll learn that he's out there joining some obscure little Tantric community in India [as part of his research] and when you ask him he says, (paraphrasing) "Yeah, of course, I do rituals." So he is entering these extended consciousness realms and then he's coming back and jamming it back into this goofy materialistic thing. That's why I think the whole thing comes out as irrelevant gobbledygook.

Dr. Richard Grego: I need to push back a little bit. I don't know if this particular guy, doing this particular kind of research on the institutional history of Scientology, feels that he is in a position to make judgements about the veracity of their beliefs?

Alex Tsakiris: ... L. Ron Hubbard and Jack Parsons were in the desert summoning the antichrist... and now Hugh Urban goes, "Well that doesn't really matter, what matters is that they believed it." No, that's completely wrong! Their "belief" is completely secondary to whether or not there is any reality to them connecting with an extended consciousness realm and that extended consciousness realm interacting with us. That's what matters most.

Dr. Richard Grego: Yeah, I agree personally...

Alex Tsakiris: ... If you cannot come to some determination as to whether or not there's a reality to that extended consciousness realm, then you need to stop everything you're doing, and you need to do as much research as possible in order to determine the reality or non-reality of that. You can't pretend like that isn't the main thing.

Dr. Richard Grego: ... On the other hand, to draw on experience from my criminal investigating days, I was a polygraph examiner as well. I did one on a big capital case and they actually called me in to testify, which doesn't usually happen because they usually don't admit polygraph evidence in court, but this time they did. I was testifying for the defense attorney and it was weird. It was at a sentencing hearing, of all things, after the verdict of guilt had been determined. I'm not really sure why he wanted this evidence entered. But I testified that this guy had essentially passed my polygraph test and interestingly, the attorney was asking me about it, and we went through the whole thing.

At the end of my statement to him in court, he said, "So, in your opinion then, this guy is innocent of the charges, right?" And I said, "Well, I'm not really qualified to attest to that." And the reason is because all I did on that particular case was I took one forensic tool... and provided testimony that came from my narrow perspective. I don't know if that's exactly analogous...

Alex Tsakiris: ... but it comes back to extended consciousness, and if you get consciousness wrong, then you wind up with all this silly, goofy stuff... What's religion? What's spirituality? ... It's all gobbledygook until you wrestle the consciousness issue to the ground.

Dr. Richard Grego: It certainly is to me, but what about people who just aren't interested in the consciousness issue and they just want to explore Scientology as an institution?

Alex Tsakiris: ... you are a professor of philosophy and I have on the screen the very famous quote from physicist Stephen Hawking, who said at Google's Zeitgeist conference that "Philosophers have not kept up with science and their art is dead." Which I think probably did more for philosophy, in terms of giving it a good kick in the butt than anything that has occurred in the last 20 years.

But I would juxtapose that with the interview you just helped me conduct with physicist Dr. Donald Hoffman, because when he comes out and says, "Well, look, space-time is doomed and every experiment we've done with deep physics, subatomic physics, and quantum physics, has proven over and over again that consciousness is fundamental," it would seem we don't have any contradiction to those experiments.

Then, and he doesn't directly say this, but I think it's a natural inference, scientists (including social scientists) who have not kept up with consciousness research, their art is dead.

(later)

Dr. Richard Grego: If Hugh Urban was to come to a conclusion, regarding what Scientology is and about the nature of consciousness, what would that be?

Alex Tsakiris: In terms of what I wanted Hugh Urban to acknowledge, is to say, "Based on the evidence at hand, the burden of proof would be on Scientology to clearly demonstrate that it is not a destructive cult that ruins people's lives, and until they can overcome that burden of proof, then we should regard them as a cult."

I think the reason he doesn't take that position is because of the box that he's in regarding consciousness... and I don't think we should allow academics to comfortably live inside that box.

Dr. Richard Grego: I actually agree with all of that, except, is that box the result of their humanist-atheist-materialist assumptions? I mean, suppose academia had deeply spiritual assumptions, as opposed to materialistic ones.

Alex Tsakiris: We'll never know, but their art is dead because they haven't kept up with the science. Until they tackle that problem and understand consciousness isn't an illusion, until they grapple with that, we won't know. It's not that they're humanists, it's not that they're atheists, it's the assumptions they're making based on that philosophy.

Dr. Richard Grego: ...is every religion a cult, every organization? ...where do you stop?

Alex Tsakiris: I think we keep asking the same questions.

(later)

Alex Tsakiris: ... that's why I love your little snippet about moral responsibility and criminal culpability. If you put yourself out there as a religious/spiritual institution, then you're claiming to uphold a certain moral responsibility and certainly a criminal culpability, and to the extent that you don't measure up you should be held accountable...

Dr. Richard Grego: A lot of philosophers and postmodernists have promoted this ideal of the clinically detached, critically detached, objective, impartial, unbiased observer, who doesn't make value judgments. Do you think this has put those people unwittingly in the service of forces that are very biased, but can hide behind that, and can enable them to hide behind that veneer of supposed objectivity to actually push an agenda?

Alex Tsakiris: I'm going to answer that question with another question, and that is something that's raised by another person that you greatly admire, Thich Nhat Hanh, who said:

"We run during the daytime, we run during our sleep, we do not know how to stop. When we can look deeply into the present moment we can look deeply into our true nature and we can discover the ultimate dimension." -- Thich Nhat Hanh

And the reason I think that quote is so significant is because it gets at the core question of spirituality that we've lost in all of this nonsense, and that is, is there an ultimate dimension to be discovered? What could we know about that ultimate dimension? How would we interact with that ultimate dimension?

So now I'm substituting ultimate dimension in the way that I normally talk about extended consciousness, and I'm suggesting that the beauty and the power of what Thich Nhat Hanh and so many others I've talked about on this show, the power of what they're doing is they're misunderstood as talking about some airy-fairy philosophical shit, when in fact they're saying, "No, there really is another dimension out there. There is another energy out there. There is another reality." And if we don't approach it, or at least ask that as a question, we'll never be able to answer the question that you asked. So I think that has to be on the table.

Dr. Richard Grego: I agree. Do you think all of this stuff, from biological robots in a meaningless universe philosophy to the distractions of our commercial culture and propagandized infotainment nature of our media and everything else, do you think that those are designed to prevent us from... Do you think these things are deliberately designed to prevent us from engaging that ultimate dimension that Thich Nhat Hanh talks about?

Alex Tsakiris: Let me turn that around and ask you, do you think it's a possibility we need to consider?

Dr. Richard Grego: Yeah, if it's even possible, it's the most important, right? But why are we being prevented from attaining that and even worse, are there forces deliberately trying to distract us because they can benefit from it?

Now, I can see where that would be the case in the academic world and in the commercial world. I don't know if those people have that profound a view of reality. They just know, if you keep them distracted, addicted, and superficial, they'll buy, and that's all we really give a damn about.

And in the academic world, we keep them scared and conformist and afraid to really do any original thinking. Just mimic the jargon we approve of. It will keep us in power and it contributes to our prestige.

But is there something more?

Like any good private investigator, Rich is good at asking tough questions. Is there something more to the denial of "evil" within academia? Is there something more than a boys-will-be-boys, one-funeral-at-a-time academic clique? Who might stand to gain by a chronically depressed and disheartened population trained to not question their role in an absurdly meaningless universe? Before we can answer those questions, we might want to consider what science is telling us about these extended consciousness realms. We'll start by looking at near-death experience science.

5
WILL YOUR NDE SEND YOU TO HELL?

> *People into the hard sciences like neurophysiology, often ignore a core philosophical question: 'What is the relationship between our unique, inner experience of conscious awareness and material substance?' The answer is: We don't know, and some people are so terrified to say, 'I don't know.'*
> *-Near-Death Experience Pioneer,* **Dr. Raymond Moody**

> **IN THIS CHAPTER**
> - is Near-Death Experience science, really science?
> - is there a hierarchy to consciousness?
> - what do NDEs tell us about evil?

I like the well-known skeptic, Dr. Michael Shermer. He's another science entertainer. But I also understand why folks like author and near-death experience expert David Sunfellow who studied and published, peer-reviewed near-death experience science for 30 years find him annoying:

Alex Tsakiris: Before we started this recording I was telling you that Dr. Michael Shermer is one of my favorite frenemies because he does have a certain style that makes these dialogues entertaining. You shot back, "I can't stomach the guy," and I get that.

I just think we need to be real about what pisses us off about these folks. I can start with myself. I feel sorry for people who have been socially engineered, and mind-controlled into this "biological robot, meaningless universe" shit. It gets drummed into them in school. Then, they grow up and it gets drummed into them every time they turn on the news… Michael Shermer is either a useful idiot in that process or a player, and that can be aggravating, but maybe we need to be open to being entertained by Michael Shermer.

David Sunfellow: Sure, I agree with that… but what's upsetting about Shermer is his refusal to look at the data. If you're going to be a true skeptic, you need to look at the data. "Where's the evidence to support this or that?" You actually have to look at the data to make the decision, you can't just say, "This data is not in my particular worldview, therefore we're not going to consider that.[16]"

Well, David's got a point there. Here's a clip from my interview with Dr. Michael Shermer on *Skeptiko* #379:

Alex Tsakiris: A couple of years ago I interviewed Dr. Jan Holden from the University of North Texas, who, along with Dr. Bruce Greyson from the University of Virginia, are two of the most prominent names in the near-death experience research community. They compiled the book, The Handbook of Near-Death Experiences. This book is primarily for people in the medical community, so they can be familiar with the topic when they encounter someone who has an NDE after cardiac arrest. At the time they first published the book, it referenced over a hundred peer-reviewed papers. Their latest edition references over 200. I don't see that in your book.

Michael Shermer: Well, look, I don't have to cite everybody that's ever written on the subject.

Alex Tsakiris: But you don't cite any of them.

Michael Shermer: Yes, I do, oh yes, I do…

Alex Tsakiris: Pim van Lommel, Sam Parnia, who else?

Michael Shermer: Yeah, yeah...

Alex Tsakiris: You misrepresented both of them, but you at least cite them.

Michael Shermer: But anyway...

Later on in the interview, Dr. Shermer claimed peer-reviewed near-death experience science was a "red herring." To which I would respond by borrowing a phrase from Michael-the-entertainer, "but anyway..."

THE NDE FEAR FACTOR

As we saw in the last chapter, the soft science's (Dr. Shermer has a Ph.D. in history by the way) reliance on the "biological robots in a meaningless universe" meme is not going to get us any closer to understanding the big picture questions we're after, but over the last 20 years, near-death experience science has done more to change the hearts and minds of materialists than anything else. So why do many scientists continue to resist the evidence? It's a question I asked well-known NDE expert and the author of, *The Purpose of Life as Revealed by Near-Death Experiences from Around the World*, David Sunfellow[17].

> **David Sunfellow:** ...most people have a more or less comfortable life... and bringing in some of the data I'm talking about would completely challenge their materialistic, humanistic worldview. That's something most are not going to do. After you've spent a lifetime building a worldview that allows you to operate in the world, the last thing you want to do is let in something that's going to tear that apart.
>
> So I understand why people are defensive... I see reflections in my own life... where I had certain ideas I thought were true. I built my life around those ideas and defended against data that suggested I was wrong. When I did open the door... it dismantled a lot of the things I thought I knew, and I had to rebuild my life in a new way.
>
> **Alex Tsakiris:** Let's hone in on that for a minute, David.

Specifically, what do you think are some of the challenges to that paradigm shift? What do you think we're holding onto with this materialistic belief system? Because at another level, the message coming from near-death experience science seems like an attractive alternative.

David Sunfellow: Well again, I think it boils down to the fact we've created a world that we're comfortable in, that our egos are comfortable in, where we can be the gods of our own worlds, the master of our own worlds, and the things that we learn from near-death experiences challenge that whole system. It's not just about us, there actually are other forces in life much bigger that we have to contend with.

I'm wondering what your answer is to that question.

Alex Tsakiris: I think it's about fear. I/we have constructed a reality that allows me to avoid the things I'm afraid of and hold onto the things that make me feel less afraid. I've built a world around not getting what I don't want and trying to get what I want. And I live in constant fear of jumping outside of that space.

(later)

Alex Tsakiris: Let's talk about "God" and the work of near-death experience researcher, Dr. Jeff Long, who's been on *Skeptiko* several times, and is known for being a radiation oncologist and a near-death experience researcher. He's also known for writing a *New York Times* bestselling book and compiling the largest database of near-death experiences.

... in Dr. Long's second book, *God and the Afterlife*, he asks near-death experiencers, "Is there a God? Is there a moral imperative to this? Is there a hierarchy to this extended consciousness?" And they say, "Absolutely." As a matter of fact, Dr. Long points out that this finding is under-reported by near-death experience researchers.[18]

David Sunfellow: Right.

DECODING: HIERARCHY OF CONSCIOUSNESS

from Skeptiko #327 with Dr. Jeffrey Long:

Dr. Jeff Long: ... we now have over 4,000... this is by far the largest near-death experience study that has ever been conducted.

Alex Tsakiris: You asked people who experienced God or some kind of supreme being about the reality of that experience. And the stat you got back was stunning. 96.2% said, "It was definitely real."

Dr. Jeff Long: Yes. I mean, that's just an amazing percentage... for 96.2% of people to come back and say it's definitely real is a profound message. That really shows how confident they are about what they encountered. That's not surprising because you see huge changes in these people's lives.

Alex Tsakiris: ... I'm not a religious person, I'm not Christian, but I do think, like you said, following the data with regard to near-death experience does bring us to "God", to the moral imperative, to a hierarchy of consciousness, however you want to say it. So let that be a launching point for any thoughts you have about the God issue.

David Sunfellow: Well, the first thought for me is, how is it that we're 40-plus years into modern near-death experience research, how is it that it's taken all of this time for a researcher, like Jeff Long, to come out and actually acknowledge the central role that God plays in these experiences? Why has it been ignored or overlooked by researchers all of these years? I think it has to do with the materialistic culture we're in, the materialistic way that science is kind of forced to look at everything.

HELLISH NDES ARE UNDERREPORTED

Alex Tsakiris: You have an article on your website that is the most comprehensible collection of hellish near-death experiences I've seen. One thing you point out is these hellish near-death experiences are significantly under-reported. They're under-reported by experiencers afraid of facing ridicule and judgement, "Hmm, why were you in hell, what have you done that I don't know about?" And hellish NDEs are also under-reported by NDE researchers who don't know what to do with the hell thing and the Christian baggage that comes with it.

David Sunfellow: Hold on, I'm not talking only about Christian experiences. I'm talking about your atheist on the corner who ends up in a hellish realm. Let's take a look at hell through the window of big data. Let's get all of these stories together, let's put them all on the table, let's do what we can to strip out the inappropriate, destructive inculturations of the various people that are coming to the table with these stories, and let's see if we can identify core truths that run through them that we need to learn from and apply to our particular life and to our particular culture.

Alex Tsakiris: Okay, I'm with you to a certain extent, but I think we've got to do a little reality check. I wanted to play a couple of these clips that I got from televangelist Sid Roth:

Sid Roth: *Now you are about to know what hell has purposely kept hidden from you, it's hell's best kept secret and I'm going to blast it now. (Sid addressing his guest Laurie Ditto) ...how bad was it?*[19]

Laurie Ditto: *Well, I was so depressed, I had planned my suicide different times, and my life just didn't feel... I had hurt and pain, rejection inside of me and I didn't know what to do with it.*

Alex Tsakiris: Here Sid is interviewing a woman named Laurie Ditto who wrote a book about her hellish experience, which is more terrifying than the worst horror movie you've ever seen.

Laurie Ditto: *To always be in pain and to know that it kept ramping up and it was going to keep getting worse and worse* *and worse and it was never going to end, that was the thing. It wasn't like you could reach a pinnacle. In hell, it worked the same as in heaven, my full brain operated. I knew every scripture that I've ever read and it made complete sense and it was completely righteous that I was in hell. And there were people there, they were just like me. They knew Jesus is the Lord God, but they refused to obey him. They say, "We love you, we love you," but the scriptures teach, if you love me then obey me.*

Alex Tsakiris: And I think that's why so many people are a little bit taken aback by these hellish accounts that primarily come from the fundamentalist Christian crowd.

David Sunfellow: ... what do you mean by that?

Alex Tsakiris: Her conclusion stands-in stark contrast to what near-death experience researchers tell us. Just listen to my interview with Jeff Long, he says exactly the opposite of what she's saying. He says, "I've compiled all of this data, I've looked at all of it, there is an infinitely loving God, not there to punish us, not there to demand that we follow his creed."

He says the data contradicts the conclusion Laurie came to. She is entitled to her experience, I'm not taking that away, but I'm just saying in the game of trying to figure out what's really going on in this extended consciousness realm we have to follow the data, this isn't the data.

David Sunfellow: ... Jeffrey Long's research very much supports the idea that there are these hellish realms. In fact, here's a quote from him, "The most frightening things that I've encountered in my life are not from fictional books or scary movies, but from near-death experiences with hellish content." So he's not saying there's no hell, he is just saying that God is not sending people to hell, which is a common theme among near-death experiences as a whole.

Alex Tsakiris: I think his data is saying something different... He's saying, there are a lot of scary movies out there, and you may have to watch a scary movie that may be on your path, but don't take the freak'n scary movie too seriously. It's a lesson. Don't go off and interpret it as some kind of reality or you've lost the path again.

Because tomorrow comes and you have to do the best you can. And you'll encounter other people who, even though they seem evil or satanic or whatever, they're doing the best they can. They're trying to figure things out and they may be making horrible mistakes and horrible decisions, but God doesn't love them any less than he loves you and he isn't waiting to freak'n punish them as soon as he gets his hands on them.

David Sunfellow: Well Alex, I agree with your main point. I think what's happening here is, using the typical Christian experiences of hell, what we're confronted with are experiences like the one you've just shared. The way that I've come to understand it is you have to separate the big picture, which is what you just shared, everything is wonderful in the universe...

Alex Tsakiris: What would you say about not getting too hung up on the hellish/evil thing?

David Sunfellow: ..I think taking a step further back, people universally report, when they have these near-death experiences and they get into a place where they become one with God, they universally describe it as wonderful, spectacular, astonishing. Everything is in its perfect place, everything is beautiful, everything serves the whole.

I think hell needs to be looked at from that perspective. Yes, hell exists. It exists just as this world does because this world also is a dream world, it's created by mental constructs of various kinds. But that said, it plays a part in the overall scheme of things, it needs to be honored and recognized. We need to understand it so we can know how to live our lives in a balanced, more healthy fashion. That's how I would say it.

Alex Tsakiris: ... I'm saying, we're never going to understand it, that's off the table. We should be incredibly humble about tightly holding on to any "lessons" we take away and avoid turning them into our cult/religion.

I would draw an analogy to parenting. You said you have four kids, I have four kids. That's wonderful. We love our kids. Every one of my kids needs a different kind of love and a different kind of life lesson. One might need a hellish experience in order to learn a lesson. Another one doesn't need that at all. What do you think about that?

David Sunfellow: Alex, I think that's exactly true and the way I think that these experiences, especially the dramatic, 'Jesus saved me, Jesus is the Lord of the world, you can't get out of hell without his help' stories. I think the correct way to understand them is as a developmental thing. We all need different things.

...I think that a part of near-death experiences is also developmental. It's not just that you go to these realms that exist independent of yourself, but it's actually that you're helping create them and you go to the realms, hell or otherwise, that are reflective of your particular state of consciousness, your particular needs at the time, in the same way you just described how our children have different needs. I think that's exactly what's happening with these Christian experiences of hell. This is what they need to help wake them up.

ENCOUNTERS WITH THE LIGHT

Alex Tsakiris: ... we've had a number of discussions on this show about the nature of evil and we all are trying to understand how we're supposed to process the horrors we see in the world. I always go to satanic ritual abuse, particularly the abuse of children, because it seems to remove some of the ambiguity we have about evil. Most of us look at drone strikes of a Yemen wedding and think it sounds pretty frickin evil, but we acknowledge there's at least some geopolitical complexity to it. But, abducting a 5-year-old from a playground, torturing him, and killing him, that's just pure evil. Do you have any thoughts on the nature of evil?

David Sunfellow: ... there are two massive life-changing forces represented in the near-death experience. The first one is encounters with the light. Everyone describes it as completely life changing. The experience tells us that God loves us unconditionally. Everything is fine in the universe, everything is unfolding beautifully, everything is perfect. The other huge pillar of near-death experiences is championed by the life review and that we need to be responsible...

My niece one time asked me, "Uncle David, with all of the research you've done on all of these different spiritual paths, what is it about near-death experiences that you've learned?" And my answer was, "...the little things in life are the big things."

Near-death experience science is a terrific bridge from the here-and-now consensus reality doctors need to work with and those experiences that transcend time and space in a way we don't understand. But as you'll see in the next chapter, it seems that many of the spiritual signposts that emerge from these more rigorous explorations of extended reality are often co-opted by those with a different agenda.

6
WHY IS THE BIBLE PRO ROMAN?

"God isn't religious."
- **Wm. Paul Young**, *progressive Christian, and author of the super bestselling book, The Shack*

> **IN THIS CHAPTER**
> - the Roman playbook
> - which Jesus?
> - are Christians to blame?

There's a clip from the movie *Gladiator* where the aging Emperor, Marcus Aurelius, chooses his beloved Roman general Maximus as his heir.[20] His son doesn't take kindly to the idea and chooses to kill his father, and condemns Maximus and his family to death. Although the movie is fiction, people who know Roman history, like Joseph Atwill, will tell you that the movie is spot on when it comes to the kind of political manipulation, mind control, and conspiracy shenanigans the Romans mastered. The only questions are how far did the Romans take it and when did it stop?

(from *Skeptiko* #464)

Alex Tsakiris: I'm going to make the case because I believe it to be true, that today's guest is the most important biblical scholar in modern times. And while that might sound like a big claim, it actually goes further than that because the

Bible, whether we like it or not, is so deeply woven into our culture, our legal system, our political system, and our collective psyche, that the most important biblical scholar is someone we should pay attention to. But again, that's just my opinion. I'm going to make the case in this show, and you can judge for yourself.

Joseph Atwill's proposition is rather simple, the Bible is pro-Roman and the best, and really the only non-metaphysical explanation for this provable historical fact, is that the Bible was just another page from the Roman well-worn playbook of political mind manipulation and control tactics.

Now, I know that's a lot for people to take in so let me clarify. The fact that the Bible was a political PSYOP doesn't mean it can't be transmitting deep spiritual truths. It can, just like many great books can. And it doesn't mean the Bible can't be the foundation for some wonderful traditions of knowledge that are transmitted through those deep spiritual truths. And it certainly doesn't mean that in some way we don't totally understand, people are connecting through the Bible with some kind of spiritually transformative experience. But what it does mean is if the Bible was from its beginning, part of a social engineering and political control mechanism, then we have to deal with that first... So Joseph Atwill, fantastic to have you back. It's always such a great treat for me to have a chance to talk with you. So welcome.

Joseph Atwill: Thank you for having me Alex, it's my pleasure.

(later)

Alex Tsakiris: ... the way I always try and explain this to people is through the pro-Roman angle. Because you just said the big switch for you was looking at the Bible as Roman literature, or we could take it one step further, as a Roman PSYOP, because that's the implications of what you're saying. But just as Roman literature, one of the key pivot points for me was this idea that the Bible is pro-Roman.

So I was listening to you and (noted biblical scholar) Dr. Bob Price, and you were talking about some of the more recent scholarships you can point to and say, "That's strangely pro-Roman."

Joseph Atwill: Well, just to explain the passage you were describing, Jesus says to his disciples, "When asked to carry the pack, go the extra mile." This is a famous expression in our vernacular and people don't understand what it means. What he's referring to is the requirement in an occupied nation. And remember, at this point, Rome is a prison of nations basically. It has conquered all of these areas, and one of the aspects of the colonization was that a Roman soldier and all Roman soldiers had this power, could ask any individual who was a member of the conquered nation to carry their backpack for one mile. And this was why they had milestones, that's what the expression means. It refers to the distance that a conscripted native would have to carry a Roman backpack. And they were heavy, they weighed like 35, 40 pounds, so it was a big deal. But Jesus said, "No, no, don't go one mile, go the extra mile."

Alex Tsakiris: ... right, it's completely out of sync with the political reality of the times. it would be like telling one of those Antifa goons, "Go shine the boots of an investment banker. And I'll tell you what, don't just shine one pair of his boots, shine two."

Joseph Atwill: This was the most violent century in the history of Israel. Rome had conquered it, surreptitiously. They were able to become basically allied with one of the native Kings, the family of Herod, who were the Roman puppets. And then they were able to basically slither into power one inch at a time. And then finally they just were the authority. The Hasmonean Kingdom was over and now you had the Herodian era. Herod was the tax collector of Rome.

Now, during this period from, the year 1 through 135 CE, the period during which you had the Ministry of Jesus purportedly, you had just one revolution after another. Rome insisted upon placing images of the Caesars inside the temples. It was the only real requirement of colonization in terms of religion. The Roman colonies could have any religion they wanted, Rome couldn't care less, but they had to permit Caesar worship. The Imperial Cult was a great propaganda tool, and so it was just mandated. Everyone had to have images of Caesar, and Herod basically was carrying out this edict inside the Temple of Jerusalem. The religious Jews saw this, of course, as completely in opposition to their religious fundamentals. And so they rebel, and there was one after another, after another.

And these weren't, a couple hundred people, you have to look at the history closely and see just how catastrophic the rebellions were to the Roman Empire. There were three major rebellions and perhaps a dozen minor ones. The famous rebellion of 66 through 73, where the temple was destroyed, in that period the Jewish revolutionaries were actually able to drive Rome out of their nation and establish an independent nation-state right in the middle of the Roman Empire. So, this was just an absolute catastrophe for Rome's colonial interests, and so this led to the Seven-Year War. But that wasn't the end of it.

Then in 112, 115, you had another rebellion and with this rebellion, there's some historical documentation, but in general, it's been swept under the rug, and it was an absolute blood bath. The Jews were able to gain military control over Cyprus, and they genocide the entire gentile population, supposedly a quarter-million people. They drove Rome completely out of Egypt for a period of time. And it's just incredible to think about this. This is Rome's breadbasket.

So, Rome was able eventually to get that under control, and then the rebellion broke out again in 133 AD. This was the one where you ended up with the diaspora, they just wouldn't let the Jews even come into Israel because they felt that the geographical aspect of the religion was part of what was fomenting rebellion. But that rebellion, again, it was just catastrophic to the Roman Empire.

THE CHUTZPAH OF CHRISTIAN APOLOGETICS

I realize that all 1st and 2nd-century history can get a little Bible geeky, but it's central to the Christian proposition. But in order to bring this conversation into the 21st century, allow me to share an interview with Joe Atwill (*Skeptiko* #386) where we deconstruct the "did Jesus exist" question as it's usually discussed by thoughtful Christians who at least care enough to give history and logic a fair shot in this debate.[21] For this we used a recent presentation from Steven Crowder's popular YouTube channel where his co-host Gerald Morgan (who we had a nice email exchange with but were never able to corral into an on-air interview) re-hashed some common Christian arguments regarding the historicity of Jesus[22]:

> **Alex Tsakiris:** ... There's this new force among Christians. They seem to have a political chutzpah now. There's Jordan Peterson, Dinesh D'Souza, Steven Crowder and I would even throw my friend Rupert Sheldrake in the category of saying, "Yeah, I'm a Christian, so what? It's not relevant. Listen to what I say and evaluate my opinions on these other topics because I'm right." That confidence, I don't think we've seen in a while and when we contrast that with some of the, I'll use the term 'libtard' silliness, there's a certain traction they get because the left and the liberal point of view has been so exaggerated and has lost any connection with logic or reason, but these Christians are standing tall in comparison. What do you think Joe?
>
> **Joe Atwill:** Well, I think that's true and I think that there are a lot of Christians who, as you say, stand against

globalism, can be seen in some way standing against globalism because they're trying to retain the culture and religion in the smaller group. They don't want to sacrifice that, their cohesiveness and their values as globalism is just evaporating all of this stuff and taking it over with this atheistic machine world.

I would just point out that Christians are actually fairly easy to herd into globalism to the extent that the slaves seldom know they're being enslaved because the controllers/globalists are very, very smart.

I'll give one really good example to show you my point — one of the first globalisms that was ever created was the feudal system whereby all of the different ethnicities, races, and cultures in Europe were globalized. You basically had a monolithic religion that was used to set up the slave state and the religion was Christianity. Christianity was the mind-control device that the oligarchs had at that time to be able to set up a system where people wouldn't rebel because they believed that there would be this workers' paradise. They just believed the representative of the Pontiff Maximus, the Pope, who was just obviously a mask for the ruling families.

Alex Tsakiris: It's a great point. The one thing I'd remind people of, what I'm really hoping to do in this dialogue we're having, is to give folks a fresh idea of how to answer this question, did Jesus exist, on a deeper level than it's normally presented, on a deeper level than Steven, despite me liking and admiring his work, a deeper level than he and other Christians are generally able to do.

With that, I'm going to move onto the second clip (from Steven Crowder 6/6/2018 Did Jesus Exist):

Steven Crowder: *I had never really heard that position, that people were legitimately out there saying that Jesus was not a historical figure.*

Alex Tsakiris: Stop right there. A smart guy. Likable guy. A Christian guy who hasn't heard that maybe the historical account of Jesus isn't what we've been told?

Joe Atwill: Well, he's not conversant with modern scholarship, where the question of Jesus' historicity is being waged.

Alex Tsakiris: The next topic that I really wanted to throw on the table, which I think is so important, and it's really a stunner when you think about it which is, should Christians care?

Gerald Morgan: Well, I mean, a lot of Christians don't think you have to go through this process to figure out, was Jesus a real person or not? They mainly just give you that and focus on, what did he do and what did he say?

Alex Tsakiris: So again, should Christians care?

Joe Atwill: Well, if they want their faith to be based on something that's real, they should care.

Alex Tsakiris: The question that I think people have to ask themselves is, am I part of an organization whose primary purpose is manipulation, control, and social structure, or am I following the wisdom of a genuine historical spiritual master who walked this world? I do not understand for a second how a Christian can claim to be a Christian and not have this question be central to what they're about. And I would go one step further, this is very Joe Atwill-ian, if you don't care, you're so far into the mind-control project that is Christianity you're probably a lost cause at the start. If this isn't a burning question to you, you've already bought into the cult aspect of the whole thing.

Joe Atwill: I couldn't agree more. I mean, if this isn't an important question that means reason has been turned off and basically you are a cult follower even though you wouldn't want to admit it publicly. But if you aren't able to defend the historicity of Jesus, in my opinion, some part of your intellect has been switched off that is central to living a rational life.

Steven Crowder: *In fact, even rabid atheist (biblical scholar and UNC professor), Bart Ehrman (acknowledged that Jesus was historical) ... read that quote.*

Gerald Morgan: *With respect to Jesus, we have numerous independent accounts of his life and the sources lying behind the gospels (and the writings of Paul). Sources that originated in Jesus' native tongue, Aramaic, that can be dated to within just a year or two of his life before the religion moved to convert pagans in droves.*

Alex Tsakiris: Let me jump in here first with the Bart Ehrman thing because this drives me nuts. It's back to what I was saying, which Jesus do you want to prove or disprove ever existed? When Christians latch onto Bart Ehrman's Jesus, I think they have no clue what they're talking about.

Here's a UNC religious scholar, who seems very keen on targeting Christians for his books, yet he has this very overt approach, he calls himself an agnostic, but anyone can see the atheist position that he holds. His conclusion with regard to Jesus is this kind of nomadic, very minor figure of the time who's this "rebel without a cause," fighting these little skirmishes just like thousands and thousands of rebels who were crucified at the time. You've got a heck of a long way to go from Bart Ehrman to Jesus Christ, son of God, savior of the world. A lot of people don't realize that and it's intellectually dishonest for people like Gerald in this argument to say, "Well, even Bart Ehrman says that Jesus existed." He's not pointing to a Jesus that any Christian would recognize.

Joe Atwill: There are three categories. You have Jesus was God, Jesus was a man and Jesus was a fictional character. The second two categories are equally destructive to the first. If he was just a man, then there shouldn't be a Christian religion at this point. If he didn't exist, it's preposterous, so it doesn't matter. If a scholar is in camp two or camp three, it's not something that can be used as the basis for a religion. They shouldn't really be citing Bart Ehrman in this way.

Alex Tsakiris: Let me go on to the next one.

Gerald Morgan: *The Bible didn't just fall out of the sky. These are writings from people over, literally thousands of years, for the Od/New Testament combined that we kind of pulled together. These are books. So, we can go to each one of these letters and say, "Is this a reliable source?" and put it under some scrutiny.*

Alex Tsakiris: What I hear Gerald saying, "Hey, it's an established fact, we know where these books came from, we know who authored them, so let's move on and take the gospels at face value." It's a preposterous claim but what are the basic arguments that we can make about that?

Joe Atwill: The statement is simply incorrect. There is no agreement, whatsoever, from scholars about when they were written or by whom. The idea that it's just self-evident and an established scholarship is preposterous.

Alex Tsakiris: Okay, let's leave it at that. Now, we're going to talk about Josephus.

Joe Atwill: Good old Josephus.

Alex Tsakiris: I have these *Skeptiko* moments that I cherish, and I still remember the moment in our last conversation I think it was where you were talking through Josephus along the lines of the accepted narrative and then at some point, you said, "You know, really Alex, it makes more sense to look at Josephus as a completely fictional character," and that was just a drop the mic kind of moment for me, but let's see what Gerald has to say here.

Gerald Morgan: *Let's just go to historians from the time period. The first entry, a Jewish historian, Josephus. He mentions Jesus in his work, The Antiquities of the Jews, in the interpolated, and that word basically means, they weren't inserted. There were some problems with the document saying* that they had been changed. They were absolutely right, they had been. But we now have documents that weren't and we know that they were totally fine. He's a first-century Jewish historian, right? He's not a Christian out there pushing his views of who Jesus was.

Alex Tsakiris: So much to pull apart and again, this is going to get a little bit Bible geeky folks, but it's the path you have to take if you care about looking at this question in a meaningful way rather than the spoon-fed way that we so often get.

Who was Josephus, Joe?

Joe Atwill: Well, as history gives him to us, he was a Jewish scholar. He had been a general, a cohort of Messianic Jews in the war against Rome that began in 66CE. He was captured by the Flavian generals. He then was a turncoat, abandoned Judaism, and basically became a follower of the Flavian Caesar government. Following the war, they brought Josephus to Rome. The Flavians then had become the royal family and Josephus was given a townhouse in the Emperor's palace and was told to write the history of the war.

So, two great works were produced. One was basically about the history of the Jews and the other was about the war between the Messianic Jews and the Romans.

The idea that Josephus was some kind of independent Jewish voice is incorrect. He was, of course, a court historian of the Flavians.

Alex Tsakiris: Let's stop right there because that's an important point. That's not disputed. I mean, no one disputes that.

Joe Atwill: No.

Alex Tsakiris: He's writing these histories under the employ of the Roman Caesar. So, that's point one. Why is Gerald repeating this narrative that we often hear?

The dismantling of the Christian narrative by means of the history of Josephus and his impossible to believe "Come, my pesky Jewish brothers give unto Caesar," is the narrative that should be front and center to every discussion of Christian apologetics. The fact that it's not suggests something more is going on.

CHRISTIAN COMPLICITY

(returning to *Skeptiko* #465)

Alex Tsakiris: I don't think Christians understand how they have become complicit in some of this evil because they don't understand the PSYOP. Do you have any thoughts on that?

DECODING: PSYOP

From our friends at the Department of Defense (with a couple of embedded comments). Psychological operations, or PSYOPS, "convey selected information and indicators to foreign (right... just foreign...never you and I) audiences to influence their emotions, motives, objective reasoning, and ultimately the behavior of foreign governments, organizations, groups, and individuals (again, only nasty foreigners). The purpose of psychological operations is to induce or reinforce attitudes and behavior favorable to the originator's objectives."[23]

Joseph Atwill: Just that it's true. If you don't understand the origin of the cult, and I think that's the correct phrase, that you're involved with, and you don't understand the purpose for the rulers, basically you cannot avoid being complicit in evil because it starts out with secrecy. I mean, you don't need secrecy if there is no evil afoot.

Since Christianity is ruled through secrecy and comes from secrecy, then there are purposes for it, which had to be kept secret. So you are complicit, and you really should, I think if you're honest with yourself, try to see if there is some way of understanding the origin of religion.

Alex Tsakiris: See, I guess I hammer on this from a couple of angles, and people don't like either one but we'll try it again. If someone was to really do a deep dive into the Christian pedo thing and the pedo pope thing, and they were to come out on the other side and say, "Wow, overwhelming evidence that at the highest level, that institution has been compromised to the extent that the burden of proof is on them to show that there isn't systematic abuse of children going on from highest down to the lowest levels of that organization." If someone was to come to that conclusion, which I think a reasonable person could, then what do you do on Sunday when you go to the Catholic Church and they pass the plate around? Well, you do what you've always done, you throw a few bucks in there, but now your complicity really becomes clear. You've put money in the plate, and you now know where some of that money is going, and that kind of hits us at another level.

But that is still not the conversation we're having; the conversation is that the Bible is Roman literature. It's pro-Roman. And you have to deal with the implications of that before you jump ahead and tackle the pedo pope thing 2000 years later.

Joseph Atwill: ... people really should take a pass through the quality of the evidence in *Caesar's Messiah* because what it does is it takes just two texts and lays them side by side. And then it says, look, here are these relationships which any normal person can see are completely linked. Everything is self-evident from that point on, Alex. You don't really need to do any kind of complicated analysis to understand why Christianity was produced by Rome. They wanted another version of Judaism, they wanted something that was pro-Roman.

Alex Tsakiris: You've done this a hundred times Joe, but just quickly go over some of those parallels between what Josephus is writing and the Bible... And most importantly, Josephus' spiritually revelatory experience in which he claims that Judaism was wrong, and that what the Messiah was really all about, what the Second Coming was really all about, was Roman Caesar, and that therefore... I mean, this was so transparent at this point. Therefore, this is why we should be pro-Roman because this is what has been prophesied all along.

Joseph Atwill: Yeah, it depends how you would want to characterize it, but there might be as many as 70 events which are linked, between the Adult Ministry of Jesus that is characterized in the Gospels and the history of the war that Josephus recorded. Some of the parallels are actually quite complicated and most of the critics of *Caesar's Messiah* would go to the most complex [portion] and say, "Look, it's a hallucination by Atwill, this is parallelomania" But the fact is, you can basically look at events which are not complicated, which are in fact, simply the historical events and see that the story of Jesus was made up of events from the war. His Adult Ministry starts at the Sea of Galilee, where he tells his disciples that if they follow him they will become fishers of men. This is the same location where Titus Flavius begins his military campaign at the Sea of Galilee. And he sinks the Jewish fishing fleet, and then they fish for the Jews with their Spears. The locations of the two stories are the same and occur in the same sequence.

So, Jesus, after the Galilean Ministry goes into Jerusalem, Titus does the same. You have a series of historical events. Basically, Jerusalem is encircled with a wall, you have the abomination of desolation. And then you have the temple being raised. I mean, these events are known to be basically from the Jewish war. These are prophecies in the Gospels but are historical events with Jesus.

You have the amazing three crucified, one survived, taken down by Joseph of Arimathea parallel, which came out in

Caesar's Messiah even though it's just so incredibly obvious that the two stories are the same. Why it had never become part of modern scholarship is just beyond me.

There was one other scholar, Cliff Carrington, an Australian autodidact who had also noticed it but he hadn't published it. So we were unaware of one another's work.

Alex Tsakiris: And we should just add so we don't get Bible geeky too quick...Big picture, these writings of Josephus, who really, you pierced through that paper-thin idea of Josephus and suggest, let's just say this is the Roman court historians, it's their version. But what's really important is among biblical scholars, if you really push them, they won't even disagree with the idea that the Gospels, they say are "dependent" on Josephus. Which means, it's kind of this flowery way of softly admitting that Josephus was used to writing the Gospels. That should be game over. And it's interesting to me that it isn't.

And why isn't it "game over"...

7
THE GOD PROGRAM VS. ECSTASY

Magneto: *Are you a God-fearing man, Senator? That is such a strange phrase. I've always thought of God as a teacher; a bringer of light, wisdom, and understanding.*
- X-men

> **IN THIS CHAPTER**
> - new boss, same as the old boss
> - cut loose and fly

Joe Atwill's examination of the co-opting of Christianity isn't an answer to the evil question, but it is a teardown of the idea that cherished religious beliefs hold exclusive rights to the answer. Few, however, are willing to take the next step and consider the possibility our modern religious institutions are part of a larger social engineering conspiracy. David Icke is an exception. I interviewed the controversial conspiracy theorist who many know as the "Lizard guy" because of what he's said and written about reptilian aliens from another planet (a claim best left for another time). As of this writing, David has been banned from YouTube for advocating free thought, free speech, and non-violent resistance. And while Icke doesn't always score 100% regarding the details of his claims and the science to support them, he's still one of the bravest, broadest thinkers of our time with a much higher-than-hall-of-fame batting average when it comes to truth-telling and fact-checking. Here's what he had to say about religion as a social engineering project:[24]

Alex Tsakiris: Some people get offended when their religious beliefs are challenged. They feel like religious beliefs are protected beliefs, but others see religion as an extension of the social engineering project.

David Icke: I call it the "God program." All of the different names and different rituals obscure the fact that it's a very simple blueprint: "What are you?" "I'm a Christian." "What does that mean?" "Well, I go to church and this man in a frock (women often now) tells me what God wants me to do." "Okay, well that's interesting." "And he tells me the consequences of me not doing what God wants me to do." "Okay, you?" "Oh, I'm a Muslim." "What does that mean?" "Well, I go to the mosque and this man in a frock, he tells me what God wants me to do, and what God will do if I don't do what God says, which is what this man in a frock tells me he says." "Okay, you?" "Oh, I follow Judaism." "What does that mean?" "Oh, I go to the synagogue and this man in a frock, he tells me what God wants me to do, and they'll be hell and damnation if I don't do what he says, and that's what Judaism is."

And so you go on and you go on and you go on. What are those people in frocks actually doing, Alex? They're getting in the spaces between the five-sense mind and expanded consciousness. They do not want a direct connection. Even the word *connection* is not correct, it's only human language…it's not even a connection because [in essence] one does not connect, it just is. And what happens is we get a disconnection of influence. It doesn't mean we're not still part of the great forever, we always are and always will be. It's that it's not influencing us because of this perceptual isolation, which religion has played a major part in.

What you had were forms of culture that for all their flaws, and there were many, practiced a direct connection with what they perceived as the creator, or what I call The One. And then religion came in and created that blueprint and we got the, "Only through this can you get to God, only through me, only through believing me and what I say, can you get there. And by the way, we're going to give you a story. We're going to give you a series of rules and regulations, and if you don't follow them, well, have you ever stoked the fires of hell? That's where you're going, mate."

And then, the impact of all of that, what was it? It was a tiny, tiny perceptual state that's being sold here. You can't question it because you're a blasphemer. If you do, you're out, you're not one of us anymore.

But as people started to reject that, [next] came mainstream science, and we went from a situation where you can only get to the state of expanded consciousness, as I would call it, if you do what we tell you, because we know what God wants...actually, there is no state of expanded consciousness. There's just you and you come out of nowhere, three score years and ten if you're lucky, and then you go back into nowhere.

And now basically, you've got these two working simultaneously, science through technology and the technocracy that's developing, controlled by technocrats, is now becoming more and more dominant, and there's a common theme. Just look at the common themes everywhere that this system, the cult behind this system, is emphasizing everywhere that you cannot have a direct connection with expanded states of consciousness.

Controversial, free-thinking figures like David Icke have an important part to play in our rebooted understanding of why evil matters because they can remind us of what we already know. Icke's take on religion is an example. We intuitively understand that our relationship with God could never be anything other than personal. It can't be brokered or mediated by sacred texts or sage-on-the-stage preachers. We know this;

we just forget it until we're reminded. I was reminded again when I interviewed the great spiritual luminaire and out-of-body experiencer, Jurgen Ziewe[25]:

> **Jurgen Ziewe:** The main issue that gets lost in religion is liberation and freedom. There's always this tendency of wanting to own people, wanting to own something.
>
> **Alex Tsakiris:** The ego.
>
> **Jurgen Ziewe:** Yeah, wanting to limit it, but the end result is liberation from all concepts, from all demarcations, it's total liberation. If that aspect is missing then I'm afraid we are not seeing the bigger picture, not fulfilling our whole potential. To me that has always been the number one thing. The freedom to go beyond out limitations, go beyond our identifications and be able to dynamically experience a new world every moment, every day without any boundaries, without saying, "Oh, this is how it is. This is what it's all about." No, we're just discovering it again and again, because we are now part of that thing we are discovering. And in discovering it we are discovering ourselves which is it.
>
> And there lies the incredible liberation and also there lies the ecstasy it brings. There's ecstasy to be found in living every moment because we are not tied up, we're not tied to one single thing, to one belief, to one theory, to one model. We transcend that and we are opening ourselves up to being explorers, not knowing what is to come next. And it's beautiful because we already know we are it and we cannot get lost. Whatever we explore and discover there is another level of our ecstasy, of our ecstatic living.
>
> And any beliefs which don't allow us this exploration of freedom, they're just limiting us. I'm not anti-religious because they create a scaffold. But once we've built the sculpture, we don't need the scaffolding. We are it. That's the thing with religions, that's why I find them always limiting. But religious people don't like to talk about freedom,

they don't like that word very much.

If the freedom and ecstasy Jurgen has experienced is available to everyone why can't more of us find it? As we'll see in the next chapter, this may be because we've been conditioned to look away by our evil-friendly pop-cultural messaging system.

8
THE MOST EVIL ALEISTER CROWLEY

> *There is a pain — so utter —*
> *It swallows substance up —*
> *Then covers the Abyss with Trance —*
> *So Memory can step*
> *Around — across — upon [sic] it —*
> *As One within a Swoon —*
> *Goes safely — where an open eye —*
> *Would drop Him — Bone by Bone —.*

- **Emily Dickinson**, *American poet, 1955*

> **IN THIS CHAPTER**
> - evil influencers
> - transgression
> - the moral imperative

When you look into evil, the name Aleister Crowley pops up a lot. Fans of the famous early 20th-century occultist see him as an iconoclastic rebel and bringer of light, while his detractors see him as... well...stick around for the next two chapters and find out.[26] We'll start with author, researcher, and former Crowley follower, Jasun Horsley:

Jasun Horsley: Where I tend to start with Crowley and it seems to me, what makes him indisputably significant is his influence, and from two perspectives. The proof of his influence is indisputable. I mean, the easy go-to is pop music of the 60s and 70s. He's on the cover of *Sgt. Pepper's Lonely Hearts Club Band*[27] and he's cited in David Bowie's *Hunky Dory*[28], which was very influential for me as an adolescent, and also on Jimmy Page and Marilyn Manson. There's just no end. He's influenced several decades and several different musical movements. From r the one side, there's that, irrefutable.

But the other side is how did he have that much influence and how intentional was that? I look at *The Vice of Kings*, and the evidence that Crowley was not what he seems, in terms of this creative occult outlier, this iconic [unclear] is pursuing these extreme transgressions in order to liberate humanity[29]. That's half the story, but it's also maybe half of a cover story. And that his influence, I think, was at least partially assisted, let's say, just as there's evidence that Crowley was an intelligence agent and an operative, and was functioning at that level.

It tends to be that the biographies have separated those two things out. On the one hand, he's just an independent artist, writer, and occultist, on the other hand, he also dabbled in intelligence work, and they're almost like separate things.

Now, the connecting areas, of course, he was a member of occult AA which was a splinter of the OTO.

DECODING: PURIFICATION THROUGH TRANSGRESSION

Acts of extreme transgression pop up a lot in occult and esoteric lore. The history of this "opposite day" ethos can be traced at least as far back as the Sabbatean Frankist cults of the 17th and 18th centuries. These nihilist groups preached "redemption through sin." They advocated "the sacred sin" and demanded the annihilation of moral religion or ethical belief systems in favor of, "if we cannot all be saints, let us all be sinners." They believed the "true way" was the path of evil in order to bring deliverance to the world.[30]

Alex Tsakiris: Hold on, before we bury people, there are so many parts of that. We bury people with all these acronyms and we bury people with the cover story. But I do want to back up because when you talk about the cover story, we also have to understand the other touchpoint that today, Crowley is inside of the magic culture that is kind of a growing subculture, a Netflix culture. It's interwoven through all that, the idea of the occult, that there's something hidden, that there's something you don't know about, but it's a deeper truth. And there's this "do what thou wilt," famous ethos that is woven through our culture in another way. We don't quite understand its origins until people tell you about Aleister Crowley, and they kind of whisper it in your ear, and then you think, "Oh, wow, you mean there's this other secret Sage of the esoteric, that I need to kind of get in touch with?"

Let me do this if I can. I pulled out some clips, from some really excellent interviews you've done. Let me play some of those.

Jasun Horsley: *My first contact with Crowley was through David Bowie, the album* Hunky Dory, *which I heard in my brother's bedroom, and that might seem like a trivial thing or an odd place to start, but how a virus enters us is very key. I think, how open we are, how vulnerable we are in that moment, is going to determine how infected we are. And I'd say that that was the case with the Crowley virus, that there was a delivery device, it was a combination of the culture and my family environment and David Bowie, who I discovered through my brother, who was never a David Bowie fan, and I was very rarely in his bedroom because he didn't let me hang around with him at all, he was an older brother. So I think, you talk about priming, like if you have a really positive experience of something the first time around, then you're going to be much more susceptible to ignoring the negative aspects of it because of that initial priming.*

> So in some weird way, I think I was primed for Crowley by that combination of hearing David Bowie sing his name in my brother's attic bedroom.

Alex Tsakiris: What are some of your thoughts listening to that again?

Jasun Horsley: Well, it's still going on, that's the thing. The reason I write these books as I do, and this latest one about Hollywood is getting much more specific, I'm trying to extract the virus.

Alex Tsakiris: What if it really is about deception? What if, not even so much part of your personal journey, it's an unnecessary step along your personal journey? Over and over again our culture has told us Crowleyan, it's cool. Maybe we don't have to go there, because there are two ways to read what you're saying. One is to say, it's there and you've got to deal with it, and the other is, let's be informed beforehand so maybe we can step around the pothole in the first place.

Jasun Horsley: It makes sense, certainly, but this is a sort of conundrum I have. I also have it around psychedelics because I feel that psychedelics was a mistake for me by and large. And therefore, maybe I can use my experience of them to help others avoid the same pitfalls. This is definitely the case with Crowley and occultism, I would warn others against it.

This is right to the core of your questioning of why evil matters. Because you're talking about the allure and the cool of Crowley and all of that stuff, very prominent in our culture since the 1960s on. It's this meme that's been generated.

...it's not really fruitful if you just dismiss evil, if you just say it's evil, stay away from it, that doesn't allow for understanding and it demonizes and it scapegoats, it just perpetuates this division. And of course, Crowley himself promoted evil, and that was part of his cool. So the people who think that Crowley's cool are not going to be discouraged by people saying he's evil. Right? That's the problem.

Alex Tsakiris: Yeah, I'm trying to draw attention to the fact that we've been put in a box. Evil is either this very narrowly defined thing that this old book tells you about, or it's completely denied. It's the "do what thou wilt" denial of evil that's not only from Crowley but if you look at it in the scientific realms it's embedded in the message of scientific materialism, "Of course there's no evil... I mean, there isn't even free will... there's nothing... you're nothing." How could there be evil in that?

DO WHAT THOU WILT VS THE MORAL IMPERATIVE

Jasun Horsley: I do believe there's an innate moral sense that we have biologically, even though we have a sense of what's right and wrong in any given moment.

And so I think that any kind of deception is sourced in self-deception.

Alex Tsakiris: That is a beautiful point. I think it's a central point to all of this -- there is a moral imperative. And again, that's my approach, which is to say that's the evidence folks, the evidence. If you look at near-death experiences, if you look at all of the wisdom traditions, if you look at all of the accumulated knowledge throughout time, most everyone's personal experience contains a sense of what's right and wrong.

And I think you just made a beautiful point that deception is violating that. I think that might get us closer to...I hate to go with the definition of evil, but that's where everyone wants to go. I think that starts creeping towards a definition of evil.

... So maybe evil is that action that wants to pull a soul into the darkness because that's where they feel most comfortable.

Jasun's experience with dark Crowley-ian forces is not unique. In fact, as we're about to learn, Alister Crowley's influence on popular culture is greater than ever.

9
SATANIC PANIC

"Shining a strong light on depravity or stupidity makes it run for cover or bare its fangs."

- **Kim**, *from the Skeptiko forum*

> **IN THIS CHAPTER**
> - Crowley apologists
> - $10 million goes a long way in West Memphis
> - the deception game

Lawyers know how the legal system really works. That's important when it comes to sorting out something like "satanic panic." On one hand, satanic panic is about the very real fact that Satan hysteria has led to innocent people being convicted of crimes they didn't commit. But on the other hand, as you'll see in this interview with attorney and investigative journalist William Ramsey, "satanic panic" has become a get-out-of-jail-free card for crimes that are... well, there's no other way to say it... satanic.[31]

Alex Tsakiris: A lot of people are super intrigued by this idea of an attorney writing books on Aleister Crowley and the West Memphis Three.[32] It's not your traditional true crime stuff.

William Ramsey: Well, I was always a person who was willing to research things that were not covered by the corporate media. I went to law school in DC and worked there from '95 to '98 and saw some very remarkable things. I've briefly worked on, what they call the suicide of Vince Foster, which was really the murder of Vince Foster. He was murdered and dumped in Fort Marcy Park.

Alex Tsakiris: ... We're going to talk about cultural influences a lot, and that's what I love about the West Memphis Three case, it puts us right in the middle of this "do what thou wilt" occult and satanic culture meme that says I can lie, cheat, steal, do whatever I have to. I can deceive you because that's part of it.

But at the same time, there's this contradiction that just isn't exposed, and that is the atheistic, you're a biological robot in a meaningless universe part of science... so of course, satanic ritual abuse could never be true.

The funny thing about our culture is we have this dual mechanism, where both are operating, where there's this Johnny Depp, Duncan Trussell, a wink and a nod, and of course, it's all happening in this extended realm. And then you've got this other side of Neil deGrasse Tyson, consciousness is an illusion.

William Ramsey: I'm impressed because I think you covered it in a general sense of the groups that are influencing the culture. You've got the occultists, you've got the materialist scientists like deGrasse Tyson or Steven Pinker or Kraus, or some of these other guys, or the Darwinists. And then you can put me right in that Christian camp, I'm comfortable with that. I don't really think that I'm promoting a specific kind of sectarian agenda within Christianity, but I definitely am a Christian, a hundred percent.

Alex Tsakiris: Okay. Let me just touch on the Christian point and then I'm going to let it go. Because I think Christians don't accept their culpability in some of this. And I mean culpability in the sense of just how the average person processes this and says, "Really? In this day, with the Catholic Church outed as a systematic sexual abuser of children, from the highest level, directed from the Pope, you're going to tell me that this folds right into Jesus on the Cross, the Son of God?? Screw you."

One way to read the Crowley biography, and I think it's the wrong way, is that he was just rebelling against an overbearing Christian father, who had taken the Christian slant to this kooky extreme. No birthday parties, no presents, no Christmas…all of this cultish kind of stuff. And of course, we can pack it back into psychology, then we never have to deal with the real stuff that's going on.

But I'd say the same kind of thing with the West Memphis Three. When you break that down, and if people haven't heard this before they are going to be stunned because you stack the evidence and it's overwhelming, these were satanic crimes. But people are still going to process it as, "Oh man, satanic panic, those damn Christians are at it again."

So I guess that's what I mean when I say complicit.

William Ramsey: I think that's fair. I'm glad that you brought up the Catholic Church because that's the exemplar that antagonists believe Christianity is. Even Crowley, too. He was part of the exclusive brethren by Darby, who you may argue isn't even an authentic Christian. So he's definitely within this wide tent of what's defined as Christianity, but that's a very generalist way to put it. I don't think Darby, I mean, he was a dispensationalist, and there were all kinds of problems with his theology.

Some of these Christian leaders in different sects are very comfortable with the occult. Supposedly, like Darby, I need to research that more, but also Joseph Smith, the guy who started The Watchtower, the Jehovah's Witnesses. There are all kinds of problems. And I think this actually happens often. You can look at the gospel as a kind of caricature and say, you're just going to throw that agenda on people.[33]

I know what happens and that's fine. I don't even describe myself as a kind of sectarian Christian. I'm just a Bible-believing Christian. So I think that the real basis of any proper definition of that faith would be to see what's in the gospels and in Paul's writings. That should be the basis point, not the church. The Catholic Church is hyper-corrupt. I mean, the kinds of things that have been going on in there and the doctrines. And even Crowley, it's interesting that you bring him up. He actually favored Catholicism. He said that the real enemies were the Protestants and the Jews. So he had this tolerance for it. Even some of his religion that he adopted, he took from Orthodox Christianity. His whole occult Gnostic mask is from the Orthodox Church and he absorbed a lot of Christian teachings and twisted it. But yeah, you're right.

I think that these critiques are common, they're fair, but I think that they can be addressed and that's fine.

You can look at me. You can look at me through whatever lens you want, but if you want to look at the facts that I've written about in those books, they're all fairly long, they're all footnoted. They're almost none of my subjective opinions, just reference points. They're properly referenced in my opinion. And then you can take it as what you want to believe.

We're all biased. We all have our own outlook. I can't detach that from my books, my personality, and the way I believe things. So I think total objectivity is unattainable. People always say, "Oh, you're biased." Well, everybody's biased, age, race, education, gender, politics… I think that's fair. I listen to the left [perspectives] and the right. I don't really mind as long as they're being honest, that's really what I want, being honest with the facts.

CROWLEY APOLOGISTS

Alex Tsakiris: I've been on the trail of the Crowley story for a while, and I have friends who admire his books. I'm not sure his ideas work in terms of my understanding of spirituality, but I respect that people have different ways of approaching it. I don't think everyone who looks at the "Occult" is damned or condemned, or even doing it for evil purposes.

With that, I just want to get to the facts. If you can sketch out the big picture of West Memphis Three. And the other thing that I'd love to have you talk about, and then I'm going to hit you with some more questions on the details because they're fantastic, is what happened to West Memphis Three. Because the general impression is, "Well, they were found innocent... and that's not the case."

William Ramsey: Right. So they're supposedly innocent. They were arrested for a crime they did not commit. These are the standard kind of PR axioms that you'll see in almost every article that is pro-West Memphis Three. There are very few anti-West Memphis Three out there.

But the true crime story really started on May 5th of 1993, after three young boys disappeared. They were eight years old, right in line with Crowley's teachings on human sacrifice in *Magick in Theory and Practice*.[34] They disappeared. They were found the next day in a ditch, in a little area called Robinhood Hills outside of West Memphis, Tennessee across the Mississippi River. Two were found later to have been drowned after a medical examination. They were tied up in a very strange manner, ankle to wrist. One had bled out after his genitals were removed. So it was a particularly graphic and brutal crime. There was blood all over the place. It was never admitted into court, but the luminol tests were taken, so there was blood all over that area.

There was an outcry trying to figure out who did this. There was a suspect that was mentioned by a probation officer by the name of Jerry Driver, who [spoke of] this young man by the name of Damien Echols (his real name). His given name was Michael Hutchison, but he changed it to his stepfather's last name and took on the name Damien.

He was investigated and according to the records, was brought into the police office. He was questioned. He failed the polygraph test. He said, "I'll tell you everything if you let me talk to my mom." So he went and talked to his mom, then he clammed up, but the investigation continued. They didn't have enough evidence to arrest any of them until they brought in another young man by the name of Jessie Misskelley on June 3rd of 1993, who then confessed and implicated Damien Echols and Jason Baldwin.

All three were arrested. They were tried separately, due to some evidence that was going to be put in the trial. And 24 jurors found them both guilty. Damien Echols was over 18. He was given capital punishment. And the other two pretty much got life sentences.

The key aspect in creating doubt in the public's mind was an HBO documentary. There was really a trilogy. The first one was titled, *Paradise Lost*, which came out in 1996. There were two others, I think [they were released] in 2001 and maybe 2004.35 I can't remember the exact dates, but they cast doubt upon their guilt. The first documentary was somewhat objective, but the second one blamed one of the stepfathers by the name of Byers, and then the third pretty much implicated another man by the name of Terry Hobbs, which created a furor. It snowballed, and other people got involved, celebrities got involved. Money was raised, a huge amount of money, $10-20 million. One of the best attorneys out there got involved and put pressure on the state government through new laws that had been created for DNA testing. There was going to be a hearing in 2011, I think in December, before a judge about whether some of this DNA could be used.

In August 2011, an agreement was reached and the three pled guilty to first-degree murder on signed documents (by this time they're adults). But there was enough evidence to possibly convict them again. They went to court. They were put under 10 years of probation and were let out while professing innocence on something called an Alford plea, which is based on a Supreme Court case Alford V North Carolina, which allows you to profess your innocence publicly while pleading guilty. So they're basically guilty. They're still guilty and under probation until next year.

Alex Tsakiris: I asked you to keep it vanilla and man, you really kept it vanilla. Let me pull you into the real stuff. Anyone who goes and Googles "West Memphis Three," I'm not exaggerating, the first 10 [results], satanic panic, satanic panic, satanic panic. That's the only thing you hear about this case. It doesn't have anything to do with the facts, and that's what's going to be so interesting as we dive into this. Why did this become the poster child for satanic panic? And why do we think that's not accidental? It can't be.

William Ramsey: Yeah, there were statements...I mean, it's all over there. Why is it satanic panic if the guy, as a member of the OTO while he's in jail, while he's also just recently admitted to being part of AA, was specifically traced to Crowley who wrote in his own writing that he was prosecuted for his love of the knowledge of Aleister Crowley specifically? Crowley's name pops up all over this, which is really what piqued my interest in this whole case.

Alex Tsakiris: Isn't it true William, we have evidence of him performing satanic rituals in a garage he set on fire?

William Ramsey: That's true. That was in the original case. They say that he was prosecuted for wearing black, but he was actually arrested before the events for moonlighting, I think, in an abandoned trailer. And there was testimony of all kinds of weird stuff he was doing. And all their statements were in the court files, which I included in my book about them hanging out at Stonehenge. Just crazy stuff, off the charts.

Alex Tsakiris: I want to touch on two things. I want to hit on the deception thing in a minute, because I think people aren't aware that is part of the ethos. Do you want to speak to that, have you found that to be true?

William Ramsey: Absolutely. I think that they lie about all of that. They lie about their secret society, associations, who their friends are, about their signals. There's a real wink and a nod, just like you mentioned, within these groups. So I think that not disclosing... What did Orwell say, "Admission is the greatest form of lie." They tell you all this stuff, that there's all kinds of weird associations. There's some dark habits. There's so much deception in this case that almost everything that's proffered by Echols in some way, it's nothing really that's honest. He said that he was sick, that he was beaten in jail all the time, that his teeth were going to fall out, that they had to take the deal because he was going to die.

Alex Tsakiris: (the following clip was added after the original recording) I just wanted to jump in for one second with a couple additional points I wish I would've asked William, but I didn't. So I'm going to try and get these in here. And these come directly out of his book, Abomination: Devil Worship and Deception in the West Memphis Three Murders. *It's really important for getting to the bottom of this question of whether Damien Echols did these horrible, evil deeds.*

I have to make the distinction because a lot of people don't get this. It doesn't speak to whether or not he should have been released. Or, whether there were some legal aspects to his prosecution, that's separate from whether the guy did it.

William has published some of the police interviews they did with Echols. And these police interviews are tricky because police in these situations do some pretty...I don't know...kind of shady things. Like one of the things they do to people is they say, "Okay, who do you imagine would have done this crime?" It is a trick to get them to say incriminating stuff they may want to get off their chest without confessing. And in this case it was revealing. Echols said he figured the killer knew the kids in the woods and even asked them to come out to the woods. He stated the boys were not big, not smart, and they could have been easy to control. He also felt the killer would not have worried about screaming due to being in the woods and close to the expressway. And then Echols added some important factual details. He said the bodies of all the boys had been mutilated and one had been mutilated a lot more than the others. This fact was not known to anyone except those at the crime scene. The police never released this information. He also said Steve Jones from the Juvenile Authority had told him about how the boy's testicles had been cut off and that someone had urinated in their mouths. Echols said that could have been the reason why their bodies were placed in the water, so that the urine could have been washed out.

This is another critical piece of evidence that was never released. Steve Jones from the Juvenile Authority had no way of knowing this and couldn't have told Echols. Only someone at the crime scene could have known that detail.

So again, I'll leave it here because I hate all this gory true crime stuff. But again, pack this back into the question of whether or not this is a case of "satanic panic."

Okay, back to the interview.

William Ramsey: You know, all kinds of crazy stuff. If you look at the totality, it's just nonsense. It's really hard for people to believe there are groups of networked people out there doing these Satanic crimes. And I think that's really the hardest part of addressing the West Memphis Three.

Alex Tsakiris: I think you're absolutely right. One of the chapters I have in my book is an interview that I did with this woman named Anneke Lucas (Chapter 14).) And she's really a lovely person, and we connected. We both like yoga and she's a yoga teacher who started a foundation for incarcerated women in Upstate New York. she's someone who's used yoga to go through this transformation in her life. And she would have to, because at six years old, she was sold by her mother to a satanic ritual occult abuse network in Belgium.

William Ramsey: Belgium, right? Was she associated with the Dutroux thing?

Alex Tsakiris: Well, she's careful about who she names, but it's very clear that is the group that had her... and that's fascinating too, right? Because talk about history repeating itself, there was this "big drain the swamp" thing that's popular right now and as I tell people who have doubts about the reality of satanic ritual abuse, you can still Google photos of kids in cages, tied up. Just the most horrible of horrible things you can see. And her account is that she was going to be killed. She had been raped, like thousands of times, six years old remember, six years old by her mother.

But the interesting thing I always alert people to, if you want to take a secular perspective on this, it doesn't work because what these people are doing, and they will tell you what they're doing, is they are trying to connect with malevolent forces in this extended realm. And they're trying to connect with that force for a reason, to bring in a certain energy into this realm. And that's why they connect with Aleister Crowley. And it's nothing unique about Aleister Crowley, it's just many people have chosen that path. They're so attached to this world and what they can get out of it, that any entity in that extended realm that connects and offers the chance, they'll do it.

William Ramsey: I'm glad you brought up that case because it was totally networked, it was covered up. There were all kinds of shenanigans that took place under the surface. Like the prosecutor got fired, and there's an incredible German documentary that traces the people who were murdered around the Dutroux case that knew too much. It's like 25 people. Like, those who said, "I know too much, they're going to kill me," end up dead. Another person says, "I got information on this," gets run over by a car. It's incredible. It's like JFK, you know, all the people who knew about that, who ended up dead. It's incredible.

The Dutroux case, if you don't think that's network evil, I'm sorry, you're just wrong because it went to the highest levels of the elite. And Dutroux was known to leave Belgium, he was moving around Europe. So they don't even know the totality of what happened and the horror show. Like two of the kids died because he was in jail and couldn't feed them in the dungeon.

So that's a real problem. People cannot connect to spiritual evil, and I'm glad you brought that up because that's what these people are doing. That's what Crowley was doing.

WINK-AND-NOD SATANISM

Alex Tsakiris: ... So, what is the play in culture? Why do we have this divide? Why do we have Neil deGrasse Tyson, who you and I think is probably just completely oblivious to evil, and then you've got the kind of Hollywood element, which you've just explored extensively, that's saying, "We're way past you guys. We're using the force."

William Ramsey: That's a good point. I mean, look at Johnny Depp. He supposedly uses these entities to inform himself on all of his roles. Like, he's fully involved in... what we call evil. People ask me, "You're an admirer of Crowley, you seem to talk about it in laudatory terms," I don't. I call him the prophet of evil. He thought he was a prophet of the new aeon. I believe that's evil because all of his ideas are antithetical towards the treatment of society, really in general. It's super selfish, like you said already, and go over this theme of our conversation, you lie, you manipulate, the slave shall serve. Crowley was kind of like a classist of the worst sort.

But I think the definition of what people are willing to do to their fellow man to get worldly benefits, whether it's money, sex, fame, set the standard for sin. They counterpoise that at least in the teaching of Christianity to be somewhat universal. It's like Christ is a servant, and you turn the other cheek and there are those teachings where you're not supposed to propagate trauma or hurt somebody else. That's what turning the other cheek is, you don't strike back. So it kind of lessens whatever harms are out there, it doesn't engender that kind of malevolence towards people hurting each other.

It's interesting too about how many of these occultists really are Christ and Christian haters, whether it's Hubbard or Crowley or Hitler, or some of these other people. How they really deliberately counterpoise themselves against the teachings of Christ.

Alex Tsakiris: And I think there's a couple of interesting things and I don't know if we can smooth this out and hit all the points. And this is in the Crowley book, maybe you can pick up on it and elaborate on it. But the "do what thou wilt" ethos, which whenever you talk to a Crowley apologist they jump on that, they go, "You don't know what that really means." And I always respond, "His whole life is about that... look at the deeds, the fruit."

William Ramsey: I think that, you know, Crowley said he got power from transgression, and I think that's a very common theme within occultists or Satanists or whatever, however you want to call them. And I think the worst crimes, are an inversion. So definitely it's there in Crowley.

Alex Tsakiris: I wanted to skip back to the Hollywood thing for a minute because we look at some of these folks, it just looks like their soul has been sucked out of them. But other ones, you feel like maybe they're just being duped and that's when you really feel sorry them. They're going to the parties and Marina Abramovic is cutting up the human sacrifice cake and isn't this cool. And they don't understand what's at play, or do you think they do?

William Ramsey: Well? I mean, I could probably analogize, like they had just a naive view of certain things. You know, I had a very naive view of American politics, and there's a lot more going on under the surface than you could imagine. And it's probably the same in Hollywood.

Alex Tsakiris: Last point and then I'll wrap it up. Russ Dizdar (Chapter 15). has a really interesting theory. It's going to sound completely wacky to a lot of people, but I have reasons to believe he's on the right track. Russ claims, a lot of times when you hear about this sexual abuse of children and pedophilia, that it's not even so much about sexual abuse. It's about traumatizing children in order to create this dissociative identity disorder, because it is a direct link to making them more vulnerable to spiritual attack. And the crazy thing is that it connects directly to stuff we've learned about MKUltra and what they were doing to weaponize that dissociative aspect of it. Because we learned that it's almost like a technology. What do you think about that?

William Ramsey: I think he's right. I think that's true. In a very dark way, a lot of the stuff that happens in the Catholic Church is to keep people in the Catholic Church. So they get traumatized, they become helpless, they become less active, so to speak, or accepting of authority. I think that's definitely believable, right? I think that's what they're doing. They're deliberately traumatizing the kids as well. For sure.

And in some of these cases, McMartin and stuff, the kids are deliberately being traumatized, or the Finders case (Chapter 17. STATE-SPONSORED EVIL), they're all using these same techniques and these strange occultists are running the whole show. Look at the Finders case man, terrifying.

Alex Tsakiris: When you get into weaponized traumatization, then just the thought someone has figured out how they can get a leg up by doing that, is really scary, especially in this extended realm.

William Ramsey: Very scary. And you know the traumatization starts and then the suggestion follows. Right? So you're traumatized and then the suggestion, and then...

Alex Tsakiris: You've opened up the door.

William Ramsey: Absolutely right. Then you have this kind of approach, this technique. It becomes a skill and they develop that.

Our culture's fascination with darkness and evil is something we've grown accustomed to. Overtly dark entertainment goes by without notice. But the cumulative effect of this desensitization may be significant. Perhaps it's part of a larger plan. A plan partially revealed by the darkness and deception of our government's dance with malevolent forces in the extended consciousness realms. We'll look at that next.

10
THE DEVIL IS A CONSPIRACY

> "And it is my contention that the name of evil should have a definite place in our lexicon. ... But without the name, we will remain limited in our capacity to help the victims of evil. And we will have no hope whatsoever of dealing with the evil ones themselves (I would add "in flesh or spirit.") For how can we heal that which we do not even dare study?"
> - **M. Scott Peck**, *from People of the Lie*

> **IN THIS CHAPTER**
> - what remote viewing reveals about science
> - is evil being hidden from us?
> - I've read the documents

Up to this point, I might have slipped a couple of conspiracy theory fast balls by you, but that's not going to be possible in this chapter. I previously referenced Project Stargate, the FOIA-documented United States Government remote viewing program, aimed at weaponizing extended consciousness in order to psychic-ly spy on enemies of the state. It's an amazing bit of history and something we've covered extensively on *Skeptiko*. But while the stories of remote viewing secret Soviet submarine bases from a comfy cubicle in Palo Alto, California are amazing, the implications for the questions of consciousness and our investigation of evil are even more intriguing. Because one undeniable fact we can glean from our remote viewing program is that by 1978 the best and brightest scientists the US government could find had moved way past "biological robot, meaningless universe" scientific materialism, and embraced the "scientific" reality of extended consciousness.

I discovered this way back in episode #166 of *Skeptiko* when I interviewed psychic spy number 001, Joseph McMoneagle. McMoneagle was an Army intelligence officer near the East Germany border during the Cold War. He was a spy.[36] One day, after lunch at a favorite Bavarian restaurant, Joe began to experience extreme tightening in his throat. Within seconds he couldn't breathe. Thoughts raced through his head as he realized he'd been poisoned like a lead actor in a spy vs spy thriller. He stumbled to the door in an effort to get help and then collapsed. Instantly, and amazingly, Joe found himself outside of his body. He watched from above as his buddies frantically loaded him into a Jeep and then an ambulance in an attempt to save his life. What followed was a dramatic near-death experience, accompanied by a transformative spiritual experience that radically altered the way Joe saw the world, but that last part would take a while.

Chief Warrant Officer McMoneagle , upon return to our space-time reality, saw Army intelligence officers leaning over his bed in an effort to debrief him. It's an amazing story that Joe tells in his book, *Memoirs of a Psychic Spy.*[37] But, as amazing as Joe's out-of-body and near-death experience was, it's only part of the story. Years later, Joe was tagged as a potential candidate for a new secret intelligence program at Stanford Research Institute. Project Stargate was training soldiers to use their consciousness to travel through space and time and spy on our enemies. They needed psychics, and they had an idea of where to look. Joe describes what happened next:

> **Alex Tsakiris:** One of the things I found interesting about your experience as a remote viewer is when you first described meeting Hal Puthoff and the folks at SRI (Stanford Research Institute) and you tell them about your NDE; they are accepting of it. You think they're going to say, "Get this guy out of here." But they're accepting. Don't they even share with you Raymond Moody's book at that point?
>
> **Joe McMoneagle:** Actually, it was the exact reverse of that.

I thought their strong interest was in the psychic functioning and that sort of thing. So when I started my interview, what I came to find out was that they had opened a package (Dr. Raymond Moody's book, *Life After Life*)[38] that was inserted in my 201 file, my personnel file.

What had happened after my NDE is all of the psychiatric reports and all of the final assessments as to what my experience was had been put into a permanently-sealed file with a red stripe across it and it said, "Not to be opened except by the Commander of the Intelligence & Security Command." When they obtained my file, the first thing that Lieutenant Atwater did was open it.

And they were very pleased to find that I had this experience in 1970 because it meant that I was one of those special people that historically were able to probably do exactly what they were looking for.

Alex Tsakiris: So they were already aware of the connection between [psychic abilities] and NDE phenomena?

Joe McMoneagle: Exactly. In my discussion with Hal Puthoff and Russell Targ at the time, the initiation of the project, they were only going to recruit three people for a three-year test and analysis program. It turned out that as a result of their selection process, they wound up with more positive reactions from people than they expected.

So they decided to go ahead and expand the program to six people instead of three. I'm glad they did because in the end of that first half of the program, I ended up being the only one left. They might not have been able to get that far without the additional three people.

PROJECT STARGATE: REMOTE VIEWING

Project Stargate is an important part of our history. It's telling that our best and brightest scientists (anyone who looks into the bona fides of Dr. Hal Puthoff and Dr. Russell Targ would put them in that category) were tasked with the job of operationalizing a phenomenon that completely contradicts the materialist, "biological robot in a meaningless universe" paradigm. It's further proof the "invisible college" is real.

This doesn't mean that every snarky science type who spouts the "consciousness is an illusion" party-line is a pawn in "the conspiracy," but it may provide a clue as to how easy it is to manipulate science with a small amount of money and the promise of prestige. Even though the Project Stargate story, as well as many of the other programs under the MKUltra umbrella, have been told many times, its history is still mostly obscured by the usual crowd of "I-wouldn't-believe-it-even-if-it were-true" deniers.

This is what made my interview with filmmaker Lance Munguia so interesting. Lance's movie, *Third Eye Spies* not only provided an excellent presentation of the Stargate history and its players, but it also contains on-the-record interviews with program insiders that, before now, have never been able to speak freely about secret aspects of the program.[39] And while this might raise legitimate questions about why such a treasure trove of previously classified documents are being released at this time, it was still interesting to take a look at what is being allowed to be told:

Alex Tsakiris: The storyline that the movie follows is Dr. Russell Targ, who is of course one of the original investigators in the Stargate Remote Viewing Program, along with Dr. Hal Puthoff, on this final mission.[40] He's an older guy, and he's going to reconnect with all of these people that have been a part of this amazing program. So, he gets these classified documents released and then the plot is, "Okay guys, we can now tell the story we wanted to tell for so long, let's do it." And you sit down with these people all over the world and they fill in the blanks of the Project Stargate story but it just gets a lot deeper than that.

Lance Mungia: I got a call from a mutual friend of Dr. Russell Targ, who was interested in speaking with me because he had seen another film that I had done called *Six String Samurai*. He literally flew out to LA and showed up at

my door with a big box full of documents that were marked
classified, and he started laying out all of these documents
on a table.[41] Even though I knew something about this, I did
not, at all, know the extent of what had happened with this
program that had gone back over 20 years.

Okay, I said there were going to be a lot of rabbit holes to follow in
this chapter and we just stumbled into one. Given everything that we
know about secrecy within our intelligence organizations, we might
be a little bit skeptical of the motivations behind the release of tens of
thousands of previously classified documents. But we'll get to that in a
minute...

Alex Tsakiris: ... your movie reminded me this was outed
25 years ago. You have film clips of Ted Koppel, who at the
time was the go-to guy in terms of serious nighttime news,
and he's saying, "Hey, there's this psychic spying thing
going on. We're in a race with the Russians, they're doing it,
we're doing it," and basically lays the whole thing out.

But part of the Project Stargate storyline is that this public
narrative inexplicably changes to where we moved to this
skeptical/denying/did-it-really-happen, kind of thing. We
don't understand why the narrative changed from openness
to denial of it.

Dang, another rabbit hole. In November of 1995, Ted Koppel's
Nightline was the most popular news show on television.[42] So when
he dedicated an entire episode to blowing the lid off of a CIA program
using psychics to spy on the Russians, people took notice. Science
should-have/could-have/secretly-did take notice as well.

In case I haven't pounded on this enough, there's absolutely *no
way* to reconcile remote viewing with "biological robots in a meaningless universe" nonsense science claims. Remote viewing is about
the manipulation of consciousness outside of space and time, which
only makes sense if consciousness is outside of time and space. This
doesn't make sense in a mind=brain, materialistic science world. And it
certainly doesn't fit Dr. Neil deGrasse Tyson's pondering about whether

consciousness exists. And maybe you can forgive me for repeating this, but at some point, and maybe now's the time, we have to face the inevitable conclusion that this silly "biological robots in a meaningless universe" outlook is not an accident, but part of a project to distract us from pondering about things beyond our shopping habits. But more on that later.

Alex Tsakiris: ...you touched on the ongoing nature of these programs. You have a bit of a tease at the end of your movie where you're interviewing Kit Green. He, of course is, one of the super-duper insiders of this program and you catch him in an elevator saying, (paraphrasing) "Oh, yeah, these programs are still ongoing. I know it from my most trusted, reliable source," which all of us who've really studied this have said, "Duh, of course." If you can easily and secretly gather information from your enemies, of course you're going to continue to do it. You're not going to stop just because some senator has some religious objections or something like that.

Wow, two more rabbit holes. First, insiders don't reveal secrets. That's what makes them insiders. More on this later, too. Secondly, and to our evil question, anyone who tries to gain a scientific understanding of the extended consciousness realms is going to smack up against a very close-minded, dogmatic religious interpretation of how extended consciousness works.

Lance Mungia: .. I would ask the people I interviewed, "Who's the villain? "Who's the bad guy in this?" And [Dr. Russel Targ] didn't even think about it, he just said, "It's the religious dogma, the scientific dogma to a certain extent, but mainly religious dogma."

... what I learned through years of going out and interviewing these people, that was one of the biggest obstacles that they had, not only a scientific skepticism, but a completely illogical skepticism that wouldn't even look at the data, that wouldn't even entertain the idea that this could be. This was something that was supernatural and spooky and scary to them.

Alex Tsakiris: One of the points that stuck out to me in *Third Eye Spies* was this point where Joe McMoneagle becomes kind of passionate talking to Russell and says, "Russell, we survived five presidential administrations," and you get the sense of what they had to put up with, all this political craziness that was often driven by a Christian kind of craziness about how we should understand this stuff from a very narrow religious perspective... and there's just no way to soften that or to make it go away. It really struck me that this was a reality in their' lives.

(later)

Alex Tsakiris: If there is an extended consciousness realm and if there are beings that have more power than we do, should we seek to marshal their forces?

... because the evidence shows that other programs under the MKUltra umbrella were willing to try and marshal those same forces, and it's also clear that in some cases they did. There's also evidence that other intelligence agencies around the world have done so.

Lance Mungia: Well, it'll sound really philosophical but I think that whatever you look for you'll probably find. I think that the only issue with that is, if you're looking to do harm, you're really harming yourself. It's like when you really start to understand where all of this kind of leads you philosophically, I am inextricably linked to you, everybody else is inextricably linked to me. So when I start trying to use my magical powers to harm someone, in effect what I'm doing is harming myself and usually that will just bounce right back at you...

Alex Tsakiris: I don't disagree, and I think that's actually deeply spiritual. I do think it's hard for people to process that inside of the country we live in. We both live in the United States of America, we both deal with the contradictions of that in terms of our history... look at our intelligence agencies and we know we've done the most horrible things...

Lance Mungia: ... you'd probably find that most modern governments are probably in some way, shape or form, using things like remote viewing and other kinds of psychic techniques. [They're] probably trying all kinds of crazy things, like you said, just to see what sticks to the wall and what works, because we know that there's something there and we don't understand it. When we don't understand something, we want to understand it. So that's what it becomes about, especially if it's useful.

We don't know how far down this rabbit hole goes, and we can talk about that all day long, but for me the more important takeaway is what does it mean to you? What does it mean to me? In other words, what does it mean for human potential? Because that's really the only reason to talk about it. This stuff's been hidden since the days of the guy on top of the Mayan Temple sacrificing victims.

Alex Tsakiris: The guy on top of the Mayan pyramid who's sacrificing human beings and pulling their heart out, is playing a different game. He's not playing the, "Be your greatest self," by transcending all of this. He's playing the, "I want what I want now" game. And why wouldn't he play that? Why would he play the spiritual, "To harm myself is to harm everyone" game?

Lance Mungia: Yeah, but we also get that people have been doing stupid things forever. You know, fear is a very, very effective tool. It's a very effective tactic of control.

The United States military approached remote viewing as a technology. A war toy. Doing a deeper dive into the MKUltra Program reveals that they were also trying to come to grips with the larger philosophical and spiritual implications of entities that transcend space and time. Some would argue they weren't doing a very good job. Some would argue, as you'll see in the next chapter, they weren't even in the game.

11
LUDDITES NEVER WIN

"If they can, they will."
- **Nick Bostrom**, *Sweedish-born Oxford philosopher who asks whether inventing artificial intelligence implies we're living in a simulation.*

> **IN THIS CHAPTER**
> - remembering how smart we're not
> - backdoor materialism

Riz Virk is a smart guy. MIT Computer Science and Stanford Business School kinda smart. He's a successful entrepreneur who has started and run several successful companies and the famous Play Lab at MIT. People like Riz who've really studied computer simulation, artificial intelligence, virtual reality, and cutting-edge computer gaming software, have a different understanding of the tenuous line between our external what-we-agree-we-see, consensus reality and the simulated/augmented reality we're beginning to experience as we stare at *Call of Duty*.[43] But what do these advances in technology, that are already light years past the Turing test, tell us about the nature of consciousness and the beings occupying these unexplored realms? Here are some excerpts from my interview[44] with Riz:

> **DECODING: TURING TEST**
>
> The Turing Test is a thought experiment developed by the famous computer scientist Alan Turing. It proposed that a computer can

be said to possess artificial intelligence if it can mimic human responses in a way that can't be identified as computer-generated.

Riz Virk: ...So getting back to Jacques Vallée and UFOs, I had lunch with him recently and he told me he investigated a case where there was supposedly a UFO and [witnesses] said it came down at a 45-degree angle, and it actually left some marks on the ground. So there was some physical evidence. Jacques went back after the original investigation, and he looked at it and said, "You said it went at a 45-degree angle. That means it would've had to go through the trees." They said, "Yeah, but we didn't want to tell anybody that because nobody would believe us." Which gets back to, is this a virtual phenomenon that gets materialized when it's needed? It's something that we see. So, I think explaining how all that works is a task that's ongoing.

(later)

Alex Tsakiris: ...you do a fantastic job of linking that back to physics and the most important experiment in quantum physics ever, the double slit experiment. You beautifully linked those two together, tell us about that.

Riz Virk: With the idea of the double slit experiment, there's this theory that a particle will go through one slit or the other, but you don't know until somebody is there to observe it. So that reminded me of how we develop video games. If you were to ask a video game developer in the 80s, "Can you render a fully 3D world like *World of Warcraft* or like *Fortnite* or like *Call of Duty*?"[45] The answer [would have been] no.[46] There wasn't enough computing power. So they optimize and only render those pixels which can be observed by your avatar. That is the golden rule for optimization, which allows form what we call "conditional rendering" in the world of video games. Now, looking at it as a video game designer, that's very similar to what quantum indeterminacy is like in the physical world. Why do things that only get rendered when they're observed? It seems like the golden rule in quantum physics is to only render pieces of the world which can be observed.

Alex Tsakiris: So if a tree falls in the forest and no one is there, well, if no one's there, we wouldn't render in the first place, right?

Riz Virk: Right, exactly. This brings up a bigger question, is there a shared rendered world that we are all seeing at the same time?

Alex Tsakiris: ...if we really take this stuff seriously, then we have to question whether we can really measure anything at all, and if we can't measure anything, isn't science somewhat obsolete?

Riz Virk: Well, I view science as trying to discover the rules of the physics engine of the game, right? When we make video games, we have a rendering engine, we have a physics engine that controls how you move, and there's some kind of a design or layout that's inherent in the system. I view most scientists as still working on discovering those rules, but they haven't necessarily asked the big questions.

Even within quantum physics, there's the famous quote, "Just shut up and calculate," don't try to think about what it means, and the double slit experiment, in various versions, gets weirder and weirder. From my perspective, one of the weirdest aspects is the delayed choice experiment, which is this idea that it's not just a matter of whether it went through slit A or slit B, but something else happens down the road. Another choice that happens in the future.

Probably a better way to explain this is if you have light from a star or a galaxy coming at us, there's a black hole in the middle. Does the light go to the left or the right of the black hole? Well, if that black hole is a thousand light years away, that decision was made a thousand years ago, but the delayed choice experiment is telling us that it doesn't actually get made until there's an observer looking at the light. Now you have this situation where it's not just a matter of slit A or slit B, but the whole path can be changed from the present moment.

So this sounds much more like what the mystics have been telling us all along, that the present moment is the only one that exists, and that consciousness is fundamental.

What I like about the simulation hypothesis is that it provides a bridge between the materialist worldview and the worldview of the mystics and people who think that consciousness is fundamental.

That's why I'm glad the first thing you brought up was this distinction between Neo and Agent Smith, because that really is the fundamental tension I tried to explore in this book: is consciousness just a reproduction of neurons, in which case consciousness can be reproduced? Or is it in fact, a conscious entity outside that's playing a role or playing a game?

That's something that I can discuss with physicists and people at MIT, and I can discuss it with Buddhist monks and I can discuss it with biblical scholars as well, because there are lots of aspects to AI -- this idea that the world around us isn't quite the real world, that perhaps there is another world we cannot see.

Alex Tsakiris: Sure, you can discuss it with them, Riz, because you like to play nice. Aren't we really just propping up these materialists because they own the mic? And because none of us are comfortable with the implications of all this... i.e., space-time is doomed. The idea that we're living in this linear day-by-day experience of space-time, well, that's out the window. Neo-Darwinism, no one ever brings this up, but that's completely out the window, too. In fact, science as we know it is out the window because we can no longer measure what we think is reality. So we're propping these guys up, right?

Riz Virk: Yeah, but that's just one way to describe it. I would describe it also as a way to provide a bridge, and to provide an even better understanding.

Now you know what I mean, Riz likes to play nice.

ARTIFICIAL INTELLIGENCE AND BACKDOOR MATERIALISM

Alex Tsakiris: Don't we get into a problem of infinite regress and "turtles all the way down?" If there are rules, if there is karma, and karma is rules for a computer gamer like you, then you might say that those rules suggest a moral imperative. And a moral imperative suggests a hierarchy of consciousness. And a hierarchy of consciousness suggests God.

So, I'm not sure where there's any room for AI other than as a tool for God.

DECODING: TURTLES ALL THE WAY DOWN

"Turtles all the way down" is an expression of the problem of infinite regress. The saying alludes to the mythological idea of a World Turtle that supports the earth on its back. It suggests that this turtle rests on the back of an even larger turtle, which itself is part of a column of increasingly large world turtles that continues indefinitely (i.e., "turtles all the way down"). The expression was supposedly coined when an astronomer rescinded to a question after his presentation: "What you have told us is rubbish. The world is really a flat plate supported on the back of a giant tortoise." The scientist gave a superior smile before replying, "What is the tortoise standing on?" "You're very clever, but it's turtles all the way down!"[47]

Riz Virk: … you do get into this idea of regress sometimes, right? If we can create a simulation where we would appear to be gods to those people inside the simulation, because we can change the rules of that simulation and make things appear in midair, for example. The people in the scene would be like, "Wow, that's a miracle. Where did that thing come from? It wasn't there a minute ago." We do it all the time in video games.

In fact, we even do conditional rendering based upon the level. If you and I are inside of a scene, and you're a level two character, and I'm a level 30 character, the server can decide that the level 30 character will see this being or angel and the level 2 character will not. They're all being rendered inside each of our computers, which is kind of like us rendering in our brains or as part of our own consciousness.

So there's this idea that would appear as supernatural to people that are stuck inside the simulation, when actually it might just be rules that are being determined by someone *outside* of the simulation.

Now, the question of levels is an interesting one, because if you say there's a level outside this, could it be that there's another simulation outside of that?

Alex Tsakiris: Well, hold on, you can't not ask that question. I mean, simulation of what? Is it a simulation of a simulation of a simulation of a simulation... eventually you're talking about God...it doesn't matter how many intermediate steps there are.

That's the other problem with what I call "backdoor materialism." It's like, we're going to get away from materialism until we need it, and then we're going to bring it back in. Now, if consciousness is fundamental, then all of this is in consciousness. The simulation is IN consciousness, the rules are IN consciousness. God is IN consciousness. We can never be outside of it if it's fundamental.

Riz Virk: That's one way to think of it, God is in consciousness. But another way to think of it, if you take the RPG version, because obviously if you take the NPC version, you're limited by computing power, and you can have only so many version simulations within simulations within simulations. But if you consider the RPG version, there's a version of us that's outside base reality, but if that's the simulation, there's another version that's outside base reality. But what is that version? My point is that it becomes less material, not necessarily more material. Although, within a lot of simulation discussions base reality means a physical world outside of the simulated world. In the RPG version it means, who is the entity that is playing us? So it's more about the consciousness of that entity.

Just like in *The Matrix*, Neo had the wire connected to the back of his head when he woke up in the pod.[48] That was the connection. It was a conscious connection between that person and another entity. And at some point you get conscious entities, and perhaps that's a better definition of God than what we get from religions. Pure consciousness is God as opposed to God is in pure consciousness. So each of the individuals are like droplets of pure consciousness. It is what's playing all of these characters in the first simulation, and each of them are allowed to go down and experience things. Just like people say to me, why would I make a simulation? I say, well, why do you play video games? We do it to experience the things that we cannot experience outside the game. I can't be a fly on a dragon and fight orcas in physical reality, but I can do it inside a fantasy type game or fly spaceships, etc.

Then the question becomes, what would be the purpose of this video game? Well, now we get into subjects like emotions and interactions, perhaps things that are not possible.

Alex Tsakiris: God forbid we talk about love or emotions or anything like that.

Riz Virk: Right, things that don't exist according to a lot of materialists. But these things may, in fact... I mean, I view most religions as [peepholes] when someone peeks outside the simulation and then they come back and tell us what they saw. It's like the three blind men and the elephant. Each of them saw a different part of the elephant and they tried to describe it and said it's like a snake, which is the trunk, or it's like a tree, which are the legs, or it's like a house, which is the body.

But they all seem to have this idea that the purpose of life is love and to be kind to each other, whereas it gets more intricate in the ideas of karma, and that you are here to create experiences, which then you have to go and resolve down the road.

So, I view it as a series of quests and achievements and the more you play, the more of these you create for yourself. That's what leads us to the Eastern traditions.

There's actually some debate, even in the Eastern traditions, between Buddhism and Hinduism. In Hinduism there's the idea of a pure, eternal soul, which could be the conscious part that comes in and it plays different lines. Within the Buddhist point of view, the thing that goes back and forth is not necessarily a soul but a bag of karma, if you will. So it's a set of information. If you think of it as increasing the size of this file but then as you remove things from it, eventually the file goes down to zero and goes back to whatever the original essence was. This gets back to this issue of what is God, what is pure consciousness in and of itself? I think that a simulated world better describes how that process works.

Alex Tsakiris: Well, yeah, or at least gives us a new way of looking at it and exploring it, which is really cool, because you're certainly hitting on all of the main points. Even the analogy of the ocean and the wave and the droplets and all of those things. A lot of people have offered the best explanation for what pure consciousness/God/spirit being would be, i.e., the ocean, and the individuated self as little droplets.

But I'm still not sure that I buy the idea of all of this being a bridge. It seems to me, with this extended consciousness question, we're just not allowed to talk about it because it's all taboo. And yet it seems the evidence is overwhelming that there's a reality to it.

I touched on NDEs because they're safe. We have all of this science published in these great journals, but the evidence for out-of-body experiences comes right along with near-death experiences. And the evidence extends beyond that, after-death communication, psi, and so forth. I always point to Dr. Dean Radin's Double Slit experiment which kinda says -- screw all that, let's go right to the end game. Here's a photon beam generator and I'm going to bring in a meditator and tell him to change the beam and he's going to do it or not do it. And low and behold he can do it. He gets six sigma results. So the evidence is all over the place.

Also with remote viewing, *Men Who Stare at Goats* and MKUltra, and all the ET stuff, which at this point, I don't know how we're even allowed to keep that out of the discussion.[49] Even the Department of Defense is coming out and throwing the holy water on it. Then we have the whole shamanic journeying, DMT experiences.

Is this "science is a bridge" idea really the way to go? Is the simulation hypothesis you're offering us a bridge, or is there a chasm you just have to jump over? That would lead to the next question, is there a reason we're not already on the other side of that chasm?

Riz Virk: So let's take ETs for example. If the model is they came here on a spaceship from another galaxy, I think a lot of scientists get lost a little bit and say, "Oh yeah, we're sure there's life out there, but we don't see how they could have possibly gotten here, because we don't know of anything that goes faster than the speed of light."

Again, we're caught inside these models, and in order to move science along we need to think of a different model.

Now, I think one of the reasons why the ET phenomenon is so weird and not accepted is because it may actually be *weirder* than that simple explanation.

One of the people I talked to in writing this book was Dr. Jacques Vallée, who has been around since the SRI days and was part of Project Blue Book.[50] One of the things he told me was that UFOs are not a purely a materialist phenomenon and they're not purely a conscious phenomenon, they're actually both. He said there are many instances where two people will be standing next to each other, one of them will see the UFO and one of them will not.

Again, there's no model in the materialist's point of view for how that happens. Either the craft is there or it's not, you can't have a situation where it's both. Well, it turns out, if you start thinking about video games and how they work, you can. I mentioned it earlier. If a person is at level 30 versus level 2, they might see the UFO and they might not.

I think they're just inexplicable, it gets to a level of inexplicability where many scientists will individually admit to be interested in these things that you're talking about, but as a group, they don't want to be the first to jump outside of this paradigm.

A great example of this, because I talk about *The Matrix*, people ask me all of the time, "How do you hack The Matrix?" I bring up the example of the spoon bending from the movie, where the little monk-like kid tells Neo, "Remember, there is no spoon."

I believe another gentleman who was involved with SRI was Jack Houck and he started to do these spoon-bending parties. One of my favorite stories is when he went to Los Alamos and hosted a spoon-bending party with a bunch of physicists and their wives, and he found that none of the physicists could bend the spoons but their wives could. Now, that was interesting because it turns out it was because the physicists were together. Any one of them individually who went to a spoon bending party with their wife, could bend the spoons sometimes. It becomes this weird morphogenetic field, if you will, that people are stuck in.

I think to get people there we have to present them with a model that makes sense. Science has been built up and has had a lot of successes in the physical world, building rockets, computers, all of these things because you create models and then you validate the models. The problem is, most scientists say, because it's something that can't be reproduced in the laboratory 100% of the time, and it's outside of our paradigm, it must not be real.

The same thing with spoon bending, people will say it doesn't exist but many people have seen it. I think it's showing us that the material world is not quite what we think it is, but it's so far out of the paradigms.

OUTSIDE THE MATRIX

Alex Tsakiris: One of the things that becomes clear to anyone who's ever meditated is we are more than our mind chatter. This becomes self-evident. As soon as you go past this monkey mind state of awareness, you're in a different world. You're outside of The Matrix.

I was listening to Eckhart Tolle not too long ago and he made a great point about the whole matrix thing. He said (paraphrasing), "Okay, maybe we live in a matrix... what we're doing here certainly does seem dreamlike. But if you are, then there you are the one who's experiencing it."

Riz Virk: I think you're getting back to Descartes, right? He said if everything was a dream or if he was being deceived by an evil demon, the only thing he knew for sure is that he's there, "I think, therefore I am." That's the fundamental idea you're talking about. This dreamlike nature of reality is quite interesting to me and I spend a lot of time on dreams because I talk about the technology that will develop to build something like The Matrix. Well, it turns out it already exists in a biological form, it's called dreams.

STRONG AI, IF THEY CAN THEY WILL

Alex Tsakiris: A lot of people are pretty worked up about Strong AI, and I think for good reason. I've been following AI for a long time and I was always a disbeliever, but there are some advancements in this technology that would make anyone wonder. As a Silicon Valley guy, as a very successful investor, entrepreneur, what's your take? Are we approaching a Simpson-esque "I, for one, welcome our new AI overlords" moment?

We have AI-driven shadow banning, and demonetization. We already have AI in the hands of people with the power to change the world. And it goes beyond Google, of course. It's in a million different places we can't see. Should we fear AI? And the second part of that is, what about the concentration of this AI power? Like we're saying, if you could, you would, if you can, you'd hold onto it, you wouldn't share it.

DECODING: STRONG AI

Weak AI -- the principal value of the computer in the study of the mind is that it gives us a very powerful tool. For example, it enables us to formulate and test hypotheses in a more rigorous and precise fashion.

Strong AI -- the computer is not merely a tool in the study of the mind; rather, the appropriately programmed computer really is a mind, in the sense that computers given the right programs can be literally said to understand and have other cognitive states. [51]

- **John Searle**

Riz Virk: I think people wonder how sophisticated AI has gotten, and if you remember back in the 90s and 2000s [AI] was not very powerful. AI has gone through several waves, there were the expert systems and ruled-based waves, then neural nets came along for a while. When I was in college in the 90s, we studied how to make neural nets and this recent wave has been more about data and machine learning and reinforcement learning. So a lot of the advances that have come recently have been because of the advances of computing power, the availability of data and the ability to crunch [data] and for machines to learn.

In the video game world, Claude Shannon, who created what I consider one of the first AIs, which was a chess playing computer back in 1950, he was at Bell Labs at MIT. Gaming and AI are intimately related, but he said the stages of [future] AI he first saw was where AI can play a rule-based game, like chess, but then eventually it can learn the rules. That's kind of where we are today.

A colleague of his, Alan Turing, has the Turing test which is this idea that if you're talking to an AI, back then it was to a computer, not necessarily software, they were thinking of it as hardware. But if you were talking to AI versus a person and you couldn't tell the difference, then the Turing test has been passed or what he called the "imitation game" back then. We're not quite there yet. In talking with an AI, you can usually tell if it's still an AI. In my opinion, there's another wave of AI that may need to come, added on to the current technology, I don't know what that is, but a lot of people are worried about super intelligence and that AI will take over the world. I actually worry not that AI is so intelligent, but if we start to hook up weapons and the AI is not that intelligent, it's more intelligent than it is now. But today's AI is very limited, it's only good at certain tasks. We don't have artificial general intelligence yet, because you have to train it along certain things.

If you're training it just to shoot, it's almost like, would you rather do a training match in karate with a brown belt or a 10th degree black belt? Well, it turns out the brown belt is more likely to hurt you than a 10th degree black belt who will make sure you don't get hurt too much when you're doing the sparring. Not only do they have the power, they also have the refinement, the control and the wisdom.

Alex Tsakiris: But it depends on what the directive is.

Riz Virk: It depends upon what the directive is and what the values are. I think eventually we will have to worry about AI and weaponized AI.

If we don't have a better handle on evil and how it functions in the extended consciousness realm, we will be incapable of evaluating the impact of the simulated and augmented consciousness technologies that are clearly coming our way. Despite our misgivings about technology, history doesn't look kindly toward the path of the luddite. Maybe it's time to confront our "if we can we will" nature. Maybe it's time to consider whether we're actually in a game of catch-up. We'll do that next.

12
THE INVISIBLE COLLEGE GOES OFF PLANET

"Without pain, without sacrifice, we would have nothing. Like the first monkey shot into space."
-- Fictional character **Tyler Durden**, *from the subtly gnostic movie,* Fight Club

> **IN THIS CHAPTER**
> - what we don't know might hurt us
> - the pursuit of terrestrial goals
> - ETs prayers

Dr. Diana Walsh Pasulka's stellar academic background didn't prepare her for Gucci-clad, Silicon Valley's billionaires and their breakaway civilization built on alien space junk harvested from the New Mexico desert. And it didn't prepare her for what she found in the secret archives of the Vatican.[52]

Alex Tsakiris: In 2012, today's guest was at a high point in her career, a well-respected Professor of Religious Studies at the University of North Carolina, Wilmington. She had research awards, a successful book with Oxford University Press and gained tenure, which is almost impossible to do these days...

...Then the universe winked. A colleague referenced a paper you published and noted that your description of a Catholic saint's encounter with an angel sounded a lot like a UFO experience. That led you to a UFO conference where you met Chris Bledsoe who told you his encounter with ETs seemed more technological than biological. Next, you're off to a UFO conference in California where you just happen to land a personal tour of Silicon Valley with none other than Dr. Jacques Vallée.

That set you off on this six-year journey taking you from your academic religious conferences with our friend Dr. Jeff Kripal at Rice University, to harvesting space junk from secret crashed UFO sites in the New Mexico desert with Silicon Valley meta-experiencers who don't think twice about ordering thousand-dollar lunches from the Ritz and hopping on a private jet like an Uber, and ultimately into the deepest walls of the library of the Vatican. Wow! What a story. What a book. Congratulations on *American Cosmic*. Tell people your opening line when someone bumps into you on the airplane and says, "Tell me about *American Cosmic*." What do you say?[53]

Dr. Diana Walsh-Pasulka: So people in my field of religious studies, this is kind of a well-known joke among us, we never tell people what we do when we're on airplanes because they will inevitably think we're ministers or priests in the formation or something, and want to know that type of stuff and that's not what we do.

We are in interdisciplinary fields with archaeologists, sociologists, historians and things like that, and we don't really weigh in on the reality of beliefs. People believe in all kinds of things. They believe in Vishnu, they believe in Jesus, they believe in Muhammad, and we don't say yes or no to those. What we do is study the effects and practices and these kinds of things.

If somebody asks me about *American Cosmic*, frankly, I'd have to figure out who they were because that book has so many different levels to it. If they were ufologists, I'd tell them about the crash site and I'd talk about that. If they were academia, I'd say, "Well, what I'm doing is basically using the UFO belief system as a case study of the changing infrastructure that's akin to the book of the *Protestant Reformation*," that the book actually changed our culture. Technology changes culture, it changes everything, and religion is not exempt from that.

If they were interested in things like *The DaVinci Code*, I'd tell them a little bit about the more unbelievable aspects of the book, which are nonetheless true, and my access to the secret archive because of my credentials and medium, Brother Guy Consolmagno.[54] He's the Director of the Vatican Observatory, which is of course a giant telescope area in Castel Gandolfo, but also one in Arizona.

He was just here to give a lecture at my university and we were hanging out and I said, "Hey, I do archival work, do you have a space archive?" And he said, "Well, as a matter of fact, anything that has to do with space from thousands of years ago comes to our place in Castel Gandolfo, it doesn't go to the Vatican."

So, I just happened to sit there and thought, "I wonder if I could get a look in your archive," and he said, "Of course. We have a place for scholars to stay, you could stay for free," and of course I had to take him up on that.

I went there and honestly, that's the end of the book. The book was done by then, I didn't think that was the last chapter. So when I got to that chapter I had to tell my editor, "Sorry, there's one more chapter to this book."

Then it got edited about, oh, I don't know, a million times and a lot of stuff was taken out. I should actually write the real story behind *American Cosmic*, but who knows? It's already caused quite a bit of controversy.

Basically, what I'm doing is I'm reporting on this new form of religiosity and to me it changed my life. As an academic, the best thing you want is to be surprised by your research. The book I wrote about purgatory, which is a Catholic dogma, I found out that people actually went to purgatory caves and that it was actually a physical kind of practice before it became a dogma of the Church. That surprised me, I didn't know. I don't think anybody really thought about it. That's the kind of stuff we do, we uncover things.

Now, I was, and still am, being daily mind blown by the research I'm doing into this field for the very reasons of the meta experiencers, the people I met who like I say, could Uber a jet. I've seen this on a number of occasions, and I've gotten hate mail about it. Like, "Who do you think you are? You're not *The DaVinci Code* person and blah blah blah." I said, "I'm sorry, but I'm not making it up. This guy can Uber a jet." And when I say "Uber," I mean he just calls up and says, "I need to be here. Can you get me a jet at the airport?" And they do, and off he goes. I'm not making that up, that actually does happen.

I know it sounds unbelievable, but if you look at what I've written so far and you look at my CV, nothing is out of the ordinary. I'm a completely ordinary professor. I move up the ranks. I'm a full professor actually, not an assistant or an associate, I'm at the top. I'm a chair of a department and like you said, I've won research awards, I've won grants. I'm a very typical, boring professor and all of a sudden, I come out with *American Cosmic*. That's not because I wanted to do it, it's because that's what presented itself to me. I felt it was my obligation to present it to an audience.

I presented it to an audience that I thought would be academics mostly, but it crossed over into the mainstream and people were fascinated. So I've been doing, on average, four interviews a week.

Alex Tsakiris: Let me just comment on that, because you were super welcoming about doing this interview and at this point, I think you would reach interview fatigue. You've done phenomenal interviews. I've listened to half a dozen of them in addition to reading the book and they're all great. You're so just unpretentious and welcoming.

I'd like to talk more about this transformation you just touched on. This is a super important book. It's one of the most important books I think you could possibly read about the current state of consciousness research, UFO research, the whole inner play with technology, which you hit on. It's also a wonderful, well-written story of this personal transformation you've gone through.

You were raised in a born-again Christian house in California. You're not religious in that way anymore, but you still attend Roman Catholic services. Again, I mention that because that's not always the case when you talk about a Professor of Religious Studies. Most of those people I have come across are pretty atheistic when you really get down to it.

So you go through this and then you go through an amazing... I can't stress it enough.... the stories that you've just mentioned are literally the tip of the iceberg. I mean, even the Uber jet thing is a minor part of that story. Tyler, the Uber jet guy, just finished showing you how to locate and retrieve fragments of a crashed alien craft in the desert. And he's explained how he reverse engineers this material in order to file patents on advanced technology that has not only made him a multi-millionaire, but wound up in biomedical devices that have saved lives...

I don't know how you go through all of that without being transformed, but it did, right?

Dr. Diana Walsh-Pasulka: It did. The thing is, I thought and hoped that I could evade that. At first, I was very suspicious, to the point of being frightened of a lot of the people that I met because they were not at a level that...they're not people that I'd ever met before. There were some who were professors and who were studying this as well, and I kind of bonded more with them, like James in the book. I bonded with James a lot more and he's a good friend of mine.

The other people that are way out there and doing that space program...

Alex Tsakiris: Can I just interject something because the weirdness never stops, right? James is what you described, but James is also an experiencer who's had multiple experiences with ET, if you want to call it that for simple terms. And the driving ambition behind his research project is to counteract this ability ET has to invade our head space. He wants to have greater control of that.

Even when you blow past that, which you should be allowed to do because your story's so huge, there's a lot of depth there that would blow people away, totally change our paradigm, and change everything we think we know about this stuff.

So, I'm sorry, please continue with your transformation.

Dr. Diana Walsh-Pasulka: Oh sure. So, I put off the meeting. I became very good friends with Christopher Bledsoe and his family. We actually happen to live about an hour and a half away and one of his kids went to my university. We would see each other often. I would go to his house and bring my kids and he would come to my house and we'd eat dinner and stuff like that. He met several of the professors in my department and he would come and talk to my students. What a sweet, nice man, and what an incredibly hospitable family.

What happened was that he became surrounded by the meta experiencers and people that were affiliated with government programs, and that was something I didn't actually want to get into at all. I was afraid of it, frankly. I thought, I'm just a normal professor, a mom, going about my business and I was worried about Chris. So, I had to kind of step away. Then I met Tyler.

Tyler was a person who I agreed to correspond with over email for about a year-and-a-half before I ever met him. When I did meet him he wanted to take me to New Mexico because he said that he wanted to know what I knew about consciousness and the religious experience, and mysticism. He said, "You don't believe in the physical aspects of the phenomenon, but I'm going to show you the physical aspects," And I thought, "Hmm. I'm not sure I want to know about that." But he insisted.

I met him in Atlanta at one of our conferences, the American Academy of Religion, and I asked Jeff Kripal who is a friend of mine and an academic at Rice University. He has an amazing body of work, and I asked him to meet [Tyler] along with me.

That was funny because here we are at this giant conference of religious studies, these scholars, they're all wearing black. You know, they're like shuffling around and looking for food and tables and everything. In walks this guy, completely cool and wearing Gucci, and I immediately knew that was Tyler. I was like, "Okay, this is not a scholar of religion."

He comes in and we introduced each other, and he looks around and says, "We can't eat here. Let's go to my hotel, the Ritz." Jeff and I said, "Sure." So, he just phones and he said, "Hey, I need a table for three," and when we got there, he was incredibly charismatic. I told Jeff, "Don't give in to his charisma. He might..." and Jeff completely did. By the end of the lunch Jeff was inviting him to his house in Houston, meeting his wife and everything and I thought, "What are you doing? You need to be more suspicious."

Tyler reiterated his invitation to go to the alleged "crash site" of these artifacts in New Mexico, and I was not going alone. I said to Jeff, "Why don't you come with me?" And Jeff said, "That's a little outside of my comfort zone," and I said, "I know." So then I decided to ask James the scientist, and James of course was all over it.

[James and I] had to wear a blindfold because it's a place that can't be known apparently. There are apparently seven crash sites that happened in that time period.

Now remember, I'm speaking as a scholar of religion, so I don't actually believe or disbelieve that there are actual crash sites of UFOs. What I'm doing is, I'm going to document this extremely elite group of people who believe that they're getting these artifacts and they're engineering them into biotechnology.

BREAKAWAY ACADEMIA

Alex Tsakiris: One of the themes I kept coming back to is this idea of a breakaway civilization, or in this case, breakaway academia. You're describing this group within academia that knows stuff nobody else knows. Is that what you're documenting here? Is there a civilization-level distance between where these folks are and where the rest of us are? Even those of us reading *American Cosmic*, we're in the minority. We're in this tiny little tribal community that's willing to accept what you're saying; what about the rest of the population? Have we reached the breakaway civilization point?

Dr. Diana Walsh-Pasulka: Okay, I know the theory and from my perspective the people who I interacted with were...this is where it gets really weird, I know that it's already weird enough, but it gets really weird. We went to the Vatican, Tyler and I, and we learned a lot because he said, "What should we do?" And I said, "The only thing we should do is keep quiet and listen. That's all we do," That's how we learn.

So we went and met people...the people we should meet, and what I learned, let's theoretically suggest there's this breakaway civilization within our species, and they are at the forefront of discovery.

By the way, I don't know if you know about this author Ted Chiang. His book was the basis for the movie *Arrival*, which is a great movie about the phenomena. He wrote a very short story about 20 years ago called, *Picking Up the Breadcrumbs* and it's basically about the breakaway civilization, but about scientists who hack into their own bodies and become super humans and are so far removed from humans that we have to just study them.

Alex Tsakiris: Just let me be clear on this because some people take the breakaway civilization in a whole other direction, in kind of a sci-fi(ish) direction, which may be the future reality. But what was amazing about *American Cosmic*, that's my literal read of your book...that you're chronicling a breakaway civilization. You're definitely chronicling it in academia where there are people who know and people who don't. Then you tell how James is secretly passed a card that says, "Call us."

Then, the kind of men-in-black-ish, not real men in black, but guys who just know stuff say, "You're invited to the Invisible College," and it's real and you've been there. You've seen *Fight Club*, the secrecy kind of thing. It's a whole different world.[55]

This is what you're documenting in the book, and then when you meet Tyler, he's in a different world, not just because he Ubers jets, but because he knows stuff that is way beyond what other people know or would ever be willing to accept. Again, I'm emphasizing the point maybe too much. Diana, you're documenting a breakaway civilization. It's not a sci-fi one, but aren't we already there?

Dr. Diana Walsh-Pasulka: I hear what you're saying. I didn't know I was doing that. I just was amazed by what I was discovering and the things that were happening. Even with Jacques Vallée [I was amazed at] his trust in me. He's got a whole library and archives of information, and I'm one of two people who have accessed it for 10 years. So, I was being given a lot of access which I didn't understand. Well, now I understand a little bit more but still don't know the full story.

Nobody knows the full story here, Alex. So that's why it's not an invisible college anymore because at least they used to talk with each other, now they can't. I want to convey the tragedy of this for these people.

Take Tyler, I wanted to convey that place in the story where he sees Judy Resnik and the whole situation of the Challenger blowing up. What I wanted to show is this guy leads a tragic life. I mean, hey, it's all cool, he can order this multimillion-dollar Uber jet and he's really awesome, he wears Gucci, and this kind of thing, but he's not a happy person. The things that he knows drives him crazy, he doesn't know how he knows these things.

I'm glad I'm not Tyler, I'm glad I have a more ordinary life. I don't even know if I ever want to get back into this thing again because of the pain and suffering of that group. When you bring it out, look what happens to you, you get targeted as a crazy person and this and that. Who wants that? And it stops academics from trying to study it because once they do, they get ridiculed and things like that, things that I don't actually want to have in my reality. It sounds glamorous, those lives, but they're tinged with pain and suffering and constant anxiety.

So… it's out there, yeah, and maybe somebody will take the banner and go and do *American Cosmic 2* or something like that, but it most likely will not be me because I've been burned by it. It hurt me.

The realizations that you see are amazing and you'll never be the same and maybe that's what life is really about, is to open up and see, not just the amazingness of it, but also the pain and suffering of it. I saw a lot and I just want to go back into my cave again for a while.

I do the interviews because my book just came out, people want to know about it, and I do like the book. I've read it a couple times now, you know, we read our books. Academics, by the time we've read our books a couple times, we're sick of them. I actually still like my book, when I read it, I go, "Yeah, I remember that experience." These are experiences I had; these aren't theoretical. I went through all these experiences.

I retain excellent relationships with James and Jacques Vallée, Jeff Kripal, Whitley Strieber, and others of the "Fight Club." I'm just like I was before. I want to retreat because I don't want to be involved again with that.

LEFT HAND PATH

Alex Tsakiris: ...Much of what you're describing sounds so left-hand path(ish), "materialism is cool, tech is cool," but your book is about a spiritually transformative experience as well. Not your own, but one of the key characters in the book. What do spiritually transformative experiences tell us about what's going on? Are they closer to a real spirituality? Is there such a thing as real spirituality? A lot of people look at organized religion, particularly Catholicism, and ask, "Was that ever real spirituality?" Even though there's no doubt that people have spiritually transformative experiences, with Catholicism as the vehicle. Tell me how we begin to pull that apart.

DECODING: LEFT HAND PATH

Beyond its roots in mysticism and esoteric literature our popular understanding of the left hand path is a path through life that pursues worldly goals and the preservation of the self. From a spiritual perspective, left-hand-pathers are not seeking to merge with God/consciousness, they are finding/creating their own divinity.

Dr. Diana Walsh-Pasulka: I think what you're getting at is this idea of, is there some kind of objective reality. When we talk about religious language, are we actually talking about something that's objectively real, outside of ourselves? And if we encounter those things, are we having genuine experiences or are we having subjective experiences? So it's this problem of other minds, it's called philosophy.

You also mentioned Jeff Kripal with respect to this, who says that it's all of us. It's all kind of us, and I'm actually not of that opinion. I think that there could be… I mean what our religions, or experiences that expand who and what we are.

Heidegger, one of the philosophers that I talk about in the book, says the age-old philosophical question which is not asked in philosophy anymore, "Why is there something rather than nothing?" Once we start to contemplate, wow, we're here and that's a little bit strange. Once we start to think about those things and think about these experiences, [we're more open].

WHO DOES ET PRAY TO?

Alex Tsakiris: If we're talking about a non-human intelligence with control of the extended consciousness realm, shouldn't we be very skeptical when we enter into this spiritually transformative stuff?

And before we even go there don't we have to begin to map this extended consciousness realm. Is there God realm, and Heaven realm? This seems to be where NDEs say. Because recently there's movement within certain some parts the UFO community, including Jeff Kripal saying (paraphrasing), "No, it's all one. Heaven and God are just different ways of contacting and accessing these same extended realms."

I framed it up as a question, who does ET pray to? You mentioned in the book, "I prayed, because I didn't know what was going to happen, and I could only expect the worst." So you prayed. Does ET pray? Who does ET pray to? That's the question. No one's asking that question.

Dr. Diana Walsh Pasulka: No, other people are. The Catholic Church has asked that question.

Alex Tsakiris: Oh, the Catholic Church. That's who I'd trust, believe me.

Dr. Diana Walsh Pasulka: I'm just saying that they've asked that question. Brother Guy Consolmagno asks in his book, *Would You Baptize an ET?* And he says that he would if she wanted to be baptized. Even when you read the Old Testament Hebrew Bible, God is referring to God's self as plural. [56]

I always like to go back to Socrates as the person who is given the honor of the smartest person...the one who said they knew nothing. I think we have to approach this with the [same] perspective of gosh, those are all good questions and we should follow through on them, but draw no conclusions.

Alex Tsakiris: ...to me, your book forces a shift in terms of burden of proof. We can no longer talk about whether there is ET, that's answered. Anyone who doesn't believe the burden of proof is on them. We can't ask whether or not they're travelling in these unbelievable tech crafts from other places far away, that's answered in your book. The burden of proof now shifts to whoever wants to prove otherwise. I'm not saying you're making these claims, I'm just saying if someone just follows your stories, this is where they lead.

And, regarding James (Diana's friend who is featured prominently in *American Cosmic*, an experiencer who has been traumatized by ET contact and very invested in stopping it or having the ability to control it) if we are going to follow the data, we've got this major divide here between what people are reporting as the "God experience" and what people are reporting as the "ET experience."

Dr. Diana Walsh Pasulka: ... by the way, part of the reason I prayed that night was James actually showed me a presentation he had done about his research and it terrified me, I couldn't sleep that night. I had terrible dreams and nightmares. He said, "You know Diana, if we were doing this research 100 years ago, we would call these angels and demons." That would be the framework, for sure, because a lot of them are pretty nasty and do nasty things. Now, do they do [those things] on purpose? I don't know. So the experiences are nasty for a lot of people and I think that a lot of people won't accept that.

There are people who want it to be all about love, but it's not. They want it to be all about cultural evolution and everybody getting along, but it's a lot more complicated. And I get into the complexity of it in the last chapter with Sister Maria of Agreda of Spain, a 16th- century nun who was reported to bilocate, which means she could be in two places at once. She believed she was by-locating from Spain to New Mexico. She goes to New Mexico and she's supposed to evangelize a local Indian tribe. There are still monuments of her if you go to these places in New Mexico. I think about her with respect to Tyler and think to myself, that was a pretty horrific thing that happened to her because she did not want any of her experiences to be put into the political ends of the Catholic Church, with respect to colonizing the indigenous population, but that's exactly how they used it. I thought, what if they're doing the same thing to Tyler? What if they're using him in this way?

Some people have said, "If you believe in ET, do you want them to come and be here?" And I'm thinking, no, because like Stephen Hawking said, "Why would we be advertising, hey, come and get our stuff, come and colonize us." Not a good idea. So if they're here already...

Alex Tsakiris: How are they not here already? This is back to the ancient aliens question. I don't know how we put together a story that doesn't have them here for a long time. I don't know how we put together a story that doesn't have them working on us as part of a genetic engineering program.

How else do you explain the way the pyramids are precisely lined up with the stars and that all the ancient tribes say they came from the sky? All of that becomes accepted until it's falsified in my opinion.

The extent of ETs/others participation in our history/ancestry remains unclear. The more pressing question may be their current agenda. The UFO community has been divided regarding ET's intention. Many see them as rescuers of a dying planet sent to save us from self-annihilation and environmental disaster. Others see them as advanced spiritual beings who bestow positive spiritually transformative experiences and healing to those willing to accept their gifts. But we may have to consider a darker aspect of the ET phenomenon. Reports of ET's unwelcome contact with humans can't be ignored. We'll tackle that next.

13
GOOD ET VERSUS EVIL ET

> *The same forces of nature which enable us to fly to the stars, enable us also to destroy our star.*
> *- "reformed" Nazi rocket scientist, and NASA space scientist,* **Wernher von Braun**

> **IN THIS CHAPTER**
> **- disclosure**
> **- when PSYOPs go political**
> **- ET angels and demons**

My oldest son saw a UFO while surfing in the Pacific Ocean a few blocks from our house. He had gone alone, but met a couple of his buddies in the water. They all saw the huge triangular UFO with colored lights rise up out of the water and fly off. My younger son, Zane, saw a similar craft a few years later. Again, while surfing. UFO sightings are not uncommon any more. Even those like me who've never seen a UFO, usually know someone who has. If you don't think so it's probably because you've never dared to ask your friends and family. Some people think UFOs and the beings that inhabit them are here to help us. Others think they're here to destroy us. Who better than one of the world's leading UFO researchers, Richard Dolan, to answer the question.[57]

Alex Tsakiris: The UFO/ET mystery is at the center of just about every big picture question we can ask. Who are we? Why are we here? And that places the UFO mystery at the center of not just our history, but also of our science and maybe even the center of our spirituality.

That's what makes Oxford-trained historian and Rhodes Scholar finalist, Richard Dolan, who's widely acknowledged as one of the most respected, authoritative, and influential researchers within the field, an important voice. Here's some clips from my interview with him:

Alex Tsakiris: You gave a presentation on The New Face of Disclosure in Copenhagen in July of 2019. Let me play a clip:

Richard Dolan: So can the establishment truly dominate the narrative if they are rolling out this disclosure narrative? I think it would be very difficult for anyone who's trying to control the narrative, really. There are a lot of questions that will come up. When we did After Disclosure 10 years ago, Bryce and I really asked about these things. For me, the big question is, if you make an acknowledgement that UFOs are real, then wouldn't it be the case that people would say, "Oh my God, how have you been lying to us all of this time?"

Richard Dolan: The first thing I'll just say is, it's funny about disclosure. I didn't want to write about disclosure, ever. Fifteen-plus years ago, people were talking about disclosure. This was back in 2002, 2003, 2004, and I would say, "Ah, way too early to talk about that. We still have to get into the nature of the cover up and disclosure is premature." The problem was, I kept getting roped into Steve Bassett's ex conferences, which are about disclosure and all of these other disclosure conversations. I was naturally brought in because of the political analysis that I used to do and have always done.

So, when we wrote *After Disclosure*, that's a book I'm really happy that I had a great co-author. Bryce Zavel is a screenwriter, producer, and he's got a lot of Hollywood experience. He did the TV show *Dark Skies*, which many still remember, and his imprint is really definitely visible on that book.[5859]

But in terms of what I was talking about in that clip from Copenhagen, I still maintain this, I've always believed that any kind of official announcement from any government body, particularly the United States Government, is going to be a really difficult one for them to control. Because with UFOs, people think they can tame this subject and it cannot be tamed. It's too big of a reality transformation and that's why I don't believe that we're seeing disclosure right now.

When the mainstream narrative changed, starting at the end of 2017, when the *New York Times* did their few pieces, and *Politico*, then all of the follow-up, [since] we have seen so much transformation, it's easy to come to the conclusion, "Oh, well, this is completely government controlled. It's a PSYOP. It's a disclosure narrative," whatever.

Alex Tsakiris: I know. You really pushed back hard on me when we were talking and I said, "Richard, to me, this is obviously a political PSYOP kind of disclosure."

Richard Dolan: No, I totally disagree.

Alex Tsakiris: You totally disagree?

Richard Dolan: I mean, I can understand the point of view, but I'll tell you why I disagree.

Alex Tsakiris: Can I ask you to pause that? Let me add a clip and then you can respond directly because I think you know and appreciate Leslie Kean, who has the byline to the *New York Times* story,[60] and I had a chance to interview her. I love Leslie, she's awesome. She's been on the show a couple of times, a lot of respect for her, but I hammered her pretty hard. Let me play this clip.

Alex Tsakiris: *...who comes forward? (Luis Elizondo) he's not a whistleblower, right? (note: Luis Elizondo originally claimed to have been working for a Department of Defense Pentagon program investigating UFOs, but later evidence suggested he* was an intelligence agent).

Leslie Kean: Yeah, he kind of is.

Alex Tsakiris: *Just looking at it from the big picture, where is an example of anyone inside the government who has come out and said anything like this? I mean, the kid who went to jail for having a picture of a submarine in his background, this is not a day and age where people inside the government with deep state secrets like this are allowed to speak freely. He was not breaking boundaries or saying all of this crazy stuff that no one wanted him to say, this is a controlled release.*

Leslie Kean: *No, I don't agree with that. I mean, none of our work ever led me to get to that conclusion, or any of us, and we talked to a lot of people.*

The point is, none of the information that he brought forward was classified information. It's about classified information, that's the distinction.

Alex Tsakiris: *That distinction is meaningless at this point. This is the biggest story probably in the history of our lives, certainly, a lot of people are saying in the history of the world, and to suggest that this somehow in some phony baloney way is not classified... I don't see it.*

Richard Dolan: It's so funny, I find myself agreeing with Leslie on this issue. I'd like to have this out.

Alex Tsakiris: Okay, first of all, the idea that Luis Elizondo is a whistleblower just doesn't add up, it doesn't pass the sniff test.

Richard Dolan: Well, I wouldn't necessarily call him a whistleblower.

Alex Tsakiris: [Leslie] just did. She said he's a whistleblower. Next, the idea that, "We met with the guy at the DOD offices, but he's a whistleblower." And then, "All of the information he revealed, well none of it is classified or top secret." It's like I've mentioned, the kid who innocently took a selfie inside his submarine, is in prison for revealing government secrets, and this, the biggest thing ever, isn't classified? No one cares that it's being released?

Richard Dolan: I wouldn't say that Elizondo necessarily classifies as a whistleblower. I don't know. All of these people are self-serving. So the folks at TTSA, it's not like they're all angels and they have no other ulterior motives.[61] They do. It's all about money, it's all about getting a piece of the action. I would hazard to guess that maybe they want some defense money, maybe they want some contracts, maybe they want access to what they know is classified technology. There may be other things going on here where it's not all philanthropic. I would be shocked if it were. So I don't know if I would call him a whistleblower.

Alex Tsakiris: Here's the alternative read on that, number one, it's political...This is clearly coming from the Podesta-Clinton camp that was trying to release it the year before. They were hooked up with Tom DeLonge and they were announcing, they were kind of preheating us for the release. They didn't win the election, so they just kind of rolled it out anyways. That's how it looked to me.

I think the whole Peter Levenda-Tom DeLonge thing, the story just never made any sense. Peter Levenda, "Well, you know, Tom DeLonge called me up and I was like, 'Wow, is this really Tom DeLonge?' He was like, 'Yeah buddy, we've got to go to the CIA and get to the bottom of the UFO story because it's never been told.'" Many holes there.

Richard Dolan: I think there's some reality and some non-reality in that. I've never believed that Hillary and Podesta were ever going to be a disclosure team, ever. I didn't believe it then, I don't believe it now. If she had been elected president, there would be no more disclosure than there is now. I don't think that was a plan.

I do believe Podesta is very smart and as a UFO-savvy

guy, which he clearly is, recognized that his candidate who was desperately in need of an additional cool factor in her campaign, could benefit from being kind of a UFO advocate. Knowing also that the *New York Times* would not trash her, since they basically own the *New York Times* coverage. She could get away with being a UFO candidate, go on Jimmy Kimmel, try her hand at that whole thing and maybe win a few votes, that's all that I've ever believed.

There's no evidence to me that in any of the DeLonge-Podesta communications that Podesta was actually serious about this. Someone please show me where Podesta [says], "Yes, we're going to do a disclosure." This is all DeLonge. Podesta allowed some communications to happen and then, of course, they turned the lights on, WikiLeaks came out and they all ran for cover and DeLonge came with his B team. But the Hillary thing, I don't believe that. I think DeLonge's people might have had these illusions, yes, I think that's entirely possible they would have thought, "Oh yes, we're going to get Hillary and Podesta to be disclosure candidates." But I seriously doubt that Hillary Clinton or John Podesta would have considered moving ahead with UFO disclosure.

ET CONSCIOUSNESS

Alex Tsakiris: I want to talk about good ET versus bad ET because one of the things I respect about your work, Richard, is even though the political side, the national security side is your specialty, you've allowed yourself to be stretched in some really important ways. I'm always surprised at how many people are unwilling to go over that next hill. Be it consciousness, be it spirituality, be it your incredible four-part interview series with UFO/ET experiencer, Chris Bledsoe.[62]

You and your wife Tracey, who is an experiencer...does she call herself an experiencer or an abductee?

Richard Dolan: She would probably call herself an

experiencer. That's her go-to. She wouldn't say that she knows she's an abductee, so I would say that she believes strongly she's had a couple of experiences with non-human intelligences.

Alex Tsakiris: Well, you guys did an incredible YouTube video on this that has like 80,000 views, and it's just impressive in terms of its breadth and covering a lot of these topics. But there's some I wanted to drill into further and I thought this would be a time to do it. I think it also pairs up well with Chris Bledsoe. Here's a guy we both know, like and respect. Grant Cameron, UFO researcher, he's been on this show, I know you're friends with him.

Let me play this clip from Grant:

Grant Cameron: *...his wife suddenly wants to talk about, I'd like to talk about entanglement, particle entanglement, and I'm thinking, why would you ask us? Your husband has a PhD in physics.*

He's right. He's run the parapsychology, the...what they called a phenomenology desk, at the CIA. And what people have to realize is that when the CIA calls it phenomenology, that is a hint as to what's going on. It is not UFOs, it's remote viewing, ghosts, parapsychology, telepathy. It's the whole ball of wax, it's all consciousness. That's the ground of being, and they know that.

That's why when the Canadian government documents said in 1950 that mental phenomenon may be involved, the top-secret Canadian Government documents, say mental phenomenon may be involved in flying saucers, that's when they started the MKUltra stuff. That's when they started all that because they were trying to figure out how consciousness works, because they had a live alien in 1947. That's how the Americans knew to tell the Canadians in 1950 that mental phenomena was involved. Nobody was talking to aliens in 1950.

Adamski and Williamson would not come forward until a couple of days after the detonation of the hydrogen bomb. Betty and Barney Hill would not become public until the mid-60's. Nobody said they were talking to aliens, in public at least. Therefore, how did they know that mental phenomenon was involved?

Because they had a live alien and they knew that the alien is telepathic and it gets in your head, and they went, wow, man, if we could discover how this worked...

Alex Tsakiris: Now, I know you're a New Yorker and you talk fast, but no one talks as fast as Grant Cameron.

Richard Dolan: In a class by himself, and he's from Winnipeg, Manitoba. How does he do that? I just want to give Grant credit because as far as I know, he's the first person to really key in on the significance of that phrase, *mental phenomena*, in the Wilbert Smith memo that he wrote to the Canadian Department of Transport way back in 1950. People have looked at other parts of that memo for years, the subject's more important than the H bomb and so forth. But Grant keyed in, below that, where this aspect of mental phenomena was considered very important by the US Government.

Alex Tsakiris: And that catapults us into a whole bunch of questions that [throws] us right into the Good ET, Bad ET topic. Richard, my approach to this whole thing, the whole *Skeptiko* approach has been about consciousness. That's what I've been interested in answering, who are we, why are we here? Let's look at what people are saying about consciousness, let's look at near-death experience, out-of-body experience, after-death communication, parapsychology.... So it was interesting when I met Grant and synched in. I think I was influential in saying, do you understand... part of the conspiracy is that science continues to tell us that we're biological robots in a meaningless universe, while at the same time they're doing Stargate, they're doing *Men Who Stare at Goats*. They're way beyond consciousness is an epiphenomenon of the brain. Then Grant, like you said, puts in the missing puzzle piece with the evidence from the 1950s where consciousness was being identified, which makes us rethink the whole MKUltra topic. We also rethink what our orientation is to evil because clearly there's evil in MKUltra where we're trying to wipe people's minds clean and reprogram them.

So, jump us into what has been your process with these deeper questions because it also gets into spirituality very quickly.

Richard Dolan: I will start by telling a story that I have told on occasion, but not that often. For me, it was a defining moment in my life. I think I was 20 or 21-years-old at the time. And, you know, I've always thought about these types of issues of free will and determinism and spirituality. I think a lot of people have. And I went through a very strong period where I was...I guess I was an atheist. I was 19, 20-years-old. I had my reasons all laid out as to why I didn't believe in any kind of transcendental reality. I thought that was all based on wish fulfillment. I just started reading Freud, I remembered, and a lot of other philosophers and existentialists. I thought, well, we believe in an afterlife because we're afraid of death, and we don't want to come to terms.

And then I had a dog. I was feeding my dog, and I can see this in my mind even now. So I've got a can of dog food out and I'm opening it, and [my dog] knows exactly what I'm doing. He's watching me. He's excited because he knows that I'm about to feed him. And I'm observing him as he's eating and I'm thinking, he's a very intelligent creature, he knows me. That can represented dog food. Plus, I knew he was aware of many things that I wasn't aware of, like smells, sounds. But I thought, here's something he doesn't know.

He doesn't know how the food got into that can. Like, he'll never grasp that because *dog brain*, it just doesn't work like that.

He doesn't know what the stars are if he looks up at them. He doesn't know that he's been taken out of his natural environment and all these other things. Then I thought, "Gee Richard, you're so damn smart. So your dog's at this level. You're at this level. What's here?" What's there, what's there, what's there? Suddenly it occurred to me, my insistence on this complete, like absolutely no transcendental reality... how ridiculously arrogant for me to say that. Then of course, as you go through life and you go back and look at people in the past and everyone's always believed that they had it all figured out.

Go back to ancient Egypt 5,000 years ago. Talk to an Egyptian peasant living on the Nile. He'd tell you, yeah, when that sun thing goes down, that's the God, Ra. And he goes below the disk of the earth. It's shaped like a coin and he's going to be battling the demons of the underworld. You better hope he wins 'cause if he doesn't, the world will end. That's what they believed. We could look back and think, well, that's really quite wrong, but we now believe we've got it all figured out. Clearly we don't.

And more fundamentally, our brains themselves are the limitation. Our brains are amazing. They can allow us to engage in all kinds of incredible ideas and realities, but they have limits. And in fact, we understand that the limits are--we organize reality spatially and temporally, but do space and time actually exist the way that our brains tell us? Even guys like Immanuel Kant 200-plus years ago said, nope, not really. And Einstein and others confirm that. So we know that our brains organize reality.

With that said, I look at anomalies in our world today. I published a couple of books by Mike Clelland, the owl guy.

Mike's amazing. His work, to me, he's the true heir to people like Jacques Vallee and John Keel, in terms of looking at this synchronistic world that we live in with this meta intelligence that really does seem at times to be guiding us, like we're characters in a video game. It's like someone out there saying, yeah, I've got Alex Tsakiris for a couple of years. I'll have Dolan. Let's have them do an interview in early 2020. Okay, cool. Let's put that on the calendar. Like I whimsically wonder about things like this, because there are *very* bizarre anomalies and synchronicities that happen in this world.[63]

And I don't pretend that I know what it is, but here's why I'm getting into this. Consciousness clearly is important in some fundamental way to the nature of our reality. There is no question in my mind anymore. We've done enough genuine scientific experimentation that supports that. Secondly, we have an enormous hole in our general understanding of reality itself. There are things we don't get. And in that hole are things like UFOs, synchronicities and spirituality...and maybe even psychic phenomena, PSI phenomenon...[they] absolutely fit in there.

So we don't get it yet. And I'm hopeful that we might one day have a better understanding of it. I don't consider it paranormal. I consider these things normal we just don't have a full understanding.

(later)

Richard Dolan: I'm going to admit that my bias is toward physical material encounters. I'm not going to deny that, but I'll also say that a lot of people who have come to me with encounter stories, I guess, all I would say is they're not always credible people. It's not something that people ever like to talk about. We don't like to discuss this in this field. We don't like to talk about the fact that there are seriously damaged individuals. They're drawn to this field sometimes because they've had experiences, but sometimes it's because they're damaged and it's hard to distinguish what is what. So I have sympathy and compassion for all of those people because you can tell they're in pain. Beyond that, I have to get what is true. I don't know how to get to the truth of some of those stories.

I've been struggling for the last decade or more in trying to incorporate a true understanding of consciousness into my understanding of ufology and of the world itself. I'm open to it. I don't throw it out, but I try to treat it carefully. I'm not ever going to be someone who's going to embrace it because it seems like a good idea. Maybe what Ray [Hernandez] is onto is a good idea. You do a survey with as many people as you can, but are all you doing is getting social prejudices and ideologies?

Alex Tsakiris: I guess I'd rewind it a little bit, back to what you said, we need both sides. We need somebody who's out there willing to collect the evidence. Because you know the issue with the God thing, the angel thing with Chris Bledsoe, or the God thing that Grant Cameron mentions, which is really, I think, a punt.

There's no good or evil and you know, look at Michael Newton "in between" lives and it all works out and we're here for a purpose. It's like...I need something more than that, buddy. You're going to have to explain the rape and torture of little kids. You're going to have to explain that to me.

Richard Dolan: That's right. Tell that to their parents.

Alex Tsakiris: Tell that to yourself, if you are a parent. Tell that to yourself, if you're a victim, tell that to yourself if this has been perpetrated on you. Don't we need to hear and respect your story? We don't need to take it and turn it into something that we imagine it to be inside of our worldview.

Richard Dolan: I think a lot of those people, I don't know about Grant in particular, and he is my friend, but I think a large number of those people who have that opinion, I really wonder how much of the world they've experienced. I really wonder, like, have they *really* experienced truly, evil people. There's a lot of folks in this world who've lived very insulated lives and exist in their own kind of bubble. So, I'm not inclined, you know? And the greater philosophical step, [you] take 10 steps back in attempts to see the bigger picture. There's no good, there's no evil? Fine. You can make that argument. But in our world, I think there is definitely good, and there's definitely evil.

Alex Tsakiris: But it does get complicated. That's why I think it's important to switch back to Chris Bledsoe's story. Here's someone who's run the gauntlet, done all the right stuff in terms of trying to understand his experience, and seems to genuinely have come to the conclusion that, unfortunately for you, is very much in line with what Rey [Hernandez] is saying. Because that is Chris Bledsoe's story. His story is repeated over and over again in Rey's research, which is, I was traumatized by this. I thought it was the worst thing in the world. Over time, I came to understand it as part of my path, part of my spiritual awakening and my spiritual journey.

And that opens us up to all sorts of abuse. We've heard that over and over again from every guy who's spinning some cult, new age religion, or even old-world religion as a means to manipulate and control us. But at the same time, I think we have to remain open to the possibility that there may be some fundamental truth to that.

That's why I've been so interested in the near-death experience because the brain is out of the equation. Science has brought us to the point where we can say that. We have resuscitation studies, we have studies of people who are under extreme anesthesia in cardiac arrest.

We know that the brain is out of the equation in those situations, and people are having these kind of encounters and experiences that have overlap with the ET experience, but also have this transcendent, Chris-Bledsoe-angel-God kind of thing going on, too. So we're stuck with having to deal with both.

Richard Dolan: Right.

Alex Tsakiris: I love that you're driving a stake in the ground on one hand, saying, we have to hold the Dolan line of evidence. At the other end, you're still doing these interviews and you're going to do part five with Chris Bledsoe. That's awesome.

Richard Dolan: And you know, it's funny, when I said a little while ago, like, there's good and there's evil.

I realize, I better be careful with that because that can be a very...I'm realizing I've contradicted myself probably countless times in this interview. By stating that there's *absolute* good and absolute evil...actually, there's relative good and evil, but I still have to be careful. When you think about international relations, for example, which is a very big interest of mine, you want to be really careful when you start equating one nation with good and another nation with evil. That's a bad mistake to make. I don't like to make that mistake. So on a personal level, there are evil things that are done. Again, this is why I don't like zealots and I don't like fanatics of any sort. They scare me.

They scare me too. As you'll see you in the next chapter, some of them scare me a lot.

14
STOP THE BASTARDS

What do all men with power want? More power.
- **The Oracle,** *from the overtly gnostic* Matrix *movie series*

> **IN THIS CHAPTER**
> - unimaginable evil
> - helplessness and psychopathy
> - removing evils power

Most everyone with a passion for yoga remembers their first class. Mine was on a racquetball court in a Dallas health club. The noisy, cramped space wasn't suited for yoga, but, when the student is ready, the teacher appears. Mine was George Purvis. George attacked yoga poses like a Dallas Cowboy football player, but his real genius was seamlessly integrating yoga philosophy into those impossible stretches. Like most yoga teachers of his day, George had made pilgrimages to India in order to learn from the masters. In this case, it was B.K.S. Iyengar. Iyengar, along with Pattabhi Jois, were the two students of Krishnamacharya who brought yoga to the West. Iyengar was a yoga celebrity, so I was excited when George told us he had arranged to bring him to Dallas for a workshop. I was expecting deep wisdom from a master, but the guy who showed up was an ill-tempered, condescending, taskmaster who didn't fit with the idealized character I imagined.

My experience with Iyengar should have made me more skeptical of sage-on-the-stage yoga teachers, but I was genuinely shocked when during my interview with Anneke Lucas on episode #441, I learned that the other giant of the western yoga tradition, Pattabhi Jois, had sexually assaulted her and dozens of other female students during his years as an exalted teacher.

But that wasn't the main reason for inviting Anneke on *Skeptiko*, because Anneke is an experiencer and survivor of satanic ritual abuse.[64] From the ages of six to eleven, Anneke was subjected to unimaginable torture and rape at the hands of a highly-sophisticated and high-level, politically connected in Belgium:

> **Alex Tsakiris:** While preparing for this interview, I was swamped with all sorts of emotions and I don't even have any direct connection with the experiences of today's guest. Then again, maybe that's the beauty of Anneke Lucas's work as an advocate for children that are subjected to the unimaginable horrors of sex crimes, sex trafficking, ritual sex abuse, and other atrocities we want to pretend don't really exist and isn't real.
>
> **Anneke Lucas:** Thank you for having me on. I guess anyone's journey inward or journey into the nature of reality would lead to the question of evil. I see evil very much in the way that it is described in the yoga scriptures, that is to say, I see evil as ignorance, ignorance of the self.
>
> **Alex Tsakiris:** You know, I totally get that, and I've had those conversations before. But the other thing I deal with is, people who want to deny extended consciousness. I mean, for yogis, it's part and parcel of what the yoga tradition is all about. I think there's confusion when we talk about evil and it's reduced down to ignorance, or a misunderstanding. There is evil, right?
>
> **Anneke Lucas:** Well, let's just say that in our realm, we all have it. We all are ignorant of ourselves or we wouldn't even have to be here. So it's all a matter of degrees.
>
> **Alex Tsakiris:** And that's good. But I want to anchor this with an interview I did with an FBI agent who investigated

these horrible sex crimes against young children. He was stunned when he had to enter this world and rub shoulders with these characters. On the show, you could see his anger and frustration. That's something a lot of people can identify with. But there's also this element of complete denial.

Anneke Lucas: I've encountered that too. I think collective denial is what's creating evil at the moment. I didn't even speak out publicly about my past until I felt ready emotionally to withstand the inevitable personal attacks.

(later)

Alex Tsakiris: When we talk about the nature of evil, we understand that sometimes we go along with things that we shouldn't go along with. There's another kind of evil associated with that, and I know you've thought deeply about this.

Anneke Lucas: Yes, absolutely. There are degrees to which people are too scared, but then there is, in the public opinion, a larger component. There are people who know and who don't say anything because they're too scared for their own skin, for their job or for their life. That's fair, understandable.

Alex Tsakiris: It's understandable, but for the deeper kind of growth, for our soul?

Anneke Lucas: No, for the soul it would be best that you do whatever it takes, within reason of course. You don't just throw your life away for nothing, but within reason, to do what is right is important and then you can die free. Then you have not committed evil. But what is the right thing? It requires a lot of courage to speak up about these things and, of course, it has cost a lot of lives.

HELPLESSNESS

Alex Tsakiris: To truly accept the reality that you're exposing, makes us feel pretty helpless. It seems impossible to imagine that we could change the kind of system you're exposing.

Anneke Lucas: I just want to address briefly the word helplessness, because I understand that when I speak, I've noticed it's harder, generally, for men who are more brainwashed than women to shoot into action and do something right away to create the change, to go and save the children. It's so upsetting to find out that this is the reality and that someone you may have voted for may be a pedophile.

So I have to address psychopathy, because it's difficult for most of us to understand what psychopathy is. It's difficult to accept that people who look really good and have a good spiel would actually be raping children. It's so dark. Most of us can't imagine getting anywhere near a child like that, we can't imagine it.

Alex Tsakiris: Well, they can't imagine, in your case, a parent who begins sexually molesting their child, and then sells them into sex slavery at six years old. That's inconceivable. People really can't wrap their head around that.

Anneke Lucas: Exactly. That degree of sickness. But my mother, I would say, is easier to accept because she's just a sick person who was never found out. But she's a regular person. When it's someone who is a trusted figure at the top of the power paradigm, that's much harder to accept. My mother only had power over me, so in that sense she was at her worst, but those people have power over the entire world.

A psychopath, especially a very successful one, is someone whose reason/intellect works very well, but in fact they're completely insane, and so all this intelligence is used to hide the insanity.

Alex Tsakiris: I just sometimes wonder if talking about psychopaths, which is a popular thing to talk about, if that doesn't deflect away from the larger part of the consciousness question. Is it a way we shut ourselves off from understanding the influence of the extended consciousness realm?

Anneke Lucas: Hold on a moment, I speak about psychopaths because the psychopaths that I dealt with were ruling the world and influencing the entire world, and they were emotionally infantile. Extremely smart people, emotionally infantile. So of course, science will be giving so much more importance [psychiatrically] and those scientists who hold those narrow views will get more screen time.

But it's important that we understand psychopathy because those are the people that are influencing us.

If you look at a psychopath, they are the ones who just get rid of people below them and just climb, climb, climb without any sense of humanity for the people that they step over. Or they kill on their way up, brown-nosing the people above them and putting down the people below them.

Alex Tsakiris: That's a very secular view of things, which is okay. But what about Russ Dizdar (Chapter 15)?) Russ has spent the last 30 years working with victims of satanic ritual abuse. A lot of people don't like the satanic ritual abuse topic. But I think it's undeniable there are these extended realms that are influencing this realm. I don't want to pack it into a very narrow biblical definition, but I don't want to deny it and talk about this exclusively in terms of secular psychopathy, and people "not getting their needs met."

Anneke Lucas: Yes, I'm a survivor of satanic ritual abuse. That's what happens in the halls of power. They're Satanists. And I also work with people who, like me, have survived this. That's most of my work now, working with survivors, and many of them are survivors of satanic ritual abuse.

Alex Tsakiris: But how do we unpack the satanic part of that? I know that's not your focus, it's not my focus either, but we have to deal with the reality of it and not just from the secular psychology standpoint.

Anneke Lucas: I see it that way because it fits the trauma pattern. It fits someone who has no sense of self, who wants power to substitute their [lack of] self-esteem. Maybe it sounds too simplistic. But I was up close and personal with those people. I see what they do. I was mind-control trained to release these powers, and I probably could still use them, but the same powers are released if we do the work of integration, of mind-body integration, and that's done through trauma work. It's the natural drug, let's say, it is spiritual work, but courage is the key. If someone remains too afraid, you'll remain attached to the physical world and you'll remain attached to getting your value from external things, and we all do that to some degree.

So it's for each of us, in our own personal way, to go within and to simply face our own trauma. We don't have to think about Satanism, other than perhaps accept that people are engaging in that. Lots of people have experiences, I had a near-death experience when I was in the network when I was a child. I went to the other side. I needed it. I needed a miracle, and it was offered, the universe is completely reciprocal. And I use the word God, I dare to use the word God, but God is everything.

So I don't want to put too much focus on the satanic because it's just part of everything. Most importantly, I don't want to give that energy any power.

Anneke has faced and overcome unimaginable evil. Her yoga foundation, Liberation Prison Yoga, has helped others find a path to healing. But as we'll see in the next chapter, our inability to understand evil has left law enforcement agencies ill-equipped to serve and protect victims of crimes of darkness.

15
HAVE WE FORGOTTEN ABOUT THE VICTIMS?

"Don't judge yourself by what others did to you."
— C. **Kennedy**, *author of,* Ómorphi

> **IN THIS CHAPTER**
> **- evil leaves clues**

As you know by now this isn't a book about evil, it's a book about why evil matters. It's a call to use our best tools of reason, logic, and even science, to orient ourselves to the reality of malevolent forces in the realms of extended consciousness. But what about the victims of evil?[65] Does our inability to objectively look at evil interfere with our ability to find the justice we claim to want. It's a topic I discussed with Russ Dizdar:

> **Russ Dizdar:** I was in Worthington, Ohio at the Police Academy called OPOTA. A law enforcement agent named Thomas Wedge, who wrote a book called *The Satan Hunter*, was published in 1987 and written for law enforcement professionals.[66] So I'm going through a training seminar with Tom and the very evening that I get home, I get a phone call from a frantic woman who said, "Somebody gave me your phone number. I have a stepdaughter that's in the psych ward. She's going to kill herself." She goes into all of

the stories about satanic stuff and rituals and blood rituals and animals being sacrificed. I sat down with a 13-year-old, she's there because she keeps writing over and over and over, "The ritual of the flames. The ritual of the flames. The ritual of the flames." When I finally got enough engagement with her to talk about it, she said it's a ritual that she had to do on her 14th birthday to prove her love for her mother, a satanic priestess.

So this little girl, as I'm engaging her, began to have other personalities come up. Again, I'm a counselor, I'm in school, I'm trained to do these things. I'm listening to this 13-year-old and I'm listening to a male personality. Then I'm listening to another personality.

(later)

Alex Tsakiris: When you say that you've worked with victims, I just want to make sure that people understand that anyone in that kind of situation...that's real stuff. What do you do with that evidence?

Russ Dizdar: You're right, you can't deny the victims. The issue is, when they start telling you stories of being in boxes with spiders and blood and a baby and an altar and people in hoods and candles and strange language...they'll talk even about demons and all of that.

So, the issue is, for police officers, you can go through 25 criminology books, there's no grid. They don't teach [about satanic and occult practices]. All of the officers that I know, when we've gotten into cases and taken content to those officers, to federal officers, it's so bizarre to them.

The issue is then, how do you investigate this? When you take a Jeffrey Dahmer, nobody brought up the fact that he had a power cone in the shape of a triangle of human skulls where you conjure [spirits]...

Alex Tsakiris: ...correct me if I'm wrong, but Dahmer directly said he was in contact with spiritual beings that were telling them to do this stuff, and I think he also said his father had similar contact.

Russ Dizdar: And that's the point. On the investigative side of this, there's no, what I call a web...

Alex Tsakiris: What I heard you say is that there's physical evidence that they have to deal with that police sometimes don't understand. They walk into a crime scene. There's an inverted pentagram, there's blood, a ritual circle, all this stuff. You can't get past that. Why do we get such misinformation and disinformation about this? Why is it completely misrepresented in the media?

Russ Dizdar: I would say the first part is the issue of the grid. In other words, if you're trying to deal with the MS-13 gang, they are real. They're a real gang and they're in my city now up here in Canton, Ohio. They have certain markings, certain hand signs, certain clothing. So there are identifiable characteristics about a real gang. And law enforcement has to become aware of this. That's why they have a gang unit, but when we deal with satanic crimes there's very little teaching on that subject.

(later)

Russ Dizdar: ... What do you do with the victims? What about the ritual sites? What about the symbolism? Again, in law enforcement, if they don't know what an inverted pentagram is, or a pinnacle, a pinnacle is witchcraft, and pagan, an inverted pentagram. That's satanic. Certain writings.

If you know the language and know the content of the Alma Elantra working of Aleister Crowley...

When law enforcement shows up with a kid or a dead body that has a tongue cut out or a left hand cut off, or a satanic justice symbol carved into their chest... they can't read any of that.

(later)

Sarah Bain was abducted out of Rochester, Pennsylvania.

She ended up here in Ohio in a backfield that was known for satanic rituals. Kathy Menendez was found a month later, slaughtered and killed in early July. When you look at the satanic calendar and the kind of ritual that is demanded, blood sacrifice, usually a girl between seven and seventeen when you begin to look you have that in the mode of operation.

Russ is a people helper. He's also an Evangelical Christian. Most of us know people like Russ who have used their Christian faith for good. But as we'll see in the next chapter, the power of organized religion is easily and often corrupted in ways that look pretty darn evil.

16
WHISTLEBLOWER OF AN EVIL CHURCH

*"You find God the moment you realize that
you don't need to seek God."*
-- **Eckhart Tolle**, *best-selling author and spiritual teacher*

> **IN THIS CHAPTER**
> - a dream job
> - the reality of large-scale conspiracies
> - why God doesn't like crowds

Kevin Annett is controversial. You won't have to search very far on Google to find people who will say some disparaging things about him. I looked into those claims. I've also looked into the evidence Kevin compiled about a now admitted conspiracy of institutionalized evil on a scale none of us want to face.

In 1992, as a newly-appointed United Church minister in British Columbia, Kevin Annett, and his young family walked into his dream job. But dream jobs don't always turn out the way we expect. Kevin's turned into a whistleblower's nightmare and a 25-year legal battle as he uncovered some of the most horrific institutional-level crimes in Canada's history. Worse yet, chances are, you've never even heard about any of them.[67]

Kevin Annett: I was like a lot of Canadians and even though from a young age I was involved in politics and social justice issues, I was still completely ignorant of the injustices in our backyard. That's not accidental, the histories have been wiped clean. It resides only in the memory of the survivors and I began to meet some of them.

I was ordained in the United Church in 1990. By 1992, my family and I were in Port Alberni, which is right on the west coast of Canada on Vancouver Island, and I'll never forget the first time anyone told me about this. It was the first week I was on the job and I was hired to go out and bring new people into the church because there was a dying congregation at St. Andrew's United Church. I got a call from a native guy, Danny Gus, who wanted to get married. I went out to talk to him, and his home was right next to the former "residential schools." These were internment camps.

Alex Tsakiris: Can I just interject? At this point you don't know any of that. You don't know that the schools were internment camps. You don't know, what you later document very carefully in proceedings submitted to the Canadian court, that the death rate at some of these schools was 50%. You didn't know, but you would later learn through direct testimony you were a witness to, that children were murdered, tortured, and sexually abused at these schools, right?

Kevin Annett: Correct. I didn't even know about the existence of these places back then. Danny Gus said when I asked him why there were no Indians in church, kind of naively, he didn't say anything for a long time. He was looking out the window at the former school because the buildings were still standing there, and finally, he said, "They killed my best friend in that school and beat him to death, then they buried him in the hill out back. That's why they don't want us in their churches."

That blew my mind. Now, I told somebody in the church right away and they said, "Well, don't believe them, they're just mad at us for taking their land. They're just making all of this stuff up." At that point, this was the summer of '92 when I first started working there, there had been no court cases. The court cases didn't start until four years later. So the churches were free to say, "Oh no, it's all made up." They only started admitting stuff when they were getting sued. Before that, they had kept it covered up.

Alex Tsakiris: You were instrumental in opening up the possibility of those lawsuits. I want to go back to that story, when this guy, this potential member of the congregation said, "I want you to marry me, but the church was responsible for murdering my best friend." One of the reasons we can ignore this guy is because he's Indian, right? Because if it's a white person who says this we at least have to pause, but in this case, he's Indian, so they "make stuff up."

Kevin Annett: That's been part of the problem because it seems to be occurring to a foreign group, most white people can't relate to it. Even though this was happening and still happens today to a lot of white children, too.

...Institutionalized murder, it's going on. But the natives were like the canary in the mineshaft. A lot of the stuff that's happening now was tested out on them first.

LARGE-SCALE CONSPIRACY

Alex Tsakiris: The topic of conspiracy is always interesting to me... I'm amazed that so many people don't believe conspiracies of this scale can even happen. One of the things that you stand witness to is that these large-scale conspiracies do exist.

Kevin Annett: The way it operates in practice, is people with money and power don't have to conspire. They just make arrangements, right? We don't know about those arrangements until we learn about them and our whole world is blown because everything is so normalized. The crime is so normal to us that it doesn't seem like a crime.

Alex Tsakiris: What does that mean to you? In this case? Most people don't find anything normal about what you're exposing. Taking these kids...forcing them to enter these schools where they know a significant portion of them are going to die. And then knowing that a significant number of kids are going to be abused, physically, sexually raped. That's not normal.

Kevin Annett: I'll give you an example. One of the first forums we held in Vancouver, a woman came and she was almost the only white person. There were all native survivors of the death camps, and her name was Mary Ann McFarlane. She described how she worked in the Alberni residential school and she got fired because she found a matron taking a piano leg and beating a little Indian girl to death with it. So Mary Ann knocks out the woman. She defends the girl. Later John Andrews, the principal of the school, fires Mary Ann McFarlane and says, "Anything that happened to that little squad would be better than losing that woman because she plays the organ in church on Sunday."

So there's a hierarchy in their mind. A little Indian kid dies. Well, those little Indian kids seem kind of odd anyway. They're different. Death becomes abstract. We can't have an organist on Sunday because we know we want pleasant music, right? So we act. We all have a small circle of experience. And when you say death and torture, it's outside of that by and large, unless you're a victim yourself.

Then, you just don't want to talk about it. You want to pretend your life is fine. That's why we need to stop talking as if it's about Aboriginal children, and we need to just say *children*, that's something people can relate to. Dead children, [people] can relate to because there's nothing more horrible than the idea of losing your own child, right? Having gone through that myself with my own children, when I spoke in a healing circle, I spoke from my heart about my own pain. People trusted me because it's something they could relate to.

But genocide, it's just a word. It doesn't mean anything to anyone unless someone gives a specific example. This child was tortured to death on this date and buried in this hole by this person. And that's what we've been saying from the very beginning and all the work here, the details of how it happened, why it happened.

WHEN INSTITUTIONAL EVIL BECOMES PERSONAL

Alex Tsakiris: What was it like sitting with victims who were giving testimony about the tremendous pain they experienced? If we're honest, most of us shield ourselves from the pain of others.

Kevin Annett: When I was in the church and people would get up and speak from the pulpit, it shocked me, but it didn't rock my world yet because it was still abstract. It's only when I lost my own children, and saw how brutal the church could be, that I began to open my heart. You need a personal experience to hang it on.

I was able to relate to their pain because I was going through the same pain of not being able to see my kids every day, and to be vilified and attacked and impoverished. So you need that personal experience to develop real empathy.

(later)

Alex Tsakiris: How do you understand evil? You were confronted with an entity in this extended consciousness realm that you identified as being evil. Right? So we get that. We've heard that too many times to ignore it. I guess what I'm trying to understand is, how do you reconcile that with the light? With positive things?

Kevin Annett: The reality is, light and darkness are part of the same phenomenon. Good and evil are part of God. For example, the men who did this to me, who took my children from me, who destroyed my name publicly, who prevented me from working, I was tempted to hate them for the hypocrisy and the evil of what they had done. Then I realized, wait a minute, it's because of them that I'm in my situation now.

In the Tibetan Book of the Dead, they say, be thankful for your enemy. He shows you who you are. And it's true. There's this kind of dance we do where we are sharpened. We are made clear by our interaction with what we call evil...

WHEN THE CHURCH IS EVIL

Alex Tsakiris: Do you believe people have spiritually transformative experiences and do you believe that those experiences can be through a spiritual being that they understand to be Christ?

Kevin Annett: Well, I can't judge, and I can't look into another person's soul, but Frederick Douglass, the slave who led the abolitionist movement in the 1860s, described in his biography how his slave master had a religious conversion and became a born again Methodist. So he expected the slave master to release all of the slaves. But no, Douglass said he became even more brutal because he had God on this side.

If you have a genuine spiritual connection, why do you need a church? Why do you need a religion to express it? You don't. The kingdom of heaven is within you or it isn't. And if it's within you, you don't need to express it on Sunday in the church, right?

Alex Tsakiris: True. Look, I'm not a Christian, I'm not religious. I'm kind of playing devil's advocate here, but I do encounter a lot of people who, when they encounter this information, are confronted with the impossible option of turning their back on a tradition that is deeply interwoven in their family tradition. They just can't do it. And I do have empathy for them.

Kevin Annett: I've never been a minister. I've worked in churches and I know exactly what you're talking about. The majority of my parishioners were there because it's a social club, it's reassuring. They've always done it, it's a sentimental family kind of thing to do. That's fine. But one's calling is a very personal thing. It's not part of a group. There's an old Quaker saying, "God gets lost in a crowd" and I think that that's true.

(later)

Kevin Annett: ...when you encounter real goodness and real evil, they're not describable. They can only be experienced. And then, there's a mystery around them, there's an ambiguity. When you're in love, you can't describe it to somebody, it's there. It's life-giving, it's beautiful. There's nothing like it, right?

Similarly, when you're in the depths of despair brought about by this evil, there's no way to understand it. It's beyond understanding, but our heart and soul never betray us. And that's why I say to people, before you start this work, you've got to do your own personal work. And every day, go there because it's your only defense against what you're going to go up against.

Alex Tsakiris: What is your practice? How do you open that heart? You're a man in this Western culture where we're programmed from the beginning to keep that damn thing closed. Then again, you reference Sun Tzu a lot, so you're a warrior too. You are a truth-seeker warrior and now you're saying that you need to take off your armor and open your heart as part of your spiritual path. How do you do that?

Kevin Annett: I sit in nature; I sit by running water. I just remember who I was as a little boy, running around in love with everyone in the world. We go back to our innocence, right?

When I lost my kids, I'd see them now and then. I'd drop them off on Sunday night and it was a very bad time for me after I dropped them off. All I'd do is get on the bus and ride around and be with people. There's more genetic variation in one troop of chimpanzees than the entire human race. We're that close. We're really the expression of that one soul. You feel that when you're in great grief. You go to people, you hang out with them. You just absorb their energy and watch the way they are and take great solace in that. So we don't isolate. I say to people, the last thing you want to do is isolate in a room, isolate in life, thinking that a counselor is going to help you.

When I tell that famous story of William Coombes, the native who, when we occupied the church, he was there with us even though it was torture. He heard the church bell and he started getting sick because of the way he'd been tortured in these places. But there he was in the church with us, the day we occupied it, and he was really happy. He was handing out flyers to people and he had no fear. He wasn't afraid of the priests. He said, "I didn't want to let you guys down, I didn't want to be left out." Now that love, that desire to be with us, helped heal him that day, not some counselor but all of us together showing we're not afraid of these people. We're not afraid of the truth. We're going to stand here and help and love each other in practice, where it counts. And he stopped drinking that week, which was a bloody miracle if you knew his situation.

Comparing evil is a lose-lose game. The trauma experienced by those who encounter soul-crushing evil can only be weighed by a consciousness beyond our earthly understanding. But that doesn't make what comes next any easier.

17
STATE-SPONSORED EVIL

I'm bonded to you and what you are. I don't know who I am. If I'm not you, no consequences, no pain, no sorrow. I don't want to feel now what I didn't feel then.
-**Nick** *from* Supernatural *on his relationship with Lucifer.*

> **IN THIS CHAPTER**
> - irresistible evil
> - the false narrative around evil

I don't like this chapter. You're not going to like it either. It's disturbing. From the introduction to my interview with independent researcher and author of an upcoming book on the Finders cult, John Brisson (*Skeptiko* #443):

> **Alex Tsakiris:** For those of you who've been following the last few episodes of *Skeptiko*, you know I've taken this deep dive into evil. Now, not all listeners have taken that dive with me. There's been a lot of unsubscribing along the way and I get that, but I still maintain that this evil question might be one of the best lenses we have for coming to grips with, and get a better understanding of, our relationship with this extended consciousness realm. And while up to this point I haven't offered my personal working hypothesis on the nature of evil, I lean on the scriptwriters from *Supernatural* and use Nick's quote, "I don't want to feel now

what I didn't feel then." Maybe that's what this evil thing is all about. Escaping feelings, escaping energy that doesn't fit the way we want it to. And if the actions and behaviors that propel us seem wicked and evil to everyone else, they at least get rid of those feelings for a little while.

But what about evil that extends beyond our personal domain? What about today's guest, John Brisson, and his extensive investigation of the Finders Cult, a group with provable links to the CIA, FBI, and high-level intelligence organizations in our government that put to use ritualized sexual abuse of young children to cultivate a sexual blackmailing network that could be used for intelligence gathering. What are we to make of this kind of CIA/FBI sponsored evil?[68]

(later)

Alex Tsakiris: I'm always impressed by independent researchers who manage to make monumental contributions to our understanding of the world, without any institutional support, and often with very little, if any, financial support while battling forces determined to keep their message under wraps. Consider today's guest, John Brisson, who runs a YouTube channel called, "We've Read the Documents," which features John reading documents, often classified material, that has been released through FOIA requests. But John is also the author of an upcoming book on the Finders Cult, an organization with provable links to satanic ritual abuse, and unfortunately provable, and I'm going to emphasize that word again, *provable* -- he's got the documents -- links to United States intelligence organizations like the CIA and the FBI, who were tapping into this evil in order to compromise intelligence targets they wanted to control through sexual blackmail. That's a topic we're going to talk a great deal about today.

So John, as we were chatting before I began recording, this interview is going to be a rough ride for a lot of people.

I know that some have already turned away. They saw the topic and they're not going to listen. I know that in my own personal life there are very few people I can talk to about this. They shut down. You can pile the data wide and high, it doesn't matter, man. They don't want to go there.

And that's what I appreciate about your approach, your methodology, you're very committed to following the data and checking your sources, but you're also willing to go there.

John Brisson: Thank you very much for having me back, Alex. I'm very grateful to come back on *Skeptiko* and discuss this issue of ritual abuse and government institutions being involved in it, and how very widespread it is. And, as you said, we do have documentation.

Alex Tsakiris: I contacted you a couple of months back and said, "Hey, I want to dig into this satanic ritual abuse thing, and I want to know if there's any reality to it...When you Google it, the first fricking 100 entries are about satanic panic."

...you referenced *The Witch-Hunt Narrative* by Brown University professor, Dr. Ross Cheit, and his work detailing criminal evidence in cases of satanic ritual abuse. Many, like McMartin preschool, are accounts that people only associate with "satanic panic." In fact, when I brought this topic up with my wife, who's a forensic psychologist, she immediately went to the McMartin case as an example of satanic panic. But Dr. Cheit presents overwhelming evidence that many of these claims of "panic" are orchestrated to divert our attention away from what's really going on.[69]

John Brisson: When you read *The Witch-Hunt Narrative*... it's going to discuss the actual forensic evidence that children were molested by Raymond Buckey.

Alex Tsakiris: There's a kid who, if I remember correctly, is three-and-a-half years old and comes home and can't even verbalize it in sexual terms, but is kind of describing these things that are going on at the school and the mom totally flips. But like we're saying, the first thing she does is what any parent would do, she takes him to a pediatrician, and the pediatrician says, "Yeah, this kid's been sexually molested."

John Brisson: But it was even more than that. She took him to Dr. Scott McGeary who was the child's regular doctor and he said, "Yeah, this is really bad because he's bleeding from the anus, you need to take him to UCLA." So they took him to the Marion Davies Children's Clinic at UCLA, and both Dr. Linda Gordon and Dr. Jean H Simpson-Savary, who are both pediatricians, Savary graduated from John Hopkins and had five years of experience in pediatrics. They come to a conclusion that was fairly significant findings of sexual abuse. And later, a doctor who was hired by the defense, came to the same conclusion as well, that Matthew Johnson was severely molested.

Alex Tsakiris: So it's like a parent taking a kid in and saying, "What's wrong with my kid?" And the doctor basically says, "Oh shit, I've seen this before, this isn't good." Then it leads to a police investigation and the police say, "Oh, we've seen this shit before, this isn't good."

So again, pulling back, because you're into documentation and proof, we also have to pull back and consider the controlled narrative. Why is the narrative so strongly pushing this idea that it's just panic?

THE FINDERS CULT

DECODING: THE FINDERS CULT

On February 5, 1987, two men in black suits were arrested on suspicion of kidnapping six children and transporting them to Tallahassee, Florida. The children were malnourished, filthy, covered in bug bites, and in a state of sublingual shock. During the subsequent investigation, police found bags full of photos of naked children, and children participating in the ritualized mutilation of animals. They also found instructions on how to "buy" children and brainwash them. However, when the mothers of the children were eventually contacted, they insisted they knew the men and asked that charges against them be dropped. Later, police investigators in Tallahassee, and customs officials in Washington D.C., were told to back-off because these activities were part of a CIA operation.

John Brisson: As far as The Finders case is concerned, I'm bringing new documents to the table that were not previously seen, like the Ramon J Martinez Whistleblower Complaint. I am interviewing people that have not previously been interviewed, like the prosecuting attorney, Willie Meggs or US Customs John Sullivan, and Ramon J Martinez's partner, Bob Harrold. So I'm moving this case further than the information that was previously given to us by other researchers.

Alex Tsakiris: Now, you've just done a brain dump on people that's going to force them to jump right in the middle of this. So let's go back and talk about, like for someone who's totally uninitiated, do government intelligence organizations, like the CIA, Mossad, FBI...do they ever use blackmail, and can we prove that?

John Brisson: Yes, we can prove that. There are many cases that involve the idea of brownstone operations or sexual blackmail. So we have the Franklin scandal, which has implicated at the highest levels of government of [people] being blackmailed. George H.W. Bush, Ronald Wilson Reagan, Bill Casey, [implications] of them being around the nexus of Lawrence E. King that had been reported both in John DeCamp, former Nebraska State Senator's book, *The FranklinScandal* Nick Bryant's *The Franklin Scandal*, him being an investigative reporter and Henry Vinson,

Confessions of a D.C. Madam, who was around the nexus of Lawrence E. King and Craig Spence. In that case, it's very well documented for those who look into it.[70,71]

Of course, there's the Jeffrey Epstein case. They've been using this template forever.

Alex Tsakiris: Why? Why would our CIA, our FBI, why would they blackmail people? That's not in the Constitution, they're not supposed to do that. Why would they blackmail people, let alone use sexual blackmail with children? Is it because if you pay somebody to do something, then they'll only go as far as that money goes?

John Brisson: Exactly.

Alex Tsakiris: Sexual blackmail of this kind is a horribly effective tool. It's almost an irresistible tool for an intelligence organization.

John Brisson: There are many different reasons why this blackmail would be used by these intelligence agencies. It's also a good tool to weed out, "Okay, so this person is willing to do this."

... it's like a nexus of total control over someone, where it's not constantly having to buy someone off. Once you have the blackmail, you can threaten to use it forever.

Alex Tsakiris: What's a brownstone operation?

John Brisson: Brownstone operations are a method where you bring someone to a certain area where there's filming equipment, or you can get some sort of documented evidence, a camera, something.

Alex Tsakiris: So you bring them into a room, there are hidden cameras, hidden microphones, they don't know they're being recorded. They're doing some illicit act that they don't want to get out. Whatever you can get them to do, whatever their weakness is, whether it's doing cocaine, or something sexual...anything that could compromise them, you're going to record it and then you're going to start in on this blackmail thing. That's a brownstone operation?

John Brisson: Yes. Even back then, taking pictures of someone with a prostitute, for example. Any evidence that they can get where it's a setup to blackmail you, is a brownstone operation. For example, instances of Craig B. Spence throwing parties at his house where it was wired up with two-way mirrors and recording devices. Famous people would go to his parties and there would be children provided by Lawrence E. King for sexual blackmail and [some] would even practice ritual satanic abuse at those parties. The same could be said about Jeffrey Epstein.

Alex Tsakiris: Hold on, that's going to throw people and what you alluded to before, it kind of becomes a slippery evil slope in that, if you caught me doing cocaine with a prostitute, then I'm in your club, right? So, when you're inviting me to your party, I may not approve of people molesting five-year-old kids, but I'm at the party because you got me with the prostitute and the cocaine and you control me now. We have a strange bedfellows kind of thing.

So this crazy brownstone blackmail tactic creates this cesspool that joins all these different people together by the force of the brownstone blackmail operation.

John Brisson: Yes, and of course, everybody who's gone to these parties may have not participated in the darkest things that occur, like ritual satanic abuse or child abuse. Some of it can be compartmentalized, I agree with you on that.

Now, to separate the wheat from the chaff can be very difficult. I seriously doubt Bill Clinton didn't do anything wrong on the Lolita Express, for example. Or Donald Trump hanging around with Epstein and going to his house frequently and everything like that, or Alan Dershowitz, just because he's an attorney.

Alex Tsakiris: I agree and in terms of the court of public opinion, the burden of proof shifts to these people needing to prove to us they weren't involved.

John Brisson: You're one hundred percent right. Of course with Prince Andrew, he claims the picture that he took of Virginia Roberts Giuffre was a doctored picture when obviously that's her and him with Ghislaine Maxwell standing behind them. It's obviously not a photoshopped picture, but that's what he's claiming.

(later)

Alex Tsakiris: So The Finders Cult, what is it? Why is it a cult, per se? And what is the connection to what we're talking about, these brownstone operations?

John Brisson: It's a cult because Marion Petty was the leader of a group of people that would give up their monetary possessions to enter the group. I have referenced it as a cult to make it more palatable to people. I do think it should be more classified as "The Finders Operation" because that seems like what it is, with Marion Petty's ties initially to the Office of Strategic Services, him being part of the Air Force and later the information that we have from the investigative leads memo of being trained in espionage at the Jesuit College, Georgetown University.

Alex Tsakiris: Take us through a timeline.

John Brisson: With Petty, he joined the Air Force and was a chauffeur to many famous people at the time. He chauffeured Harry S. Truman, Dwight D. Eisenhower, Hap Arnold... He chauffeured many high-level, elite people around the time of World War II and afterward. He's had connections to the government at the highest levels, even back then.

Now, he claims that the money used to start the Finders Cult, to buy apartment buildings that would later be used for intelligence operations, hundreds of acres of land, was from winning poker games while he was in the military.

Alex Tsakiris: Right, and that would be consistent with what we're seeing with the latest Jeffrey Epstein story. Maybe you want to talk about that because the folks who are doing deep research into Epstein, he appears to be a lot more like a frontman, a fall guy.

John Brisson: Yes, yes.

Alex Tsakiris: One of the telltale signs is whose name is on the assets. No one puts their name on anything when they're doing those kinds of deeds, and I think the same is true with Petty and the Finders Cult. Whenever we see somebody say, "I own the land, I own the apartments..." it's probably just a front man because no one who's doing nefarious acts would have their name on the line. What do you think about that? And maybe fill people in on anything with the Epstein situation that I might be leaving out.

John Brisson: I agree with you, one hundred percent. According to Epstein, I think he was lower on the rung. There are people higher up within these organizations. Craig Spence and Lawrence E. King were fall guys. Jeffrey Epstein was a fall guy.

Alex Tsakiris: Guilty though...

John Brisson: Of course, I'm just saying those people go down, the higher-ups keep their hands clean. People that are higher up than Jeffrey Epstein would be Ghislaine Maxwell, Les Wexner, the billionaire who gave Epstein his New York City mansion for one dollar. Supposedly that mansion was wired up for the brownstone operation that was occurring.

Alex Tsakiris: Okay. So we have Petty, he's chauffeuring around all these super high-level presidents and the highest level in the military. How does that lead to the Finders Cult?

John Brisson: I guess I should start with Tallahassee... so in 1987, two men were arrested, Douglas Edward Ammerman and James Michael Hollowell, when a concerned citizen called in and said they noticed many disheveled, dirty children that were behaving like wild animals in Myers Park in Tallahassee, Florida. Two cops, Tony Mashburn and Judy Shokeen arrived at the scene.

They witnessed the children, two adults, and a blue sportsman van they were living out of.

Alex Tsakiris: What do the adults look like?

John Brisson: They're wearing suits.

Alex Tsakiris: So the kids are disheveled and dirty, and the adults are wearing suits in Tallahassee, Florida.

John Brisson: Police officers are automatically suspicious. Like, what is this? So they move to arrest. Ammerman and Halliwell take the children into custody. And when they do, Hollowell refuses to talk and he planks on the ground, and there's actually video of this.

Alex Tsakiris: This is bizarre. What happens next?

John Brisson: They're both charged with child abuse and were given a hundred thousand-dollar bonds each. From there, the Tallahassee Police Department starts an investigation.

Alex Tsakiris: They found child pornography in the van, right? They're cops. They're on this case now?

John Brisson: And they're trying to track down the parents of the kids. When they take the kids into the police station, they start noticing that the children don't understand modern objects, like clocks.

Alex Tsakiris: So we can imagine at this point the Tallahassee police might be saying, "Hey, we're just trying to reunite these kids [with their parents]." But you gotta believe that deep down they know there's much more to this.

And again, folks, John Brisson interviewed officers from the Tallahassee Police Department who remember this case. This is a real researcher-investigator who has unique information to bring to this.

Here's the really interesting part of this story, because the Tallahassee police are still investigating this when they're called off the case.

John Brisson: Skip Clements gave an interview and told me that the FBI in Jacksonville told the Tallahassee PD to wrap up their case.

(later)

Alex Tsakiris: So the children lead the police back to Washington, D.C. And the D.C. police say, "We investigated the same crime."

John Brisson: They raid the w street apartments. And in there they find Finder's numbers...computers, printers, and numerous documents.

Alex Tsakiris: Don't they also find information on instruction manuals and how to groom children for sexual abuse and other consistent information?

John Brisson: They find books on mind control and information on the impregnation of women in the Finders Cult.

Alex Tsakiris: As horrific as this is, people should know. Among some of these groups that commit these horrible crimes against children, are done at a very young age. Newborns, infants, you know, it's prime property to this kind of evil.

John Brisson: And they also found a summary of the events of Tallahassee that was being communicated by the Finders.

Alex Tsakiris: So we have a direct connection between the Tallahassee case and again, it's what pisses me off about the false narrative stuff.

And we'll talk about extended consciousness. Maybe we'll even talk about Christianity and Satanism. But this is evil, right? This, anyone would say, is evil.

These are defenseless human beings. Their entire lives are destroyed, their psyche is destroyed. How does that connect to the CIA and the FBI?

John Brisson: Investigators have forced documents to be released that show both the CIA and the FBI know about the Finders Cult.

Alex Tsakiris: What other evidence do we have that the Finders were using children to entrap people and blackmail them? How do we establish that?

John Brisson: Because of the equipment that was found at the warehouse. Customs officers Martinez and Harold reported that video cassettes and pictures that contained child pornography were taken out of the warehouse. But as Martinez reports, the FBI was bearing it.

Alex Tsakiris: What other information? That's circumstantial evidence. It's good, but what other evidence do we have?

John Brisson: Clements giving testimony that customs agents were told by intelligence operations to stand down on the second day of their investigation.

Alex Tsakiris: They're told, if I remember correctly, that this is a CIA operation?

John Brisson: Yes. They're told directly it's CIA and to stand down.

Alex Tsakiris: So you're writing this book on the Finders Cult/Operation. What are you trying to reveal?

John Brisson: The biggest thing that I'm trying to do with this book is as a way to clear Ramon J Martinez. He's been slandered and lost everything. The Customs Department railroaded him. When you read his whistleblower complaint, they shut him down. Destroyed his career. This is my main objective with the book, other than to get down to the bottom of what really happened, is to clear Ramon J Martinez's name to the best of my ability.

SATANIC BY ANY OTHER NAME

Alex Tsakiris: In a way that gets us to that next level, because you're a Christian and I don't respect anyone's religious beliefs because we're not supposed to. We're supposed to follow the data. We've just had a two-hour discussion and you didn't bring up Christianity once. You just talked about the evidence, followed by a police report, followed by this investigator who you interviewed. You haven't demonstrated that you're following any agenda so why the hell do you want to jam this back into a Christian narrative?

John Brisson: And I'd ask you, why don't you frame it as, why do you use the term satanic? Why wouldn't you just use ritual abuse? Why wouldn't you just use religious ritual abuse? Those people look at it objectively who are not Christian and see it as such with the inverted pentagrams, the references, "Satan" is the word the elite use.

Alex Tsakiris: Thank you for teeing up an excellent question in this vast, unplowed field between atheism, Christianity, and other dogmatic religious beliefs. John, I have a ton of respect for the work you've done. Here's where I'm coming from, I accept science's conclusion that consciousness does exist. We are not biological robots in a meaningless universe. Near-death experience science is real. And that then leads us to take seriously the accounts of near-death experiencers. Now, as you know, many of those accounts point to the reality of a Christian experience…to an experience with Christ consciousness. Since I'm a "follow the data" guy, I'm forced to accept the reality of Christ consciousness even though I'm not completely sure what that means.

But if you take the full body of near-death experience science, it's not an exclusive club. What seems to emerge is that we are co-creators of reality, and there is this "greater good." There is this light that we can access and a co-creator within it. So of course, Christianity, and in particular

Christ consciousness, I think is all any Christian can ever talk about because the Bible is hopelessly flawed.

John Brisson: But you're framing it as Christ consciousness and that is narcissism.

Alex Tsakiris: That's your understanding of my word, Christ consciousness.

John Brisson: You're just defining it as human consciousness?

Alex Tsakiris: No, here's what I was trying to say --

John Brisson: That we have a soul, we have a spirit, that there is an afterlife of some sort. Right? Or am I mistaken?

Alex Tsakiris: No, mistaken. What I'm saying is I don't understand consciousness. I do understand from the data that it's obvious we have an awareness of what we are, which is what I would call consciousness. I'm also persuaded by the data that awareness extends beyond bodily death and extends beyond our body. That realm of extension, I call extended consciousness.

Now, in that extended consciousness realm, people are consistently reporting that they are encountering all kinds of spiritual beings. Some of them appear to be benevolent, guardian angels; relatives that seem to be cooperating and helping people in meaningful ways; they come back and their life is transformed or their life is healed. So based on these reports, just as common-sense people, we would say, "Gee, that seems like the benevolent cooperation of a spirit in an extended realm," without jamming it into some fricking Christian or Muslim or Buddhist thing, that seems to be happening.

My use of the term Christ consciousness is derived from the fact that in this extended realm, people have reported meeting a spiritual being that they understand at that time to be Jesus Christ, of the Christian tradition, of the Bible.

That is the way I'm using Christ consciousness, for those specific people, for whom that is their experience. I don't know what to make of their report. Then I'm leaping to the next level and saying, it doesn't take a genius to see there seems to be good and bad in this extended consciousness realm. We seem to be co-creators of this extended consciousness realm. We can create good, we can look to the light, we can ascend and do good things with our spirit. Or it seems to be, based on what we just talked about, that we can connect and identify with this need for over-indulging in material existence, this wanting of things, power, sex, money, control. Service of self. And this fear of death, this fear of annihilation of the egoic, mini-me that I've created, that seems to be so much broader than this narrowly defined, one religion kind of thing. One assumes the other.

John Brisson: Let me ask you a question then. Explain to me satanic ritual abuse without using a Christian lens, [without accounting for] people saying that inverted pentagrams are used, satanism is involved, that they're invoking demons. If it's not that, then I want to know how you see it. Because there are many people who are giving that narrative.

Alex Tsakiris: Let me try. The last thing I want to do is sound like I know anything here because I don't. Are you familiar with a book by Richard Smoley, *How God Became God* (see Chapter 2.)?) One of the things that I think is interesting about this Oxford-trained theologian, is he goes back and traces the oldest Judaic writings and finds no Satan. So he finds all of the stories that wind up in the Old Testament with Satan in them but finds them with no Satan.

John Brisson: Let me ask you a question about that. Does he bring up Job possibly being written first and how Satan is shown as an agent of God to challenge Job? Because I have not listened to the interview or read his books, so I don't know. But I would assume that is one of the conclusions that he makes.

Alex Tsakiris: I can't tell you that off the top of my head, but that wouldn't directly answer your question. The answer is, of course, Satan is real because we are co-creators of that reality. This idea is repeated over and over in a lot of the great spiritual traditions and in a lot of esoteric traditions, and it just seems to be a reality of the universe. We are co-creators. So if your thoughtform goes to Satan, yes, you will find a connection. The way I always put it is, "As below, so above." Can you find creepy people who want to do horribly, pathetic, psychopathic things in this world? You certainly can. Can you in the extended realm? Probably.

John Brisson: Do you believe in a higher power, in a God, or in a creator? I'm just curious. Do you believe in a divine being that created...

Alex Tsakiris: See, that's the problem with Christianity. Who am I to presuppose that I understand the mind of God?

John Brisson: No, I'm saying, is there a creator separate from yours that's not just from the Christian lens but that is from many different religions?

Alex Tsakiris: One of the things I take stock in is the fact that so many people who reach this extended consciousness realm have this download of information, have this all-knowing, but then they're not able to maintain it. I'm very suspicious of people who say they have been able to maintain and process definitive answers to these kinds of questions while in human form. I don't think I'm able to understand the mind of God in this form. But I do think the secret to the ascent is to always look up. And that answers the question for me. I need to ascend. My soul needs to ascend. I need to do good things, have good thoughts. I need to emanate the love that I see coming through these people that are transformed in a positive way by these experiences.

That's where I need to be. And it's really that simple. It's just not that complicated. I don't need to understand God. I just need to be more like these people that are emanating all that stuff that seems to be God-like, and I need to not do the stuff that all these people do, that seems to be emanating this satanic, devilish, bad stuff. It ain't that freaking complicated.

John Brisson: I'm not saying that you can't do good, an atheist can do good works. That happens. But the only difference between me and you is that faith in God.

Alex Tsakiris: Why would you want to have faith? Why not have doubt? Doubt is the most spiritual thing. Faith is decided. I just spoke with a woman who's in the Ramtha cult. I told her, *Skeptiko* is about inquiry to perpetuate doubt, and she said, "Oh, no, I don't have any doubt... I know... I know." Sure she knows because she's in a cult.

The realization/reminder that our government has actively engaged in evil is hard to take. Harder still is the realization they've sought to weaponize evil on our behalf. To what extent are we complicit? Maybe we can start answering that question by looking at the one place we can make a difference, ourselves.

18
BARGAINING WITH THE DEVIL

*"I got a soul that I won't sell
and I don't read postcards from hell"*
— The Woods Brothers

> **IN THIS CHAPTER**
> - what do you have to offer evil?

Chris Knowles is an author and influential blogger at *The Secret Sun* where he's radically and sometimes brutally changed the conversation about our occulted pop culture. I talked to Chris about his new fact-tion book that explores the tension that arises when government intelligence agencies are tasked with operationalizing and weaponizing extended consciousness.[72,73]

Chris Knowles: I was a remote viewing skeptic until I met people like Russell Targ and Dean Radin and Ed May, and had a chance to talk to them privately and listen to these presentations that they gave privately.

Alex Tsakiris: I want to talk about evil.

Chris Knowles: It's interesting you brought this up because it's something I've been thinking about quite a bit, and I think that the descent into evil, into evil thinking, goes in steps. It's sort of like an initiatory process, so to speak.

I don't think people, except for the weirdos who are into Satanism or whatever, nobody sets out thinking, "I'm going to be evil." I think that the seduction is, "I am going to be better than you and I am going to solve the problems that you cannot solve. I'm going to solve the problems of the world," and that old Stalin phrase, "If you have to crack a few eggs to make this beautiful omelet, so be it." I think that the ends justify the means is kind of the gateway, that's the doorway to evil…evil acts, to evil intentions.

But I think that the process of descending into that kind of thinking, there's another cliché, "The road to hell is paved with good intentions," and that's what I really wanted to explore. I wanted to understand how people who descend into what we would see as the ultimate evil, how would they justify themselves? This is something I've thought a lot about for many years because I think about comic book supervillains, like Lex Luthor, Dr. Doom, and so on. They always see themselves, not only as above the rest of us, but they see themselves as the good guy. I think the worst villains are the ones who see themselves as the good guy.

One of the things that I find so troubling is the way this is being presented in the public, where Satanists, many of whom have extremely unwholesome sexual appetites, they're the heroes of free speech and constitutional rights. That's how it's couched now. And you'll have girl's magazines aimed at tweens and young girls, how to summon a demon. It's like, I'm sorry, what?

Alex Tsakiris: Why are you laughing about that?

Chris Knowles: You tell cautionary tales of people who take the leap and dabble in occultism and magic rituals. And you're not doing it from this heavy-duty, Christian Bible way, you're just saying, "Hey, my life experience tells me that a lot of people get into stuff that they didn't anticipate." Well, all of that presupposes that there's a certain reality to it. Because as much as you're talking about the hip, pop culture thing, the part that gives me pause is people who are connecting with these extended consciousness realms in order to seek power and to seek personal gain. We have that recorded throughout history, and you've recorded it in your books and on your blog.

Alex Tsakiris: Don't we need to address that? To what extent can you use spirit forces to improve your life? That's the claim being made. Is there any truth to it?

Chris Knowles: This is something that I've written about quite a bit, particularly in the past couple of years. My basic advice is just to stay away from it. If you think you can summon a demon and control it, first of all, there are two possibilities. One is that it's just absolute fantasy on your part, absolute delusion. Secondly, there is this reality, there is a reality to summoning these energies and these forces, whether it's psychological or paraphysical.

Alex Tsakiris: I've got to pin you down there. Is it all psychological or is it paraphysical?

Chris Knowles: Well, I believe it's paraphysical.

Alex Tsakiris: I do too.

Chris Knowles: The point being, if you could summon a creature that's powerful enough to change your life or to curse somebody, whatever you think you want, what do you have to offer them? What could you possibly give in return if it's some disembodied spirit that is immortal or eternal or what have you? What do you have to offer them? You have nothing to offer.

Alex Tsakiris: But that is what's being sold in the magic community. They're saying, "Well, if you just do this grimoire properly with the sharpened sword at this angle, drawn in this way, the demon will then be compelled to..." How are you going to compel that kind of force? It seems such a shill deal that people fall for. I don't get how people can be so naive.

Chris Knowles: People are naive because they don't have real-life experience. You're talking about a cohort of people who are incredibly privileged, who grew up in an era of wealth and privilege, absolutely unparalleled in human history. [They led] a sheltered existence, and they were programmed by the media, by a lot of these shows on television, kid's shows, that taught them they could do these things. I've really come to the point in my life where I'm like, don't mess around with any of it. It's interesting to study, it's interesting to watch from a distance, but I'm really at a point right now, and I've said this on a number of interviews and podcasts over the past several years, don't do it.

Alex Tsakiris: Can we really say don't do it? When we say that, it also feels a little bit churchy, mind of God, kind of thing. Like I understand the nature of the order of the extended consciousness realm. I understand the mind of God and therefore don't do it. You know what I mean?

Chris Knowles: I don't even need to go that far. I would tell them to just do a little research. I mean, read Colin Wilson's book *The Occult*, and he details how many of these stories of great magicians in history end very, very badly.[74]

There's another book I read a number of years ago that had a tremendous influence on me that I've talked about. It's a book by a gentleman named Kairo, who was one of these figures in the 20s and 30s, who were very theatrical, almost like stage magicians, but incorporate a lot of occultism. He wrote a book about magicians and sorcerers throughout history, and it's one of the grimmest damn things you've ever read. Every single story, every single chapter ends badly. Of course, we've seen how Crowley ended up, how Jack Parsons ended up. Anton LeVay was a miserable husk of a man for the last 15, 20 years of his life. Kenneth Anger seems to be hanging in there but I've spoken to the man and I've dealt with his people. He's had some unbelievably hard times that none of us would inspire to duplicate.

So I don't think you need to appeal to biblical authority, you just need to look at how people who have pursued these courses of action, how their story ended.

I think that it's just...don't do it, don't mess around with it. If you think you can control a force that has the power to curse somebody, again, what do you have to offer in return? You don't have anything to offer them.

We may want to think twice before making a deal with evil entities, but what do we do when those evil entities come to the doorway of our divided mind? We'll look at that next.

19
THE DIFFERENCE BETWEEN DARKNESS AND EVIL

"the line dividing good and evil cuts through the heart of every human being"
- **Aleksandr Solzhenitsyn**, *author of, The Gulag Archipelago*

> **IN THIS CHAPTER**
> - a clinical psychologist confronts evil
> - a protocol for combating evil
> - non-binding contracts

I had been poking around this evil question for a couple of years when I got an email from a *Skeptiko* listener named Dr. Tom Zinser. Tom was polite but direct. He said that I was heading down the wrong path because I hadn't understood the difference between darkness and evil. What he told me about his 25-year career as a clinical psychologist helping traumatized victims of evil forever changed what I thought I knew.[75]

Alex Tsakiris: In 1987, Dr. Tom Zinser was a clinical psychologist and hypnotherapist in Grand Rapids, Michigan. Like all good therapists, Tom wanted to see his patients get better, but they weren't. At least they weren't getting better as quickly or as often as he felt they should. So, Tom, as he tells it, was almost to the point of giving up when a part-time secretary in his office named Katherine came to him with a rather remarkable proposal that we're going to hear about. What followed was a 15-year collaboration that changed Tom's practice, and certainly changed the lives of hundreds of his clients, and completely changed his worldview as well.

Now, I'm not so sure what it did for his reputation as a clinical psychologist among his colleagues, but that's another story, maybe one we will get into. Because Tom's 15-year collaboration turned out to be with a spirit entity named Gerod, who consulted with Tom about the problems his patients were facing and suggested specific ways to help them overcome traumas, relieve anxieties, and generally live happier, more fulfilling lives.

Dr. Zinser's book is titled, *Soul-Centered Healing: A Psychologist's Extraordinary Journey Into the Realms of Sub-Personalities, Spirits and Past Lives*. I use the term game-changer too often, but it's an unbelievably significant piece of work and I'm super excited to have him here today.[76]

One thing I wanted to get out there right off the bat, is you're a clinician, a highly trained professional doing all of the stuff psychologists do. Dr. Zinser, tell people a little bit about your professional background, your training, your credentials, just so people know that's part of who you are.

Dr. Tom Zinser: Well, I did my undergraduate work at the University of Notre Dame and that was called The Great Books Program, a very broad field of humanities. Then I went on to get my master's degree with emotionally disturbed children. After I gained my master's and taught for a year, I went on for my doctoral studies at Texas A&M in counseling psychology.

I finished my dissertation and began to practice as an intern here in Grand Rapids in 1975, and then worked at the psychiatric hospital for several years before entering private practice. And it's in private practice that I really practiced hypnosis and attempted to work with people who had been traumatized, whether in childhood or adolescence or even later.

Alex Tsakiris: That led you, as you just mentioned a little bit ago, into this work with dissociative disorders, which is in and of itself, highly controversial. I kind of gleaned from your book that it wasn't quite as controversial when you first started. It's not like you were jumping into some trend, you had just kind of discovered it on your own.

So dissociative disorder, split personality, or multiple personality as it's portrayed in the movies, is how it's been popularized. But from a straight-on, clinical perspective, it's now recognized that people do have different kinds of dissociative disorders that lead to stress in their life.

Alex Tsakiris: Do you want to help people understand that whole thing?

Dr. Tom Zinser: When I began, I learned about an approach called *ego-state therapy*, which recognizes that we all have sub-personalities. Multiple personality, which was the term back then, is an extreme case of sub-personalities. So the issue was treating people through hypnosis, making contact with these sub-personalities, and helping these sub-personalities to relieve the pain or hurt or distress or fear that they carry. And it's these personalities that we were bringing back to integrate with the self. So multiple personality is an extreme [form of dissociation], but it's basically saying we all have sub-personalities created.

Alex Tsakiris: I kind of gleaned from the book that there was this continuum, we all have ego-states, we all have the gatekeeper of our ego, we all have the protector part...or is that not a good way to look at it?

Dr. Tom Zinser: No. We are talking about a continuum, and most of the people that I worked with as clients were not multiple personality or [had] dissociative identity disorder. But in childhood and in adolescence especially, the ego-self/identity is not well-formed and those are very vulnerable times. So when a child or an adolescent is overwhelmed by, say they got embarrassed or humiliated at eight years old, or they've had an accident, just normal traumas. If they are overwhelmed, then a part may be created to take over until things can re-stabilize.

I think one of the questions you're implying, Alex, is we can't predict what sub-personality will be created for a person. It's a unique creation out of that individual's own mind. The situation, what kind of distress is involved, you just can't predict.

Alex Tsakiris: That part of the book was very empowering to me in terms of understanding general psychology, why I get angry when my Chrome doesn't refresh as fast as I think it should, and I think, "That's rather irrational." Or why I think the weather should be the way that I need it to be. I look at the irrationality of that and step back and go, "Wow, what was that reaction?" And I think your book, because I wasn't familiar with this egocentric approach, it clicked for me in a very normal way that didn't scare me or make me feel like I was strange in any way. This was just a normal process that consciousness does to deal with things that come up.

I don't want to make too big of a deal out of it, but I think it's the foundation for this clinical work that you do. Again, folks, I can't stress enough, Dr. Zinser is doing clinical work. He's trying to make these patients more effective in their life. What I love about this guy is he's constantly looking for new protocols and he's testing them in an appropriate way with clients to see if it's more efficacious than the last. I think we need to get all that out there.

Dr. Tom Zinser: I would agree with you completely.

Sub-personalities, I think, is an extremely important concept for understanding ourselves. But I would emphasize that sub-personalities, what we might call ego-states, all the way to multiple personality, where you have extreme alter personalities and that whole continuum, is not necessarily accepted fully by psychology or psychiatry.

...I would make the distinction first between the clinician and the academician. There are a number of therapies that accept sub-personalities, and they call it parts therapy, they call it transactional therapy, Assagioli called it psychosynthesis. There are a number of approaches that have recognized sub-personalities, but almost all of them come out of the clinical tradition. When you're actually working with people, you see these people kind of split. The academic and the empirical scientists' side of psychology, can't get a handle on this unless they want to come into the clinical. You're going to find less acceptance in the academic and empirical science schools than you're going to find in the clinical.

That's one big distinction. In the clinical area of psychology, you're going to see sub-personality be a more accepted concept.

Alex Tsakiris: I'm glad you made that distinction between the clinical and the academic. The boots on the ground folks, they're not inclined to completely deny it and pretend like their experience doesn't matter, so they're trying to explain it.

We see the same thing with near-death experiences, where the people who are really making headway, is the cardiologist who says, "I can't deny the fact that the person was dead, that their heart stopped, and I can't deny the fact that they came back and recounted their resuscitation in a way that doesn't make any sense. So I have to investigate that." Meanwhile, you have the cognitive science people and other neuroscientists, "That just doesn't fit into our paradigm, so we don't have to deal with it."

The related question, and this is something I hammer on all of the time on *Skeptiko*, but I really want to get your take, how do they manage to hold on to such a silly, ridiculous, outdated view of consciousness?

Dr. Tom Zinser: When it comes to the psychic and spirit dimensions of self and reality, it leads to an all or none kind of line. You're either all in or you're hedging. And the empirical scientists today, the cognitive psychologists, the people who really fight against these other dimensions, are facing that all or none line. If they cross it, their world is going to turn upside down. If you consider yourself to be a soul who has past lives, has lived past lives, that is going to change your way of thinking about who you are, where you're headed. All of that changes if you cross the line and say, "Yeah, I think I've been around for more than one lifetime."

I really believe that line is implicitly known by these folks at an unconscious level, it's known and it scares them. They resist it.

Alex Tsakiris: Do you think it might be known at a conscious level and it's not crossed because of the implications for social engineering, social control, and manipulation in either a positive or negative way?

Dr. Tom Zinser: Yes, I believe that ultimately there's concern that if people really began to understand the power they have as conscious beings, the powers that be would not want [that awareness] to be given full freedom.

Alex Tsakiris: It's funny, I totally hear you. And I'm jumping ahead here but I can't resist. Speak to the responsibility that goes with that power.

Dr. Tom Zinser: Yeah, that's a big jump. Gerod's message is that we, each one of us, is a beam of light. We are a soul and that is in itself, powerful. We are powerful as a soul. Gerod's view is that we come and live our lifetimes in order to awaken as souls and by that he's talking about awakening to one's own power. He's talking about the power of light, the power of knowledge. Not a power to use against others, but the power to create, to be that pure light that we are.

So yes, there is a responsibility. I guess I approach it a different way which is, each of us is born/created with absolute free choice. Our responsibility is to not violate another's free choice. We have free choice, we keep that free choice. So the issue in terms of responsibility is that we do not violate another's free choice.

Alex Tsakiris: Awesome, and we did take a big jump. Let's back up and go back to the beginning of this story. You're a practicing clinical psychologist, hypnotherapist, and this woman who you know because she works in your office, but you don't know her that well, approaches you because you're an open-minded guy and you're exploring hypnotherapy. Some of the guys in the office are talking about Robert Monroe and out-of-body experiences and you played around with that. And she hears that and sees an opening. What happens next?

Dr. Tom Zinser: Well, Katherine offered me an opportunity to have a session with the spirit entity that she channeled.

Alex Tsakiris: How does that conversation go? How does somebody sit down with you and say, "I've been channeling this spirit and he might be willing to talk to you"?

Dr. Tom Zinser: It's something I never considered. But she came in, said she had overheard the conversation in the lunchroom, and it brought back that as a much younger woman, she had an experience where Gerod had approached her mentally and she had shut it down. When she heard me talking about out-of-body experiences and these kinds of things, she said she sat down with her husband and went into trance and Gerod was right there. She wasn't quite sure what to make of it, so she approached me as a way to maybe validate or help her be clear on what exactly this Gerod [communication] was. Meanwhile, she was offering me an opportunity with one of these paranormal or anomalous sorts of experiences. So, I was open, I sat down. What did I have to lose?

Alex Tsakiris: You were open Tom, but let's dive into that a little bit further. Because you're a smart guy, you're thinking about a lot of things, you're reading a ton of books. So I'm sure at this point you're also leery, skeptical, and careful about channeling spirits. We've all heard this, it can lead to a lot of confusion. At the very least, it can lead to misinformation and being trickster-ed or even worse.

As you approach this, what kind of, not just safeguards, but how are you thinking you will approach this as a clinician?

Dr. Tom Zinser: Well, let me give an example of my first conversation with Gerod and the case that came up. A fellow I was working with, he was around 40, and in the process of trying to identify his sub-personalities that were getting in the way, I was getting communication from the inner world.

Alex Tsakiris: Would you go ahead and explain to people what this particular kind of hypnotherapy technique is?

Dr. Tom Zinser: The ideo-motor response is an old, hypnotic technique, and a way of communicating with the unconscious through signals rather than verbal interaction.

Alex Tsakiris: So we want to put people in a deep trance so we can get to that deeper part of the subconscious. Even though we don't know what any of these terms mean, we don't really know what hypnotherapy is doing, we don't know what deep consciousness would be, any of that. But as a clinician, you're saying, "Hey, this is effective. Get to a deep trance state. Get the verbal part of the brain out of it and just see if I can get really simple kinds of signals," right?

Dr. Tom Zinser: Right. Asking yes or no questions, and getting signals, yes, no, stop, or I don't know. And with this technique using signals, I use finger signals, it's a very quick way to bypass the conscious mind. The ideo-motor response is what I was using with clients back then.

Alex Tsakiris: So you go to talk to Gerod and how does that go?

Dr. Tom Zinser: Well, it took a while for Gerod and me to develop a language and understanding. But in that first session, I did bring up a case, the one where I kept getting contradictory answers, and he gave me information and said that there was a spirit presence with this client who was interfering with him and confusing him. And that was a bit of a shock to me, but I did take it back in the next therapy session with this client, and I started asking questions as if Gerod's information was correct, that there was a spirit present.

Alex Tsakiris: Hold on right there, Tom. This is a huge leap, and you alluded to this at the very beginning of the interview, it almost sounded like you felt a little guilty that you went off-reservation like this, in terms of the normal protocol. But I love the clinician in you, in the way that you approach this. You're going to take this information and with all your training, background, and experience, which is very substantial at this point, you're going to test this in a real way. Did you worry at this point that you might be leading yourself into a state of where you might be deluding yourself when you go and talk to your clients?

Dr. Tom Zinser: As I said, I'd been communicating with this client, trying to [work with] the unconscious, getting these contradictory responses. And when Gerod gave me this information and I went back to my client, I was already in the habit of questioning and working with him. Before, when it was all contradictions, I did not feel I was communicating. All of a sudden, with Gerod's information, reframing it, and asking the questions, I began to get responses that made sense.

Alex Tsakiris: Now, let's make sure we're explicit about this reframing because as I understand it, and again, please correct me because I might've misinterpreted things. The hypnotherapy technique that you're using, the signaling, you now shift from talking to the ego part of this person to actually talking to a separate spirit entity that is somehow communicating through this person. What does it lead to?

Dr. Tom Zinser: Wow, we're talking 33 years ago. I went through communication with this spirit when my client was in trance, but he was also consciously getting things. So he would intermittently report things to me verbally, and he could feel this, he could feel what was happening. He also had his own sense that this was not him. So he was shocked as well. We both were shocked by this because he wasn't expecting it, that's for sure.

It was my first attempt to engage and communicate with what appeared to be a separate entity. I felt that I received enough confirmation, enough back and forth communication with this entity, and the information we finally had is that it was willing to leave.

So it's not like I came out of that 100% convinced, but it had talked to me when for so many sessions it hadn't. That was a step forward.

Alex Tsakiris: That begins this process that you enter into with Gerod where you were actually consulting with him about clients. As strange as that might sound, for some people, it might sound unprofessional like you've crossed some boundary that you're not supposed to cross. Although, I would again say, what boundary do you we think we're creating? If this is the greater reality, and we found a way to access that greater reality and possibly apply scientific methods to it, why would we want to hold off from doing that for some arbitrary reasons we've set? But I don't want to bury the lead here.

As you document in this incredible book, you get specific information from Gerod about clients that you're then able to use clinically. What was that process like? I'm sure it was confirming to you, like we just talked about in the first case, but you have hundreds and hundreds of cases, right?

Dr. Tom Zinser: Yes. Basically, after my first session with Gerod and taking it back to my clients, I was so intrigued with this possibility, I asked Katherine a month later for another session, which she agreed to. I talked with Gerod again and this was done in automatic writing, it wasn't done verbally.

After that second session, a month later, I asked Katherine if she would have another one because this information, it just was right on. So about four months after I met Gerod, Kathy and I agreed on forming this collaboration with him.

I began meeting with Katherine once a week. During the week with clients, I kept a list of questions on my legal pad. I would write down questions about where we got stuck with the client, what was happening. I also wrote down metaphysical questions. then at the end of the week, I would meet with Gerod with my questions and go over [each one]. I would go home and during the week I would transcribe that session and take that information back to the sessions with my clients, using the information with each of those individual clients. Then I would take that communication, that hypnotherapy work, and see if I could engage and get a communication. And it happened over and over.

Alex Tsakiris: That leads to, as we learn in the book, you developing more of an intuitive sense of what might be going on. So your questions to Gerod, as we read in the book, are more pointed. Like, "Hey, I think this is going on. Can you confirm that?" Rather than, "What the heck is going on?" Let's just stop there.

Dr. Tom Zinser: Well, it was the process of Gerod identifying something and me testing it out. You've got people with past life stuff, you've got people with spirit attachment, you've got people with just their own sub-personalities...all of these different clients, and I would follow up with him. Then I'd take that information back and all the different situations and see if I could have ongoing communication. But he would identify something first.

I feel a need to bring in here that one of the things [Gerod] identified was that part of us, that he called the higher self. And that higher self, according to Gerod, knew so much of the person's inner world, was aware of their soul history, and was able to be a conduit of light for each of us in our present life. This higher self became more and more a central figure that I worked with each client, so I would establish communication with their higher self.

Now, Gerod had said, and I explored this deeply with him, he pictured the higher self as though the soul projected a piece of itself into the present life when the person is born. And in projecting that piece of itself, that higher self knew it was part of the light. It knew it was part of the soul for this person's lifetime. In a sense, a beacon of light, an inner guide. And I began to work with that higher self to explore and identify parts of the self that were in trouble or had problems.

To make it even more impressive, the higher self could communicate directly to the ego-states, the sub-personality. It's as if the higher self could go to the sub-personality and communicate to it directly. The higher self could also bring divine light from the soul and from the creator, and bring the light to that sub-personality.

And this is another one of those confirmation [moments] because it was the most powerful. I have worked with thousands and thousands of sub-personalities and 99% of the time, once higher self brought the light to a sub-personality, it changed its attitude and its perception almost immediately. When you see something like that happen 99% of the time, to me that's a scientific finding. It's a consistent finding, the significance is out of the ballpark.

Alex Tsakiris: You're going to trigger a lot of people with divine, certainly with God, with the creator, with the higher self. These are all words that are highly charged in our society and our culture, particularly because of the religious connotations to them. How do you understand religion fitting into what became your larger worldview, your larger understanding of the extended consciousness realms?

Dr. Tom Zinser: I think in terms of spirituality and spiritual realms. I look at religions, plural, as forms attempting to help humans come to know and understand their divinity, their own divine light, their soul.

Alex Tsakiris: I just talked to a guy maybe two weeks ago, David Ditchfield. He's from the UK. He had this incredible near-death experience where he was dragged under a train and left his body, and he met God and saw Jesus. I was talking to David, and aid, "How do you understand that idea that you've met Jesus? Because if we look for Jesus historically, we don't always find him, and if we look at what some people have done with their Jesus, we don't really feel so great about that."

And yet, he felt very confident that this was his experience in this extended realm, and that experience was mediated by a higher spirit guide that was interested in his [higher] good. He didn't come back and do a bunch of evil stuff. To the contrary, he came back and seemed to be changed for the positive.

How are we to understand, for example, David's experience or millions of other people's experience with a Jesus that may or may not be historical in the sense that we think about?

Dr. Tom Zinser: You're asking big questions, Alex. In the spirit realm of light where souls exist there are spirit guides. There are those departed loved ones that all of us have who have passed on. Those souls in the light can also be aware of us. And Gerod said from the beginning, and he used the term light or God, that the promise was made that each of us who incarnated, every soul would have a spirit guide.

So in my view, we all have at least one spirit guide. We may have different guides during our lifetime, and at times we may have more than one guide involved with us.

When we talk about, in the near-death experience, when we talk about people who are close to death in hospice, who are getting ready to make the transition, they will see departed family members. That is so common. The thing is, in the spirit realm and at our unconscious soul level, there's more that's known than we know consciously. The person who sees Jesus, as opposed to the person who sees Muhammed, as opposed to the person who sees another being of light, that presentation is for the person who's having the experience.

Alex Tsakiris: Hold on. Pause right there and tell me... we've heard that so many times. Tell me specifically how that fits into what you learned working with your clients. Because there does seem to be a little bit of a disconnect for me, in terms of who this Jesus figure is. I've talked to a number of well-meaning spiritual people who have a direct experience with Jesus, which I'm always okay with but when I say, "Well, as I understand it, you had an experience with Christ consciousness," they're like, "No, Alex, you don't get it. I had an experience with Jesus. Jesus of the Bible, and that's just it, don't tell me otherwise."

Dr. Tom Zinser: I would say that these beings who come to meet us in different situations are conditioned by the person who's having the encounter. If you grew up with Jesus, in your own mind and heart Jesus becomes a symbolic figure, and by that I mean a sacred, symbolic figure for this person. That figure is imbued with energy, and it makes connection to the spirit realm. When that person, whatever situation that calls for that kind of encounter, especially near-death or death itself, or an out-of-body trauma, Jesus may be the one. I'm not even sure that this figure comes forward and says, "I'm Jesus," but it may come forward and appear to the person as what their symbol is calling for.

Working with people, I don't need to answer the question whether this being of light is in fact Jesus, personally. There are all kinds of beings of light who've come to meet the people I've worked with, and there are all kinds of beings of light who come to meet these people with near-death experience.

I guess I would say it's more conditioned by what the person is ready for, or the way they perceive things, or the way they need to see things in order to make the contact.

THE PROTOCOL

Alex Tsakiris: So you're saying, past lives, as with near-death experiences, there are too many reports from too many sources and too many reputable studies to just be flukes or fantasies. I want to move on to what I call a "level three" discussion. The level one discussion is whether this stuff is true. Can we rely on the University of Virginia and Jim Tucker who did the follow-up work from Ian Stevenson, and compiled thousands of past life accounts and published them in an organized systematic way and were totally open to review and criticism?

That's level one. And it stands up. If you don't understand that, there's nothing I can do. There's the data. You are going to have to deal with it.

Level two is, "Why are we conditioned to look away?" If this is solid why aren't more scientists on board with it?

But level three is what really gets me excited. It's the reason why your book and the possibilities of your work get me so energized. Because level three says, "Okay, I'm not going to worry about proving whether there's an extended realm, that's really an answered question." And I don't need to worry about what other people in the psychology community and academicians are publishing. You've jumped to level three and said, "How can I develop a protocol that might be efficacious for helping my clients move forward?" I think that is so awesome and so important and so unique.

I want to move onto talking about your protocol because you have some very specific approaches that you've developed over time, in terms of how to deal with people who are experiencing this trauma, how to deal with these different entities, however we want to understand or identify them. And then in particular, how to deal with the darkness-evil issue, which is the original reason I contacted you. There's a very important distinction that you make between darkness and evil, and that's what I want to talk about next. But I want to start with talking about your protocol that you developed and why you developed it the way you did.

Dr. Tom Zinser: Well, I have to go back again and emphasize the clinical nature because all of these start with the client's own story.

My work, and with Gerod, is basically identifying those things within or about a person that blocks the light from them. Ego-states, and sub-personalities are often blocking the light because they carry pain or hurt or fear or distress. If you bring them light, they can refuse it because they are part of the soul and therefore they have some level of choice. They often refuse this light/love energy because it brings up their pain, and if you're going to bring up their pain, you're going to have to be able to offer them relief or else forget it. Don't bring up their pain just to have them be in pain.

So the protocol developed for the ego-stages is, make contact, communicate with them, make it safe for them to receive this light/love energy. Once they receive it, as I said, 99% say, "Whoopee, I love this. I don't want to be without it." And then they will move through the sharing and release of what happened to them.

For spirit attachment, an outside entity, it's a different protocol. They don't belong with the person; they need to leave. Again, working with Gerod, it was understanding how to approach these spirits to gain their cooperation to leave my client. In the worst cases, protocols designed to get to a point where they could be removed forcibly.

Alex Tsakiris: Hey Tom, can you help folks link those two? Because I think they're also related in some important ways that you talk about in the book, in terms of trauma, frustration, anxiety, and this separation that we feel, which can be an entry point for some of these other entities that hang around and disrupt people. Do you want to speak to that at all?

Dr. Tom Zinser: There are a number of ways people might be vulnerable to external intrusion or attachment or interference, but one of the primary ways is through sub-personalities. Some personalities carry pain and stay away from the light, and these outside entities can connect with them through their pain. As I said, guides, the higher self, can communicate to sub-personalities. Well, these entities can communicate to them also. And if they fall into a sub-personality that they can threaten, intimidate, trick, or offer them something, that is an entree into this person's energy through the sub-personality.

I had one, I wrote about in the book, a young kid, maybe 12-years-old, who was offered a pocket-knife by a spirit. He took that knife and felt he could protect himself, and he was stronger now with this knife. But it turned out that the knife was a device used to keep the door open.

So we had to convince him to give up the knife before we could break the connection with that spirit. As long as the kid kept the knife, he was giving permission for the spirit to stay connected.

Alex Tsakiris: One of the things that really came through in your book is that this is not a quick fix, 30-minute exorcism, walk out like a new person. It's more about the journey that you're on. It's a process and you engage in it, and you keep moving forward and realize decisions that you've made and you remake decisions.

Dr. Tom Zinser: In terms of the healing method itself, it begins with hearing from the client about what their difficulties are, what the symptoms are, what the struggles are. The first thing I do, and I learned this from Gerod, is to contact what I call the protective part of the mind. The protective part of the mind is a part of ourselves that is conscious in the present. We think of our conscious self as able to think forward and back, past to future. The protective part of ourselves is a consciousness, but this consciousness is limited to the present. It's not thinking about what we're going to do tonight or what we did yesterday. Its focus is in the present. That's where its consciousness is.

When I work with somebody, I learn to contact the protective part first to get permission to go forward and work with trauma. I found out that the protective part was often the part blocking me before I met Gerod, because it saw me as a bull in a China shop. Bringing up trauma, bringing up pain.

Once the protective part agrees, then I will make contact with higher self. When I make contact with higher self, there are a number of steps in the protocol to make sure the communication is with higher self.

When I'm assured of that, I will start with higher self, looking inside and start to review these issues or problems or symptoms that the client has talked about. And it's through the higher self that we will see if it can identify a source.

So if a person, let's say, has intense anxiety, panic attacks, we will ask higher self to look inside and see if it is able to locate the source of those attacks. You may find, by the time it's done, six or seven sub-personalities that are involved in an anxiety pattern, but from different experiences. You might find that there is also a spirit present who kind of gets all these sub-personalities afraid and upset. You just don't know.

Alex Tsakiris: This is going to freak people out a little bit, right? I'm sure you go to conferences and meet with colleagues and they think it sounds flaky.

Dr. Tom Zinser: I'm afraid that's part of the issue. If you cross the line, you're looking at a whole different kind of reality. And this goes back to sub-personalities also.

I came to the point in my work with Gerod, where I came to understand sub-personalities. In my mind, I best understand them as psychic beings. They're not just memories, they're not just associated states, they are actually psychic beings. They are able to communicate, they are able to receive light, they are able to make a choice when you tell them they have a choice. They do have feelings. They are beings. And the issue is helping this being be relieved of whatever pain or distress it has so that it can integrate with the conscious self.

I know this challenges people because talking about the protective part is a different consciousness. Talking about sub-personalities, those are different consciousnesses of ourselves. The higher self is a different consciousness of ourselves. These are all different levels of consciousness, and our modern psychology wants a unified identity. It's an egocentric paradigm. And when you get past the ego, they just want to reject that.

EVIL AND THE DARKNESS

Alex Tsakiris: So with that, let's talk about something really controversial because we haven't yet. Let's talk about evil and darkness. And this is a huge topic to explore. Your book is very systematic. You methodically go through the protocol. You go through your experiences and how one leads to another.

One of the things that comes up in your work, there are some spirit attachments that are basically confusion. The spirit is attached and is harassing this person, but it isn't malevolent in the way that, like you're saying. If you were able to connect with that spirit and communicate and offer them a better option, which is to go for the light, which is always shining and willing to accept that spirit, they go, "Wow, that really is better. I'm sorry, I was confused and stuck here. I'm ready to move on."

But then you experience some that are not. You say, "Go to the light," and they basically respond, "No. I know the light's there, I'm not going there."

Dr. Tom Zinser: Where to start about darkness. The reason I sent you the email originally was about the distinction between darkness and evil. We all have to deal with darkness. Gerod's information to me was that this physical reality, created by the light, by the creator, whatever you want to call it, made a level playing field between the light and the dark and that level playing field is what gives souls free choice.

Alex Tsakiris: Your understanding of evil though is truly unique and for me, truly revolutionary in terms of understanding some of the subtle ways that evil comes into play and interacts with that darkness.

Dr. Tom Zinser: Going from darkness to these spirits who have entered darkness and operate from darkness, and have become evil in the sense that it's their intention to violate souls, they can violate souls who have incarnated. As Gerod pointed out, every soul in darkness is a soul of light. That light may have become very covered over, very buried, but every soul is a soul of light.

Alex Tsakiris: Let's talk about the case of the 12-year-old boy with the knife. We think, "That's terrible. Why would you do that? Why would you create this false contract with someone?" Which we've heard over and over again. People are convinced that they've made some deal with Satan, "I've sold my soul," and what Gerod tells us, very importantly, "No, you can't sell your soul, it's just another form of deception." Beings that are attracted to the darkness like deception, they like to screw with people, drag them down. So they will create these ideas that you have this obligation, but you don't have an obligation. That's a very important point from your work.

Speak to that but also speak to, more broadly, why there is this connection to the darkness?

Dr. Tom Zinser: Well, there are souls that have died with tremendous feelings of guilt, whether it's because they've murdered people, whether they've laid waste to people, or betrayed loved ones. There are different reasons like that. They were in war and became enraged and violent. And when they die in that state, they may be afraid of being judged, afraid of being condemned by this God they believe in. They may be angry at God for what God allowed to happen. So there's something that originally separates them from the light, their anger, their hurt, their confusion.

But the issue here is that there are souls in a hierarchy of darkness. They've been in darkness a long time and they've learned to operate that way. And in that operation they gather to themselves these souls that have gotten into the dark and they're confused, kind of floating around or not sure what's going on. These dark souls that know more will, in one way or another, attempt to entangle them. And this is where, what we would call the higher-level dark ones, are able to [control them]...like a mafia, the mafia is a very good analogy.

Alex Tsakiris: As below, so above.

Dr. Tom Zinser: Yes.

Alex Tsakiris: We all know the expression, "As above, so below," but this is a "As below, so above" kind of thing. I struggle with people who have a problem with that or want to explain it away. I'm like, are you kidding? Just look at our planet. Look at the worst parts of our existence. We see hierarchies of evil all the time. We see people that do horrible things and grow so comfortable with it that they don't feel comfortable being normal. It makes sense that would be what's going on in these extended realms.

Dr. Tom Zinser: I would say in working with clients where these dark spirits were present, it was in trying to remove them or get their cooperation to leave that we found as they got closer to maybe agreeing to take the light, they were starting to be threatened. And that's when I would ask them, "Are you being threatened?" I would get a yes. They're being threatened by those up above who want them to stay in line.

Alex Tsakiris: Or further below.

Dr. Tom Zinser: Yeah. And I have to work with those spirits to let them know that's all a ruse. They don't have the power to keep them. If these ones I'm working with want to go to the light, they have every power and right to do that. You're kind of breaking the chain.

Alex Tsakiris: Could you think of a case when that came about? Again, your protocol is to first, "Do you see the light?" And then the next step is, "Well, if you can't see the light out there, do you see the light within you?" Sometimes that works. And then sometimes you bring in spirit guides or loved ones and say, "Would you be willing to talk to one of your loved ones, and they'll help you see the light?" And then you keep going down the protocol, which just gets awesome. Give us a case that brings that to life.

Dr. Tom Zinser: Well, the clearest examples for me have been my work with cult victims, cult victims who have been intentionally and in an organized way abused, for specific purposes. And that abuse is the intentional creation of a dissociative personality.

When I worked with cult victims, many of these personalities were created and many of were entangled with dark spirits. I could understand exactly how cult activity damaged these children, to create trauma, dissociate them and create a fragment so that these dark spirits would have an open door into these children and their souls.

Alex Tsakiris: So you're saying, what I've heard over and over, is some people in these cult groups and groups where they label themselves as "satanic," whatever that means, because it's kind of a tricky word historically, but they actually have a systematic way where they say, "If we can create this disassociation that is going to serve our goals at this extended consciousness level."

Now, I had never made that connection. I had heard about it, but never made the connection until I read your book. And you're offering confirmation about that, that there would be a reason for them to do that.

Dr. Tom Zinser: Absolutely, and some of them consciously know what they're doing and why they're doing it as part of their allegiance to these dark souls. There are others who don't know. They carry out this dissociative trauma for the child for the purpose of bringing that child under their control, so that in the future these abusers can control a sub-personality. And they have techniques and methods developed to control people in that way, through their sub-personalities. They're not necessarily aware of the other level, where there are dark souls involved, but some people are. Some of these abusers are aware of that level.

Alex Tsakiris: What has the process been like in terms of working with these people? And again, I really appreciate that you can look at this from a broader perspective. Everyone is of the light. Everyone has the ability to return to the light. People can get off the path. We have the whole past life aspect to work into [this]. Sometimes children are entering into this because of some stuff they're bringing from a past life. I'm complicating things, but I don't think straightforward, simple questions work here.

But I'll go back to that first question. How effective have you been in terms of helping people overcome this really severe spiritual interference and spiritual disruption?

Dr. Tom Zinser: I would say it's been very successful, it's very methodical. Basically, what you're doing is working with higher self to find any obstructions or interference of the light. That's the process.

Alex Tsakiris: Have you had clients, in particular cult victims, who you've been able to effectively treat and have told you, "Gee, I've been trying to work with this, with therapists that aren't looking at this from a deeper extended consciousness realm, and I haven't had any luck."

Dr. Tom Zinser: Yes. Learning from Gerod and going through this with him, I was able to learn the ins and outs of dealing with this kind of trauma and entanglement. So yes, I believe I've been very successful helping these cult victims break the ties, break the chains and connections to these dark souls.

Alex Tsakiris: One of the things you have to say about the darkness is it's there for a reason, it's a part of our growth. And the way you describe your clients, regardless of the level of trauma they've experienced, are moving into and out of the darkness. The trick, I guess, is to maybe not get too drawn into it? What would you say with regard to that?

Dr. Tom Zinser: I would agree, and this is again, one of these things about the distinction between darkness and evil. Souls that are evil do intend to violate us. The darkness itself would like to destroy the light. But the darkness has to, in a sense, obey the boundaries, and it will not violate those boundaries or else the light will have recourse.

So the darkness, in some sense, it might want to seduce you, or convince you or draw you in, or you may want to make a deal with darkness, which will cost you. But it won't come in and violate because if it tries to violate the light, which is also a soul, it will have repercussions, and it is aware of that. Unlike souls who do intend to violate, they are trying to take other soul's energies and harness other souls and use them. The darkness won't do that. It will shelter the evil ones, it will draw them, and this is probably part of the problem, it will draw those evil ones in, deeper and deeper, until those dark ones really have no sense of themselves as the light. They've forgotten who they are. The darkness is more than happy to do that. But the darkness is not an angry, violent, kind of force, it just is what it is.

SUICIDE

Alex Tsakiris: Here's what Gerod had to say from your book. This is communicated to you about the dark spot in all of us, and he's talking about suicide. He said, "People who are prone to suicide or contemplating suicide are usually locked into that dark side. They're not moving well enough towards the light. They have stopped so much in that dark place that they can't get out. It doesn't mean they are evil. It doesn't mean that they are bad. It oftentimes means they have abandoned hope and they've let go of the idea that they are purposeful and that they have meaning."

Do you want to speak to that at all?

Dr. Tom Zinser: I think when we look today, just as somebody who has suffered long-term depression, when you live in depression, you're living in darkness. And Gerod defined darkness as the place that lacks light, love, and knowledge. He said in the darkness there is no trust. These dark spirits don't trust each other. It's a network based on power.

So living in depression can be living in darkness. It's not that you're bad and evil, but you've lacked that feeling of love maybe, or that lack of connection, or lack of connection to a higher power, or you've lost hope.

You take a young kid who has grown up in a family where one or both parents are abusive, and every day that child has to be afraid of what's going to come at him. That's living in a dark place. Darkness is that place where you don't have love and light and knowledge.

Living in ignorance, there's a darkness there. When we learn we're gaining light. Darkness is understood as the place that lacks light, love and knowledge. We know there are a lot of people who live in such a place for different reasons. A lot of it is trauma, the result of trauma.

Alex Tsakiris: Where do you see clinical psychology fitting into this transformation that people might go through in connecting with extended consciousness? When we step back, this has always been the domain of churches, very cultish churches, that are more interested in controlling and manipulating people than doing much else. But it's always been in their domain. Now we have a kind of a shamanistic kind of thing, or the magic and occult realm. They'll tell you how to deal with these extended consciousness realms.

Do you think there's something unique that clinical psychology can bring to that?

Dr. Tom Zinser: My feeling is clinical psychology is in the same dilemma we talked about with others, and that is they're facing this line and crossing this line. As I said earlier, we have a very egocentric psychology and psychiatry, and we're talking about something that transcends the ego. When you start threatening the ego like that, with the loss of power, that it's not the end all and be all, the ego gets pretty threatened. So, the soul-centered approach is saying to the ego, "You've got a place, you've got a very important place in this incarnation, but from a soul level, you are playing a part."

And when we cross over, one of the most important things is for people to understand there is no death, that when the body dies, we basically walk through a door into another level of consciousness.

Tom Zinser has been a frontline warrior against evil hiding in the realms of extended consciousness. His approach may be a jumping off point for developing a new understanding about how we can help others navigate this complex landscape. But most of us are more interested in practical advice about avoiding evil and finding good in our own life. That's next.

20
TRANSCENDING EVIL

*"...there is nothing noble in being superior to some other man.
The true nobility is in being superior to your previous self."
- Although often attributed to Ernest Hemingway, it's from
a sermon of* **W. L. Sheldon** *in 1897*

> **IN THIS CHAPTER**
> - who am I? who have I become?
> - our role in transcending evil
> - the path is easy for one with no preferences

In Chapter One I told you about my friend Rick Archer who has masterfully compiled hundreds of interviews with many of the world's famous, and not-so-famous, spiritual teachers/thinkers/practitioners. I've listened to hundreds, but one that really sticks out was Rick's interview with Norio Kushi. Norio is a long-haul truck driver without any guru credentials. Norio discovered his spiritual path during long, cross-country hauls through the deserts of California and Arizona. His big insight can be summed up in six words: It's not going to work out.

All of our scheming and plotting, all of our worrying, hoping and bargaining, will ultimately fail. Sure, you might hit the lottery, get the girl/guy or perfect family, but the little ego person you've created at the center of your cosmos will eventually collapse. Maybe this is what all this fuss about evil was to begin with. One of the many topics I talked about with the very insightful and wise psychic- medium, Claire Broad.

Alex Tsakiris: It almost sounds cliché when you say that all your life people have been telling me you'll write a book for the spirit world, but the story unfolds that way. At four years old you're having experiences at the grave of your grandfather.

Claire Broad: Well, that's the thing, I don't want anyone to believe me. Belief, like you were saying earlier, is the last thing I want. I'm trying to encourage people to explore for themselves, because that's what I've had to do.

Basically, what I tried to do was just understand my truth as this happened to me. The experiences that I've had are part of human experience. I'm not crazy. And so how do I understand this?

And as I write in *What the Dead Are Dying to Teach Us*, that I doubted for years, even though I was exploring after-death communication. But there came a time when I just knew, "Come on now, you've got to own your truth."

I don't know about you Alex, but I've always got someone over the back of my shoulders, almost like this non-physical voice that is from the human world, telling me, "You've got it wrong, you're delusional, and you're leading people down the garden path and materialistic science knows there's nothing in this." It's always nagging away at me, "Don't do the wrong thing." But there comes this point when I have to realize, no one's got the answers, and I've had these experiences and they're valuable. They helped me and they've helped others, so let's just own them and start a conversation, because I'm not daft and I'm not fraudulent. So what's going on?

(later)

Claire Broad: I'm trying to create a bit of a shift in our perception. I don't believe that materialistic science has got all of the answers. And so, the scientists and researchers who are willing to explore consciousness studies, human potential and the true-life experiences of people, I'm working with them because I want to understand this myself. Even though I'm having an experience that I know is real for me, sometimes you need to connect with people outside of yourself to see, what are they thinking? What are they finding? I truly am open to changing my mind.

THE SPIRITUAL PATH

Alex Tsakiris: One of the things that I thought was just terrific about your book, it revealed your spiritual path. It really fascinated me that this first and foremost is a spiritual journey for you that just so happens to include communication with the dead.

Claire Broad: Sure. I guess I'll just start at the beginning. You touched on it, the fact that when I was four-years-old. I was standing in a cemetery with my mother and my grandmother. We were tidying up my grandfather's plot, he'd only been dead about a year. I was just playing, as a four-year-old does, totally in the moment, just in my imagination with some stones and some water and a vase that was there for people to use, and I felt my grandfather come around me. The experience was totally overwhelming. He just almost...became me for a moment or I became him. And in my childlike inability to logically think about this, I just accepted the experience.

So, as I get older and realize, "Hey, I don't think we have understood human experience as well as we might," I go back to that moment as a four-year-old in a state of complete clear-mindedness and open-mindedness. And it's a beautiful place. It's a place where anything is possible, where I wasn't in a state of fear. I was just open to life and being there, experiencing it.

For me, a spiritual pathway means getting back to that space, where all is possible and I can be in touch with the greater reality, and that sounds trite but it's peace.

Alex Tsakiris: It doesn't sound trite as much as it sounds unique and beautiful. When we think about the spiritual path, as it's generally termed, we think about religious people because that's what we're told to think about. But that's not how I think about it. Do you have any thoughts on the different spiritual paths that people find out there?

Claire Broad: I actually don't know if they are too different. I know that might sound impossible. But the likes of Eckhart Tolle for instance, he's a huge spiritual influence in my life too, because I recognize the truth in what he's saying, about entering into the now, being in the moment. That's what I experienced with my grandad. When I was in the moment as a child and not in my logical thinking brain, I was open to a transformative experience, and I hear them saying the same thing. I've heard the likes of Eckhart saying he heard a voice say to him, "Resist nothing," when he went into a place of stillness and surrendered his mind.

And mediums, that's exactly how they get trained. The terminology is different, but a medium is taught to sit in their power. You become still, you learn to feel and sense your own energy, "Who am I? What do I feel like? How are my emotions? How does my physical body feel? What is my energy like?" When you understand who you are and how you feel, as you expand your awareness or your mind, in the same way that Yogi's do, then you become aware of a greater reality.

I hear in the East, the talk in yoga for instance, of opening up the chakras, the energy, chi, whatever you want to call it, pulling that energy up and out through you. It's exactly the same in mediumship. You're doing the same thing. You're learning to be in your power, draw upon your own energy, expand your energy and awareness, and then somewhere in there, the mind settles. It expands to a greater reality and you sense and feel the energies of others around you.

Sometimes spiritual teachers stop there. They're reticent of describing an afterlife these days. They see the power in being able to get people in the moment and that's enough, because we don't have all of the answers for what happens next, but they're all saying the same thing. They're all saying there is something more, greater than ourselves, some intelligence that goes beyond our own understanding.

Now I can read many of the spiritual texts, going right across, from the Hermetica to Kabbalah to Christianity to Buddhism, and I can see the common threads. I will say it's in the mystical texts, so I say Kabbalah rather than Jewish. I'm very drawn to the Gnostics rather than the Christians, because they're the traditions that actually put people, from my perspective, in touch with the spiritual dimensions.

For instance, if you go into a church, as I did a lot when I was a child, you're told to pray, but you're not told how. You just put your hands together and send your thoughts out. Whereas a lot of the old traditions, like the Gnostics, and I write about this in the book, actually explain about connecting to the afterlife and communicating and meditation and spirit contact. It's all in there. There's nothing new here that I'm saying. So to me, it's not a contradiction.

DEAD

Alex Tsakiris: You do a beautiful job in the book of talking about how our understanding of death is flawed from the onset. You say we've already experienced death by virtue of the fact that we're talking with people who have passed.

What do you understand dead to be and how do you understand it inside of this larger term that we throw around called consciousness?

Claire Broad: I hate the word dead. To me, it's redundant. Dead to me means annihilation and from my personal experiences life is a continuum. So when you hear, I suppose, mediums talking about "the dead," they've built an idea in their mind of literally, a heavenly realm where people are living and where we go and meet our loved ones. I'm not saying it isn't that, but I think it's a whole lot more than that. I'm much more interested in what that implies about consciousness and the nature of reality. What is reality?

Alex Tsakiris: I think that you take a dramatic shift in terms of perspective, challenging the idea that we're here and the dead are over there. This is something we frequently hear from different sources, whether it's near-death experience where they say, "I felt like I was arriving home" or whether we hear about an after death communication and they say, "You know, they kind of talk down to us a little bit, like we have to lower our vibration to get down to you." So, this whole thing is shifted when we start digging into these extended realms. It's like they're saying, "You guys are kind of playing the small game over there and there's a much bigger game."

Claire Broad: Absolutely. When I wrote *Answers from Heaven*, I was quite shocked that physicists contacted me saying, "Claire, we've read your book because we're interested in your perception...we know that the universe is holographic in nature multi-dimensional."

REINCARNATION AND SCIENCE

Alex Tsakiris: Tell us about your understanding of reincarnation, how it fits into this larger question of the dead.

Claire Broad: Yes, I do understand why spiritualist mediums have traditionally and even now are reticent to cover reincarnation. It's because they can't prove it. We're at a position where we proved the afterlife scientifically...

Alex Tsakiris: ...let me jump in for a minute. You've talked about something that is really important to me. One thing I would disagree with you about, we don't have to prove this to science, because remember, science has completely dropped the ball on consciousness. They've driven their foot in the ground and taken the position that consciousness is 100% a product of the brain. Which means, let's be clear, it's an illusion. And once you get question A wrong, you're not allowed to move on to question B, C, or D.

So, no, it's not that we can't prove reincarnation. Ian Stevenson proved it when he was at the University of Virginia. And Dr. Jim Tucker, who looked at children and reincarnation, added more evidence. The burden of proof lies with anyone who says that reincarnation isn't true. They've published enough substantial, solid peer-reviewed data that the Occam's razor now cuts on their side.

I think we have to get out of this rut in the road where we bow down to science and say "Oh science, you've been wrong so many times, but please let me convince you." That's not the game we should be playing. What we should be doing is to say, "Okay, you guys have been wrong. That's okay. Let's take your tools. Let's take your techniques and see if we can catapult you to the next level of understanding of what this means."

Claire Broad: I totally agree with you. We have this idea that we need to make sure we're proving everything, which I still believe is very valuable to the client sitting in front of me.

Alex Tsakiris: You and other people are doing really thoughtful work in that you're in service to other people, but also thoughtful in terms of analyzing and trying to understand your experience. I think you need to take an even stronger stance in saying the science is on your side because science *is* on your side and we have to stop taking the defensive position. So, I totally applaud where you're coming from.

Claire Broad: And I think that's what I'm trying to get. I do not believe once you actually look at the research in this field and see the credible, intelligent minds behind it that you could possibly come away and say, "I still absolutely think there's nothing to it."

DARKNESS VS. LIGHT

Alex Tsakiris: You do an awesome job of talking about how you can recognize the dark, acknowledge the dark and yet understand that the mission is to transcend that darkness.

Claire Broad: I believe consciousness is evolving all the time and in order to evolve, we have to choose or reach upwards towards higher emotions.

Most people are doing something because they feel it's the right course of action. The other day somebody heard me say there's light and dark in all of us and they asked, "Do you then believe God is evil?" I believe it's a choice. We either choose to stay in [evil] or we choose to move forward from it. Whether we do that in this world, or we do it in the next life, the choice is ours.

I know evil exists. I've experienced it. But do I have to get stuck in it? Do I have to be identified with it? Do I have to be ruled by it? Do I have to fear it? No, I don't. I can move myself away from it. I write in the book about intention. And when you are owning your own power, owning your own mind and your own intention, you move away. It has no control over you anymore.

HIGHER EVOLVED BEINGS (HEBs)

Alex Tsakiris: You talk about HEBs, your acronym for higher evolved beings. Lay out a whole gamut; spirit guides, ascended masters, angels, God...what's going on there? While you're at it maybe you want to talk about lower evolved beings.

Claire Broad: The thing is for me, I always have to keep coming back to the word consciousness, which is going to become like the word mindfulness where it gets overused and loses its meaning. For me, I feel that these are archetypal descriptions of different levels of awareness/consciousness.

So, a spirit guardian seems to be an intelligence that has had a physical incarnation that has some understanding of what it's like to be in physical form and is wanting to reach out or reach back or forward...however we want to look at this whole time thing, and help others through experience. We all know how good it feels when we help someone else. It lifts us higher. We feel good about ourselves. It's the same thing. They're reaching out to others here because it makes them feel good. There's a benefit to them. So, guardians are spirit beings who walk with us through life and spirit guides seem to be teachers that come in at certain moments when we need them. Then I move on to higher evolved beings, this implies some sort of hierarchy, and I don't believe that's the case. I just think there are different states of being but a higher evolved being to me is some intelligence that could have been incarnate on this planet or on other planets out there. It's a big universe out there with multiple dimensions. Actually, what is a spirit person? They're certainly not living on Earth. So, they could be deemed as higher evolved beings or even alien/extraterrestrial. We're limiting ourselves. In my viewpoint, even animals go on.

Alex Tsakiris: Let's talk about the tricksters and the hungry ghost idea. It's scary. It raises fear in terms of if that can happen in this spiritual realm that seems to be so powerful, then what can I as a mere human do?

Claire Broad: I want to stop you there, Alex. The whole mission behind what I'm doing is to change the idea that people hold about themselves. We are not mere human beings. We are something much more than this physical experience. This temporary form that, as you said earlier, isn't even real at the quantum level, it's all smoke and mirrors. We are much more than mere human beings. So why would I need to fear something if I'm already it?

We give our power away. If we give our power away even to guides and teachers, we need to understand that we are just as valuable and just as much a part of everything as they are. So, with trickster spirits, it comes down to the idea that we are no longer sensing and being aware of our environment, and they're being opportunistic. But I have never experienced a trickster spirit.

It's not as if I haven't experienced evil contact from Spirit, I'm not saying that. I've had some negative experiences. Few and far between, but it's really come down to my fear of what happened, my interpretation of what happened, and my own imagination rather than the reality of it.

I have found that the more I own myself, my mental well-being, my own ideas, I am happier, content.

21
CONCLUSION

> "When I despair, I remember that all through history the way of truth and love have always won."
> — Mahatma Gandhi

As you can see, the evil question is simple. Nope! Nothing I have offered is simple, definitive, or conclusive. I wouldn't have it any other way. After all, this is a *Skeptiko*, "inquiry to perpetuate doubt" project. So, I want to hold on to my beliefs and ideas about evil loosely. I want to leave room for different opinions. And I want to continue learning and diving deeper into these topics I've only been able to fly by. I want to make a conscious, intelligent effort to come to grips with evil because evil matters. It matters to our collective culture, and it matters to my personal journey of discovering who I am and why I'm here. Since this chapter is titled "Conclusion," I'll offer two tentative/provisional ones of my own:

YOU ARE MORE

We will never know for sure why we fell for the "biological robot in meaningless universe" meme science has jammed down our throats. Maybe we became mesmerized by our technical achievements. It could also be – check that – it certainly is, because the alternative, "You are more" worldview is not good for business-as-usual and not good for controlling the pitch-fork-in-hand mobs that occasionally storm the castle.

But the best scientific evidence, as well as the most well-reasoned philosophy, clearly stacks up on the side of you being more. You are more than your brain. You are more than your body. You are, for lack of a better term, a spirit being. And as awesome as that is, it comes with some tough realizations. The toughest may be that you are more than a collection of likes and dislikes. You are more than someone who likes sunny days. You are more than someone who hates when it rains all weekend. You are more, much more, than your opinions and gee-I-really-hope-that-works-out wishes. In sum, you are more than your attempts to soothe your fundamental discontentment by liking and not liking stuff. And there's a responsibility that comes with that.

YOU ARE GOOD

Evil is a lens. It can teach us a lot, but its greatest lesson may be that we are not it. The best evidence suggests there is a divine spark burning in each of us. It's there waiting for us to join the addition by subtraction game of moving beyond self-constructed, negative blockages and allowing the light to shine through us. We may have grown accustomed to the displaced energy of darkness, but it's not our true nature. The secret of the ascent is to always look up.

SOURCES

1 *Skeptiko* Episode No. 378 "Bernardo Kastrup, Mainstreaming Controversial Philosophy of Mind Theories" (Apr. 18, 2018)

2 Kastrup, Bernardo; (2014) *Why Materialism is Baloney: How True Skeptics Know There is No Death and Fathom Answers to Life, the Universe and Everything;* Hampshire, UK; Iff Books

3 *Skeptiko* Episode No. 461 "What Split Personality Tells Us" (August 25, 2020)

4 Kastrup, Bernardo, Crabtree, Adam. "Could Multiple Personality Disorder Explain Life, the Universe and Everything?" *Scientific American,* June 18. 2018

5 Schlumpf, Yolanda; Chalavi, Sima; Nijenhuis,Ellert; Weder Ekaterina; "Dissociative Part-Dependent Biopsychosocial Reactions to Backward Masked Angry and Neutral Faces: An fMRI Study of Dissociative Identity Disorder; PubMed (July 2013)

6 Strasburger, Hans; Waldvogel Bruno; "Sight and blindness in the same person: Gating in the visual system"; National Library of Medicine; October 15, 2015

7 *Skeptiko* Episode No. 377 "Dr. Dean Radin Brings Real Magic to the Psi Lab" (April 3, 2018)

8 "Interview with Hugh Urban on Scientology;" The Apollo Series Blog

9 Hayden, Brian; (2003) *Shamans, Sorcerers and Saints: A Prehistory of Religion*; Smithsonian Books

10 Muehlhauser, Luke; 014: Bryan Hayden: Prehistoric Religion (January 2010)

11 *Skeptiko* Episode No. 395 "Why Shamans Don't Do iPhones" (Nov. 27, 2018)

12 *Skeptiko* Episode No. 445 "Can Academia Handle the Evil Question?" (April 7, 2020)

13 *Skeptiko* Episode No. 168 "Parapsychology Researcher Dr. Hoyt Edge Explores Cross-Cultural Views of Consciousness" [*?*]

14 *Skeptiko* Episode No. 114 "Near-Death Experience Critic Dr. Susan Blackmore Responds to Critics" [?]

15 *Skeptiko* Episode No. 444 "Social Science's Blind Spot Regarding Cults" (March 2020)

16 *Skeptiko* Episode No. 413 "Can the Scientific Study of NDEs Reveal the Purose of Life?" (June 4, 2019)

17 Sunfellow, David; (2019) *The Purpose of Life as Revealed by Near-Death Experiences from Around the World;* Self-Published

18 Long, Jeffrey; (2017) *God and the Afterlife;* New York, NY, USA, Harper Collins

19 Roth, Sid. *It's Supernatural;* Laurie Diitto, April 7, 2019; (https://sidroth.org/television/tv-archives/laurie-ditto/)

20 Franzioni, D., Wick, D, Lustig, B. (Producers), Scott, R. (Director), 2000, USA, DreamWorks

21 *Skeptiko* Episode No. 386 "Did Jesus Exist?" (Aug. 7, 2018)

22 Crowder, Steven, *Louder with Crowde*r; https://www.youtube.com/c/StevenCrowder/search?query=did%20jesus%20exist

23 GoArmy.com, "History of Psychological Operations", https://www.goarmy.com/careers-and-jobs/special-operations/psyop/psyop-history.html

24 *Skeptiko* Episode No. 460 "Love, Not Fear, Is the Answer" (Aug. 18, 2020)

25 *Skeptiko* Episode No. 465

26 *Skeptiko* Episode No. 457 "How Culture Shapers Spin Aleister Crowley" (July 21, 2010)

27 The Beatles, *Sgt. Pepper's Lonely Hearts Club Band*; Capitol, 1967

28 Bowie, David; *Hunky Dory;* RCA Records; 1971

29 Horsley, Jasun. (2019). *The Vice of Kings: How Socialism, Occultism and the Sexual Revolution Engineered a Culture of Abuse;* AEON Books

30 Mueller, Antony. "What's Behind the Frankist Sabbatean Movement and its Cult of the Evil?" *Medium* (February 2020)

31 *Skeptiko* Episode No. 463 "The Satanic Panic Head Fake" (Sep. 16, 2020)

32 Ramsey, William. (2012) *Abomination: Devil Worship and Deception in the West Memphis Three Murders*; Independent

33 *Encyclopedia Britannica*; https://www.britannica.com/biography/Joseph-Smith-American-religious-leader-1805-1844

34 Crowley, Aleister. (1992) *Magick in Theory and Practice*; Castle Books; Sixth Edition

35 Berlinger, J; Sinofsky, B. (Producers); *Paradise Lost: The Child Murders at Robin Hood Hills*; HBO, 1992

36 *Skeptiko* Episode No. 166 "Psychic Spy Joe McMoneagle Tells How His Near-Death Experience Led to Remote Viewing" (April 3, 2012)

37 McMoneagle, Joe. (2006) *Memoirs of a Psychic Spy*; Hampton Roads Publishing

38 Moody, Raymond. (1975). *Life After Life;* Miockingbird Books

39 Mungia, L.; Targ, R. (Producers); Mungia, Lance (Director), 2019, *Third Eye Spies*, USA, Lions Gate, Dimension Films

40 Project Star Gate; https://www.cia.gov/library/readingroom/docs/CIA-RDP96-00789R003300210001-2.pdf

41 Burns, M; Creel, L (Producers), Mungia, L. (Director) 1998 Six-String Samurai, USA, Palm Pictures

42 Baker, S, Goldston, J. (Producers), *Nightline*, ABC News

43 Primary Infinity Ward; Treyarch; Sledgehammer Games' Raven Software *Call of Duty*, 2003-[?] Activision

44 *Skeptiko* Episode No. 442 "The Simulation Hypothesis Beyond Materialism" (Feb. 25, 2020)

45 *World of Warcraft*; 2004, Blizzard Entertainment

46 *Fornite*; 2017; Epic Games, People Can Fly

47 Turtles All the Way Down; Carnegie Science; https://cosmology.carnegiescience.edu/timeline/1610/turtles-all-the-way-down

48 Silver, J (Producer), Wachowski, A, L. (Directors) 1999 *The Matrix*, USA, Warner Bros.

49 Heslov, G, Lister, P., Clooney, G., (Producers), Heslov, G. (Director) 2009 *Men Who Stare at Goats*, USA, Smoke House Pictures

50 *National Archives*; Project Blue Book; https://www.archives.gov/research/military/air-force/ufos

51 *Stanford Encyclopedia of Philosophy*. "The Chinese Room Argument" https://plato.stanford.edu/entries/chinese-room/

52 *Skeptiko* Episode No. 417 "American Cosmic's Breakaway Civilization" (July 2, 2019)

53 Pasulka, D.W. (2019) *American Cosmic: UFOs, Religion, Technology*, Oxford University Press

54 Brown, Dan. (2009) *The DaVinci Code*, New York, NY, Anchor Books

55 Chaffin. C., Grasyon Bell, R., Linson, A. (Producers), Fincher, D. (Director) 1999 *Fight Club*, USA, Fox 2000 Pictures

56 Consolmagno, Guy (2014) *Would You Baptize an Extraterrestrial? And Other Questions From the In-Box at Vatican Observatory*

57 *Skeptiko* Episode No. 438 "UFO Disclosure, Toothpaste Out of the Tube?" (Jan. 21, 2020)

58 Dolan, R., Zavel, B. (2012), *AD: After Disclosure: When the Government Finally Reveals the Truth About Alien Contact*, Weiser

59 Blum, J. (Producer), Stewart,, S. (Director), 2013 *Dark Skies*, USA Alliance Films

60 Blumenthal, Ralph, Cooper, Helene, Kean, Leslie, "Glowing Auras and Black Money: The Pentagon's Mysterious U.F.O. Program" *New York Times*, December 16, 2017

61 To The Stars Academy; https://home.tothestarsacademy.com/

62 Richard Dolan, "Chris Bledsoe Interview Part 4" https://www.youtube.com/watch?v=E4ww3VcMKNg

63 Clelland, Mike, Doland, Richard (2015), *The Messengers: Owls, Synchronicity and the UFO Abductee*, USA, First Edition, Richard Dolan Press

64 *Skeptiko* Episode No. 441" Recovering from Unimaginable Evil" (Feb, 18, 2020)

65 *Skeptiko* Episode No. 440 "Are Christians Less Wrong About Ritual Abuse?" (Feb. 11, 2020)

66 Wedge, Thomas (1987) *The Satan Hunter*, 2nd Edition, Daring Books

67 *Skeptiko* Episode No.439 "On the Nature of Evil" (Feb. 4, 2020)

68 *Skeptiko* Episode No. 443 "Finders Cult or Another Epsteinesque Browstone Op" (March 10, 202_)

69 Cheit, Ross (2016), *The Witch-Hunt Narrative: Politics, Psychology, and the Sexual Abuse of Children*, Reprint Edition, Oxford University Press

70 Bryant, Nick (2012) *The Franklin Scandal: A Story of Powerbrokers, Child-Abuse and Betrayal*. Revised Edition, Trine Day

71 Vinson, Henry (2015) *Confessions of a D.C. Madam: The Politics of Sex, Lies, and Blackmail*, Trine Day

72 The Secret Sun; https://secretsun.blogspot.com/

73 *Skeptiko* Episode No. 450 "The Descent into Evil Thinking" (June 2, 2020)

74 Wilson, Colin (2015), *The Occult: The Ultimate Guide for Those Who Would Walk with The Gods*, Reprint Edition, Watkins Publishing

75 *Skeptiko* Episode No. 451 "Clinical Psychologist on Difference Between Darkness and Evil" (June 10, 2020)

76 Zinser, Tom. (2011) *Soul-Centered Healing: A Psychologist's Extraordinary Journey Into the Realms of Sub-Personalities, Spirits and Past Lives*, Union Street Press

INDEX

A

AI 39, 148, 149, 156, 157, 158
Aleister Crowley 66, 115, 117, 127, 130, 197, 274
angels 28, 61, 172, 175, 179, 220, 266
atheist 77, 80, 90, 102, 183, 223
atheistic 19, 22, 46, 100, 122, 163

B

Bhagavad Gita 43
Bible 24, 27, 29, 43, 96, 99, 103, 104, 106, 107, 108, 124, 171, 220, 226, 244
Bob Hamer 15, 16, 17, 18, 19, 20, 22
brownstone operation 212, 213, 215

C

Catholic Church 17, 106, 123, 124, 133, 171, 172
Chris Knowles 225, 226, 227, 228
Chris Shelton 77
CIA 66, 139, 179, 181, 208, 211, 212, 218, 275
Claire Broad 259, 260, 261, 262, 263, 264, 265, 266, 267
consciousness 10, 11, 12, 16, 17, 18, 19, 20, 21, 22, 23, 25, 26, 31, 32, 33, 34, 35, 36, 37, 38, 39, 40, 42, 43, 44, 45, 47, 48, 49, 50, 52, 54, 56, 57, 58, 59, 60, 62, 63, 65, 67, 69, 70, 71, 73, 77, 78, 79, 80, 81, 83, 85, 88, 89, 91, 93, 110, 111, 122, 134, 135, 136, 138, 139, 140, 141, 145, 148, 149, 150, 151, 152, 153, 158, 163, 165, 170, 180, 181, 182, 186, 190, 192, 195, 203, 206, 207, 217, 219, 220, 221, 222, 225, 227, 228, 234, 236, 238, 243, 244, 248, 249, 253, 254, 256, 257, 260, 263, 264, 265, 266, 267
cult 80, 93, 101, 105, 111, 187, 207, 214, 223, 253, 254

D

Damien Echols 126, 128
David Icke 109, 110, 111
David Sunfellow 85, 86, 87, 88, 89, 90, 91, 92, 93, 94
DeLonge 179, 180
demons 61, 172, 175, 184, 196, 221
disassociation 55, 253
DMT 54, 153

do what thou wilt 22, 117, 119, 122, 132
Dr. Bernardo Kastrup 31, 37, 38, 39, 50, 55, 56, 57, 58, 59, 60
Dr. Brian Hayden 67, 68, 69, 70, 71, 72
Dr. Daryl Bem 76
Dr. David Nutt 54
Dr. Dean Radin 61, 62, 68, 153, 273
Dr. Diana Walsh Pasulka 159, 171, 172
Dr. Donald Hoffman 34, 35, 37, 39, 40, 42, 44, 45, 46, 47, 48, 50, 79
dream 54, 92, 155, 199
Dr. Hal Puthoff 39, 137, 138
Dr. Hoyt Edge 73, 74, 273
Dr. Hugh Urban 65, 66, 67, 77
Dr. Jan Holden 86
Dr. Jeff Kripal 160
Dr. Jeffrey Long 89
Dr. Michael Shermer 85, 86
Dr. Raymond Moody 85, 137
Dr. Richard Grego 73, 74, 75, 76, 78, 79, 80, 81, 82
Dr. Rupert Sheldrake 74
Dr. Russell Targ 39, 137, 138
Dr. Sean Carroll 32
Dr. Susan Blackmore 74, 274
Dr. Tom Zinser 12, 55, 59, 231

E

Eckhart Tolle 43, 44, 45, 155, 199, 262
Einstein 34, 41, 42, 184
empirical 51, 235, 236
E.T. 48
ET 12, 26, 153, 154, 164, 170, 171, 172, 173, 175, 180, 182, 188
extended consciousness 10, 11, 48, 69, 70, 78, 136, 140, 193, 220, 221, 256

F

Fight Club 167
Finders 134, 207, 208, 211, 214, 215, 217, 218
fMRI 54, 273
Frankist 116, 274

G

Gerald Morgan 99, 101, 102, 103
Gnostic 24, 124
God 19, 24, 25, 27, 28, 42, 46, 47, 88, 89, 91, 92, 94, 95, 102, 109, 110, 111, 123, 149, 150, 151, 152, 170, 171, 172, 176, 184, 186, 188, 194, 199, 203, 204, 205, 221, 222, 223, 228, 243, 244, 251, 266, 274
Greek Orthodox Church 24, 46

H

hell 27, 46, 90, 91, 92, 93, 110, 111, 219, 225, 226
hellish near-death experiences 89

J

Jack Parsons 66, 78, 228
Jacques Vallée 146, 154, 160, 168, 169
Jasun Horsley 115, 117, 118, 119
Jeffrey Epstein 17, 212, 213, 215
John Brisson 207, 208, 209, 210, 211, 212, 213, 214, 215, 216, 217, 218, 219, 220, 221, 222, 223
Josephus 103, 104, 105, 106, 107, 108
Jung 26, 60, 61
Jurgen Ziewe 112

K

Kevin Annett 199, 200, 201, 202, 203, 204, 205
Koran 43

L

Lance Munguia 138
left hand path 170
Leslie Kean 177, 178
L. Ron Hubbard 66, 78
LSD 54

M

materialism 22, 32, 34, 39, 40, 52, 55, 56, 58, 59, 62, 63, 65, 68, 69, 119, 136, 145, 150, 169
Materialism 34, 51, 273
meditation 44, 46, 263
mediums 55, 262, 264
Miguel Conner 24, 25, 26, 27, 28, 29
mind control 45, 46, 67, 95, 217
MKUltra 66, 133, 138, 141, 142, 153, 181, 183
moral imperative 16, 88, 89, 115, 119, 149

N

NDE 11, 18, 85, 86, 87, 90, 136, 137
near-death experience 11, 18, 19, 26, 48, 49, 74, 83, 85, 86, 87, 88, 89, 91, 94, 136, 182, 187, 194, 219, 243, 244, 245, 264
Neil deGrasse Tyson 31, 37, 38, 39, 122, 131, 139

O

occult 19, 21, 66, 116, 117, 122, 123, 124, 130, 196, 256

Occult 125, 228
out-of-body 26, 48, 136, 153, 182, 237, 245

P

paradigms 32, 155
paranormal 48, 49, 52, 185, 238
parapsychology 11, 16, 61, 73, 75, 76, 181, 182
physicalism 39, 52
Pizzagate 19, 20, 21, 22
Podesta 20, 179, 180
Project Stargate 138
psychedelics 11, 54, 55, 118
psychic 26, 29, 48, 67, 135, 136, 137, 139, 142, 185, 236, 249, 259
PSYOP 96, 105, 177

Q

quantum physics 40, 41

R

reincarnation 11, 264, 265
Remote Viewing 138, 275
Richard Dolan 175, 176, 177, 178, 179, 180, 182, 183, 185, 186, 188
Richard Smoley 24, 28, 29, 221
Richard Wiseman 74, 75, 76
Rick Archer 20, 259
Russ Dizdar 27, 133, 193, 195, 196, 197

S

Sabbatean 116, 274
Sam Harris 76
Satan 10, 22, 23, 27, 28, 29, 121, 195, 219, 221, 222, 251
satanic ritual abuse 12, 27, 29, 93, 122, 130, 190, 193, 208, 209, 221
Scientology 66, 77, 78, 79, 80, 273
Skeptiko 7, 12, 16, 17, 21, 24, 27, 29, 31, 32, 34, 35, 48, 50, 55, 61, 65, 67, 73, 74, 75, 76, 86, 88, 89, 95, 99, 103, 105, 121, 135, 136, 182, 190, 207, 209, 223, 231, 236, 269, 273, 274, 275
spirit cooking 20, 21
Stanford Research Institute 39, 136
Stargate 11, 67, 135, 136, 137, 138, 139, 183
Steven Crowder 99, 100, 102
Strong AI 156
suicide 90, 122, 255
supernatural 62, 67, 68, 69, 70, 71, 72, 141, 150

T

transgression 115, 116, 132

U

UFO 12, 146, 154, 160, 161, 163, 171, 173, 175, 179, 180, 181, 276

United Church 199, 200

W

West Memphis Three 121, 122, 123, 125, 127, 128, 129, 275

WikiLeaks 180

Y

yoga 130, 189, 190, 194, 262

www.ingramcontent.com/pod-product-compliance
Lightning Source LLC
Chambersburg PA
CBHW020902080526
44589CB00011B/405